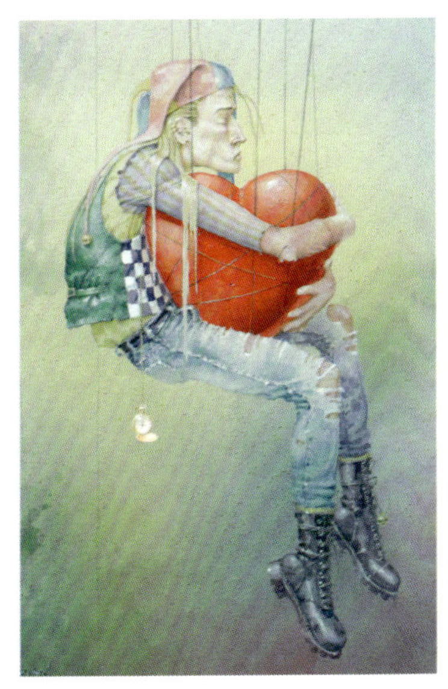

To: Amy
Live life to its fullest
Daniel B. Merriam

THE ART OF DANIEL MERRIAM

THE IMPETUS OF DREAMS

Editor
Yale Beebee

Book Designer
Kevin MacIvor

Production Coordinator
Padraic Callaghan

Copy Editor
Mary Nadler

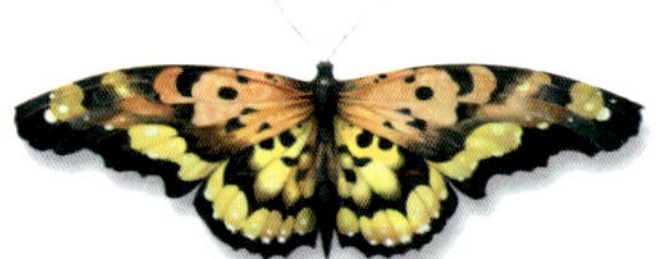

Monarch Editions, Inc.
1081A Ashbury Street
San Francisco, CA 94117
U.S.A.
415.731.7566

First Edition
printed in China

ISBN 0-9658347-0-0
LCCN 97-73074

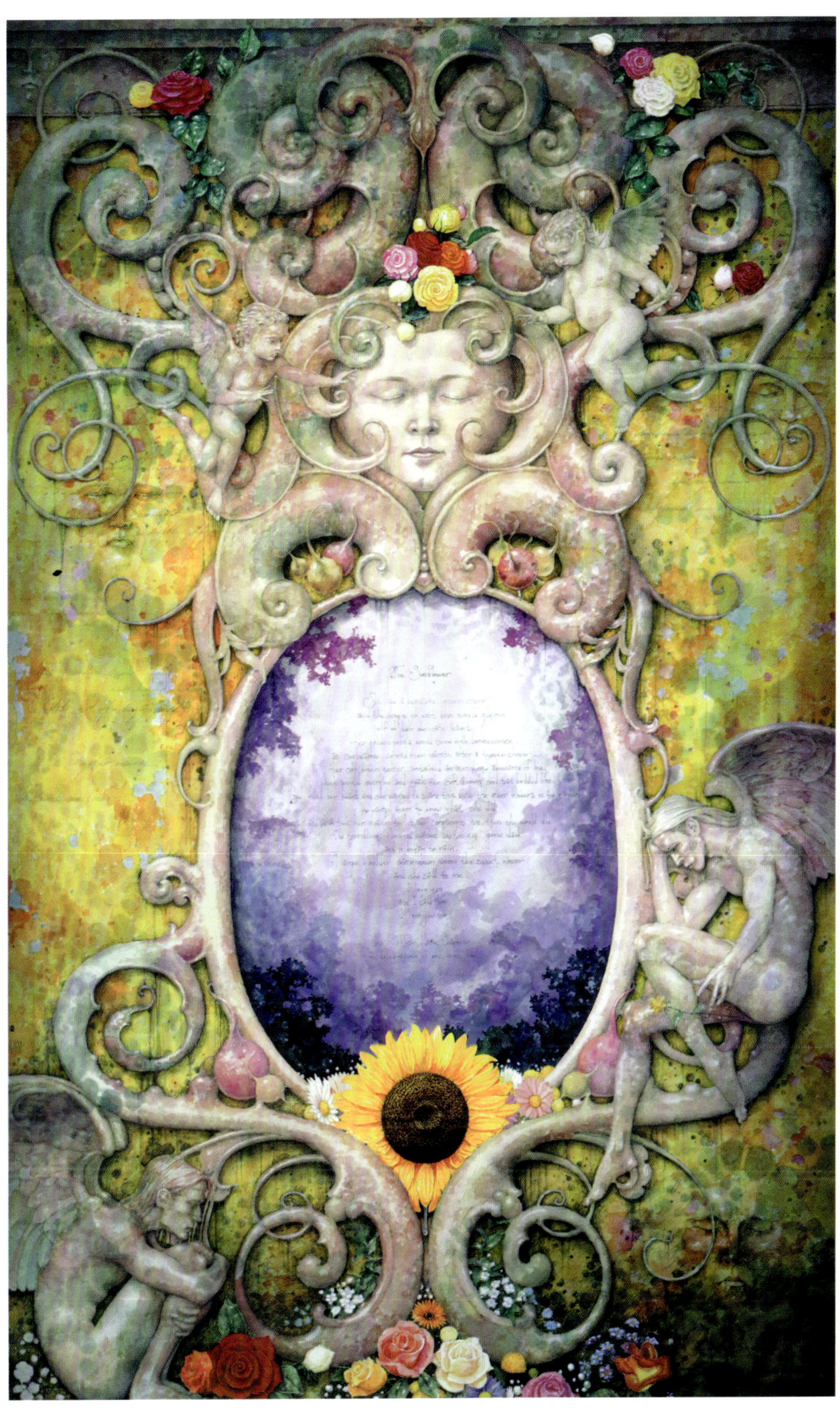

THE SUNFLOWER
1996, WATERCOLOR ON PAPER
38.5" X 23.75"

I would like to dedicate this book to the person I have most looked up to my entire life: my older sister, Tamber Chapman, whom I lost to a tragic automobile accident in the spring of 1996. She was the most loving, honest, and beautiful person I've ever known. She is my angel. The poem "The Sunflower" (page 128, and centered in the image above) was written by the elder of her two daughters, Tiffany, who miraculously survived the accident.

FOREWORD

THE LANGUAGE OF UNCONSCIOUS EXPERIENCE

by

William D. Bauer, Ph.D.

Doctor of Clinical Psychology and Psychoanalysis
Southern California Psychoanalytic Institute

Our conscious experiences -- the everyday, ongoing flow of thoughts, feelings, and images -- are actually the final end products in a series of complex stages of perception, selection, and organization. Much of this process occurs quickly, automatically, and totally outside our conscious awareness or volition. We get a glimpse of this more inclusive, automatic, less "logical" form of early thought during altered states of consciousness, like dreaming.

Almost one hundred years ago, Freud began to articulate the language of this unconscious thought process. In his study of dreaming, Freud outlined a realm of human experience where "primary process" thinking predominates. Within the surrealistic context of primary process thought, there is ample room for multiple levels of meaning, and opposites can comfortably coexist.

Primary process thought is both more inclusive and more malleable than conscious thought. It has its own unique contents and form. As a brief reflection upon our dream life confirms, primary process is a language scripted in images and powerful emotions.

Daniel Merriam's art initiates an immediate emotional relationship with the observer by communicating within the language and structure of primary process thought. Each painting presents a supersaturated rendering of the artist's inner experience. Some of Merriam's images directly portray the purity of primary process thinking characteristic of the dream state, and they immediately stimulate the imagination and unconscious of the observer. In others, a more conventional image draws the observer into the scene further to discover a more subtle interpenetration of multiple images and emotions. We inhabit a place where clocks appear to signify timelessness, where flying fish comfortably embody contradiction, and where trees with personalities reach deeper into the roots of our imagination, as their branches swirl into the heavens.

In each of Merriam's paintings, there is the paradoxical and captivating marriage of the boundlessness of primary process thinking, and the highly defined, expertly crafted image within which that thinking is sculpted and contained. Each level holds its own idea and resonates its own feeling tone. Together, they blend to form a complex visual and emotional tapestry. By communicating in the language and structure of the unconscious, Merriam's work invites us to reflect, to feel, and to play within a co-created waking dream.

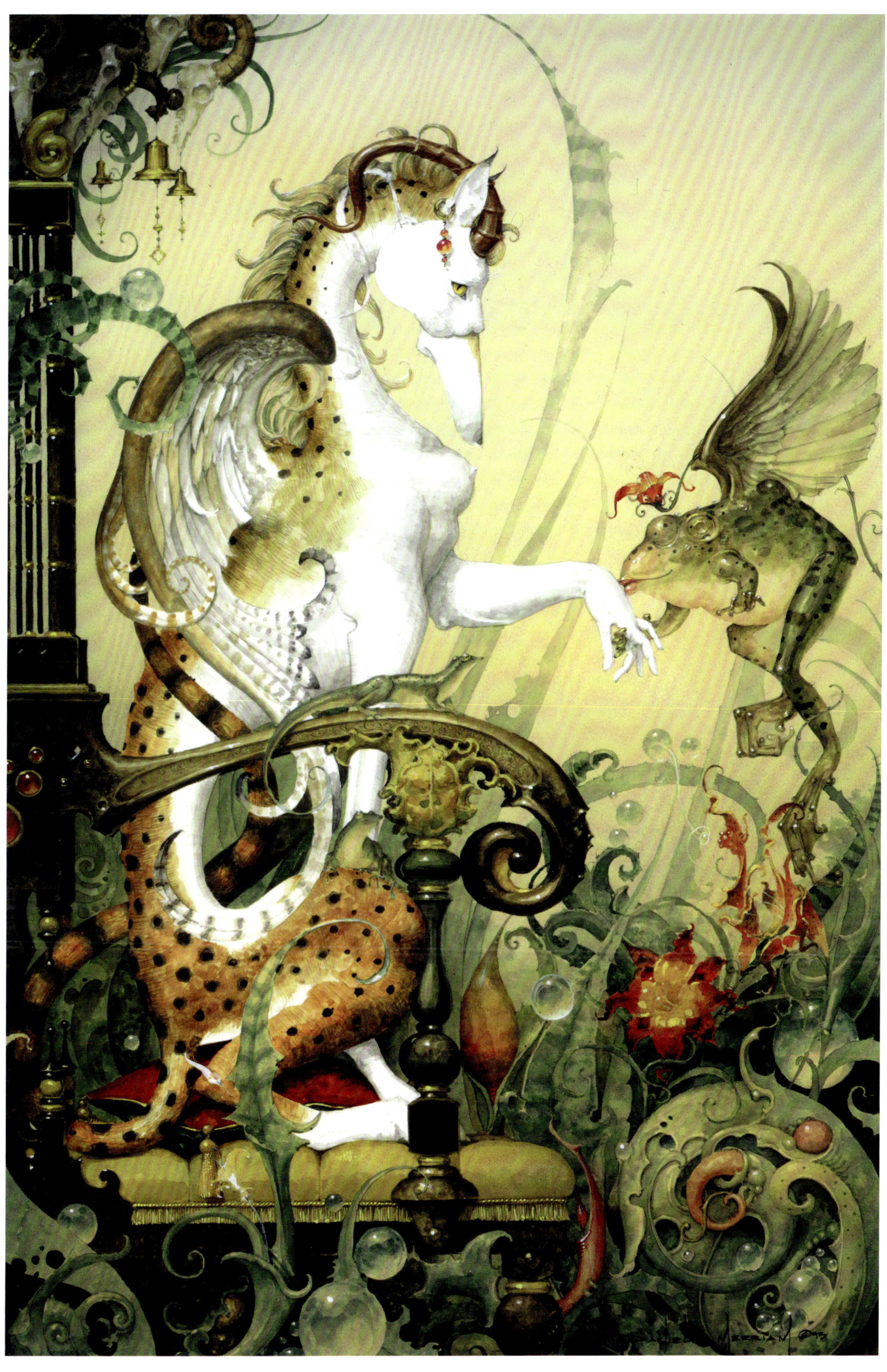

Kiss of the Winged Frog
1995, watercolor on paper
20.5" x 14"

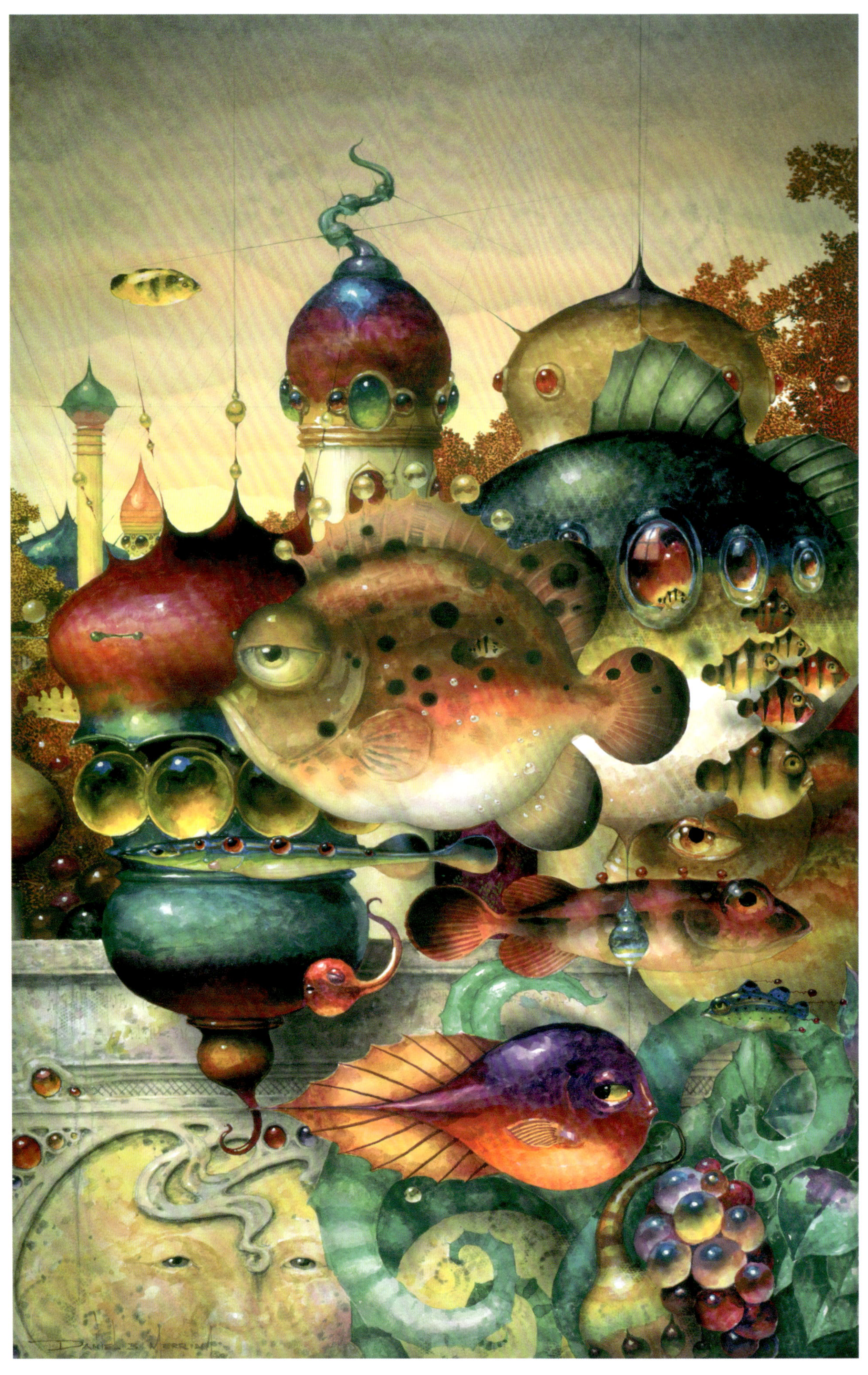

Zeppelin Tonic
1995, watercolor on paper
19.75" x 12.75"

Introduction

More than ten years have passed since Daniel Merriam first entered the professional fine art realm. In tribute to that milestone, this book presents an exquisite collection of his watercolor images, along with an intimate look at the artist's background and at the personal philosophy that infuses his art.

Daniel Merriam is a highly regarded contemporary surrealist and a master of the unforgiving medium of transparent watercolor. His work is in the collections of museums, major corporations, galleries, and private collectors throughout the world.

Merriam's many accomplishments include two Broderson Awards, the New England Scholastic Press Association first place award, and an honorary master's of humane letters from the University of New England (Biddeford, Maine) in recognition of the potential social contribution of his art and for his efforts to change perceptions of the creative mind within the traditional educational system.

Merriam's work has been featured in many publications, including *The World&I* (a publication of the *Washington Times*), *Art & Antiques*, *Sun Storm Fine Art*, *ArtNews*, *Art Business News*, *On the Boulevard*, and many major newpapers.

The December 1996 issue of *U.S.Art*, which proclaimed Merriam one of the artists to watch in 1997, stated:

> *Daniel Merriam's paintings are dreams in full color. They beckon the viewer to join a journey into the imagination, where the worlds of reality and fantasy collide in an explosion of color, shapes, and symbolism. Merriam communicates his ideas with such an original, refreshing touch that we couldn't help but be mesmerized by his work.*
>
> *His unique style is the product of solid technical skills, an illustrator's precision, and a storyteller's sense of pace. Anyone with a sense of adventure and humor who enjoys exploring a work of art will find Daniel Merriam's art a journey worth taking.*

I became aware of Merriam's work four years ago and was captivated from the very first glance. I consider his versatility, creative output, and masterful consistency to be unparalleled. His art is a variable combination of multiple influences, including Hieronymus Bosch, Maxfield Parrish, Salvador Dali, M.C. Escher, John James Audubon, Walt Disney, Norman Rockwell, Andrew Wyeth, Michael Parkes, and H.R. Giger. With their many layerings of subject and color, Merriam's astonishing paintings are unique among the works of classic and contemporary artists.

When not traveling the world searching for inspiration, Merriam divides his time between California and Maine.

You are about to embark on an incredible adventure. So take your time, and enjoy your voyage through *The Art of Daniel Merriam: The Impetus of Dreams.*

Yale Beebee
Director / Editor
Monarch Editions, Inc.
November 1997

The quotation is reprinted by permission of U.S.Art.

Between Two Worlds

New England towns echo the images of early American architecture. Gingerbread, Colonial, and Victorian houses built by ships' carpenters speckle the jagged landscape. I was born there on February 1, 1963 in York Harbor, a small village on the coast of Maine, where I grew up as the middle child in a family of two girls and five boys.

Creativity filled the air. Our house was full of a variety of musical instruments. Two pianos played constantly as seven siblings practiced daily. My mother would throw open the windows and sing while playing hymns, serenading the neighborhood. We often sat around the kitchen table and sketched on paper bags until they were covered inside and out with pictures of anything we could imagine. Hours were spent in my father's woodworking shop carving toy boats and other fun things to play with.

My family spent summers at a little cottage on Mousam Lake. I remember neighborhood games, rowboating, fishing, building sandcastles, and making campfires on the beach at night. We ran about the woods barefoot playing hide-and-seek, and didn't put on a pair of shoes until school began in the fall. Our cellar was filled with aquariums and buckets filled with pollywogs, sea monkeys, and turtles collected from a nearby cranberry bog.

My favorite escape was climbing trees. I'd search for the tallest tree I could find, pull myself up into its branches, and begin to climb. I pushed upward from limb to limb until the voices of children playing below faded into the rustling of leaves. I ventured higher and higher, testing my faith as the branches grew progressively thinner. Once near the top, I perched precariously on a limb, braced against the trunk as it swayed in the wind. This was my own world, and from here I could see forever.

When I wasn't playing I'd follow my father, Fremont, around while he worked and ask him question after question, watching his every move -- so methodical and efficient. I remember the smell of fresh-cut lumber and the sound of his voice as he explained his craft. He was a structural engineer and worked very hard starting his own construction company. My father was delighted that I took such interest in his work and soon had me working right alongside him. He gave me carpenter's tools as gifts for birthdays and Christmas. I learned to saw wood without it splintering, and to swing a hammer with the rhythm of a drummer. While in his den at night, I would watch as he drew the plans for the houses he was to build. These were his dreams, and I witnessed the magic of his making them a reality.

At the age of twelve, I was working in the woods with my father, building log cabins -- hewing logs with an axe, draw blade, and chain saw. Our family moved to a new home in the heart of the Sebago Lakes region. Majestic cathedral pines towered over the large Dutch Colonial house that faced northwest over eleven miles of lake, with a view of Mount Washington in the distance. This lonesome house had no foundation and no septic system, and it was not insulated for the long Maine winters. We dug the foundation by hand, crawling on our hands and knees, chipping bedrock from narrow trenches. My father had grown up on a farm and believed in the virtues of good, hard work. I continued to work for him in my early teens, but I found myself spending more and more time in the sanctuary of my bedroom.

It was there at my little oak desk next to the window that I began to pass blissful hours drawing and painting. With a pencil and a fresh stack of locally milled paper given to me by a friend, I had soon drawn enough fanciful images to wallpaper my entire room. I remember occasionally looking down to see my father hard at work in the yard. Though I knew he wanted my help, I prayed he would pass without calling for me. Eventually, he noticed my drawings and would call

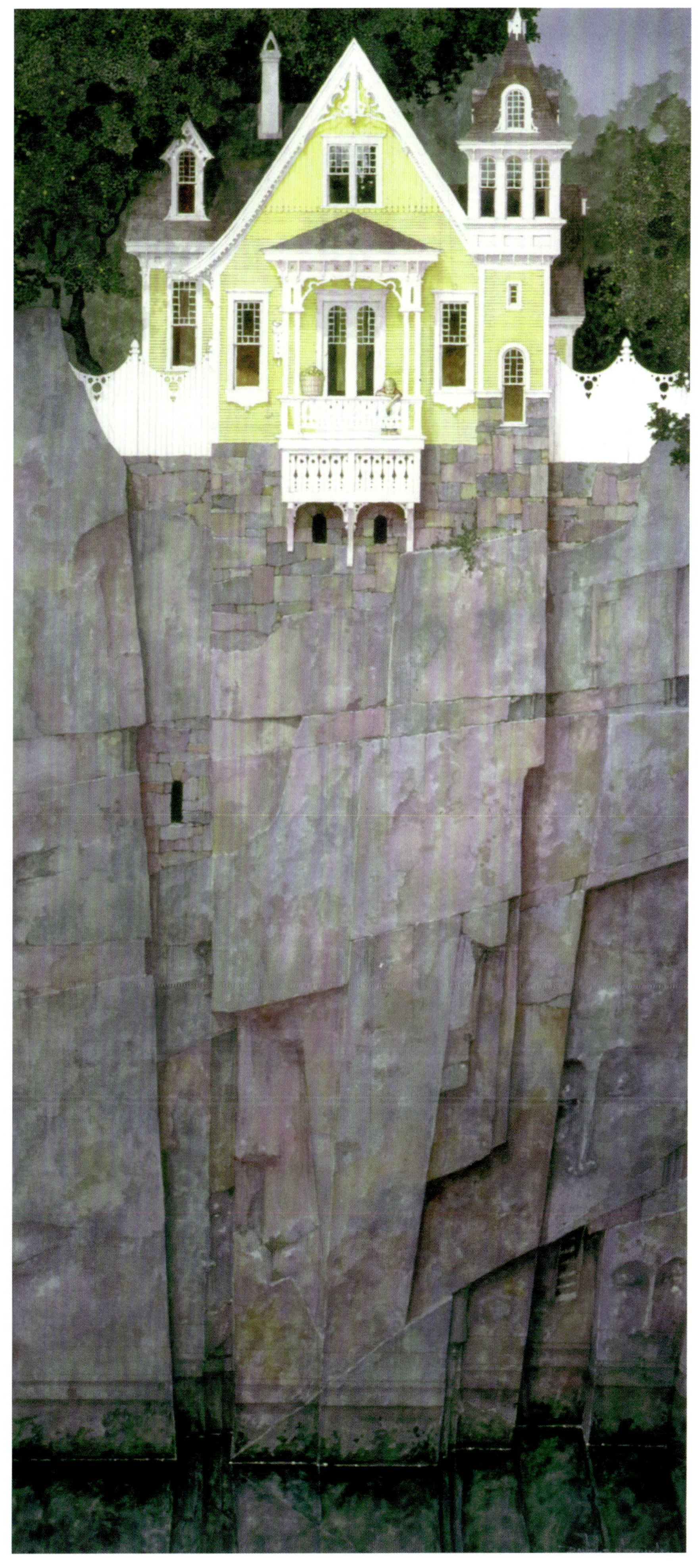

Apple Drop
1994, watercolor on paper
a. 36" x 16"

me down from my room to proudly show them to his friends. However, it was difficult for my father to accept art as a viable vocation. I recall his struggle with its intangibility. To further torment him, all five of his sons were artistically inclined.

School was difficult for me. My attention span wavered as a focus on the rote memory of dates and names somehow eluded my grasp. My teachers would say I "just wasn't there." I'd spend most of my time staring out of the classroom window, daydreaming, traveling in time through distant worlds. In spite of my erratic grades and lack of interest, my artistic edge somehow gained the support of some of my teachers.

I entered the Bridgton Art Show when I was fifteen and won first place in the student category. At the awards ceremony, I was introduced to Alan Magee who won the grand prize for his painting entitled *Stones*. I was amazed by his technique -- such great realism, done so simply. Alan spent a great deal of time talking with me and set a standard of excellence not only in his work, but in his person. I have never been able to match his skills, but I have instead cultivated merits of my own. Throughout my career I have remembered that meeting with Alan and always offer an ear or a little advice to aspiring artists.

I felt I had led a rather sheltered life in the rural climate of Maine, and the reality of attending a college for the arts seemed out of reach. Perhaps I lacked confidence, or perhaps I lacked encouragement. In any case, I never went to a formal art school. I studied for two years at the Central Maine Vocational Technical Institute for mechanical and architectural design, and I then began working for architects and builders.

My father often baffled me with his complex understanding of calculus and formulas that went on for pages. He would deliberate them for what seemed like hours, assuming I was able to follow along. Although I did not inherit my father's mathmatical proficiency, my eye for perspective and my knack for illustrating architecture proved very helpful during my first few years of working with architects and developers. After I had proved my abilities, my father invited me to work in his company. I gladly accepted his offer, as working in the family business seemed to promise greater rewards.

As the business grew, I found myself burdened with more and more responsibilities. In time I became depressed, and my senses began to numb. Eventually I reached a point where I became overwhelmed and riddled with guilt. Realizing that I was never going to achieve excellence in the construction business, I decided that I should do what I had most desired. My father had a heart-to-heart talk with me and revealed a side of him I'd never seen before. He said he felt he was letting my talents go to waste. It felt strange hearing this strong, burly man suggest I pursue a career in the arts. This began what was to become a lifelong vision quest, one that gave my life a whole new meaning.

I determined to cultivate my art and learn to survive from it. Taking on any other type of work would certainly have been a distraction, as I had not kept up my painting during my previous employment. I worked in my studio day and night, seven days a week, stopping only to sleep for a couple of hours atop my homemade drawing board. I rented out my house because I could not afford the mortgage payment and was never home, anyway. Home was in my head, and my head was in my studio. Taking no time off for leisure, I diligently kept up this pace for two years.

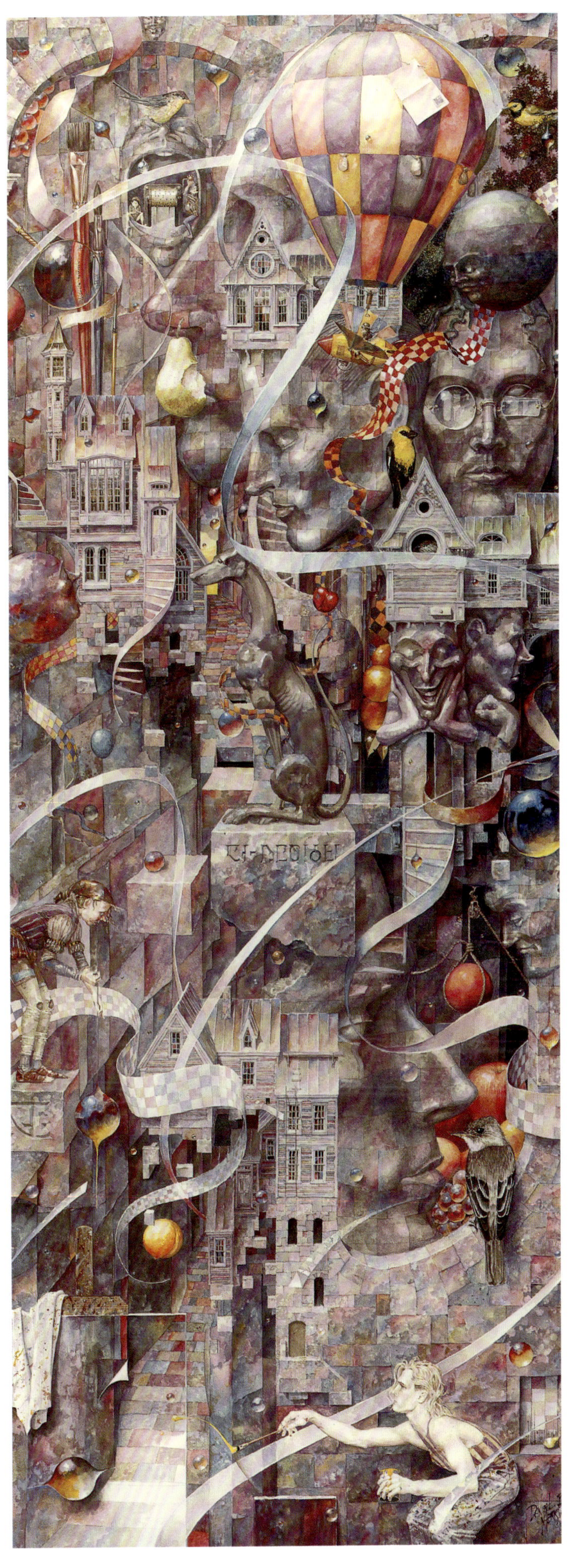

The Edge of Innocence
1989, watercolor on paper
50" x 28"

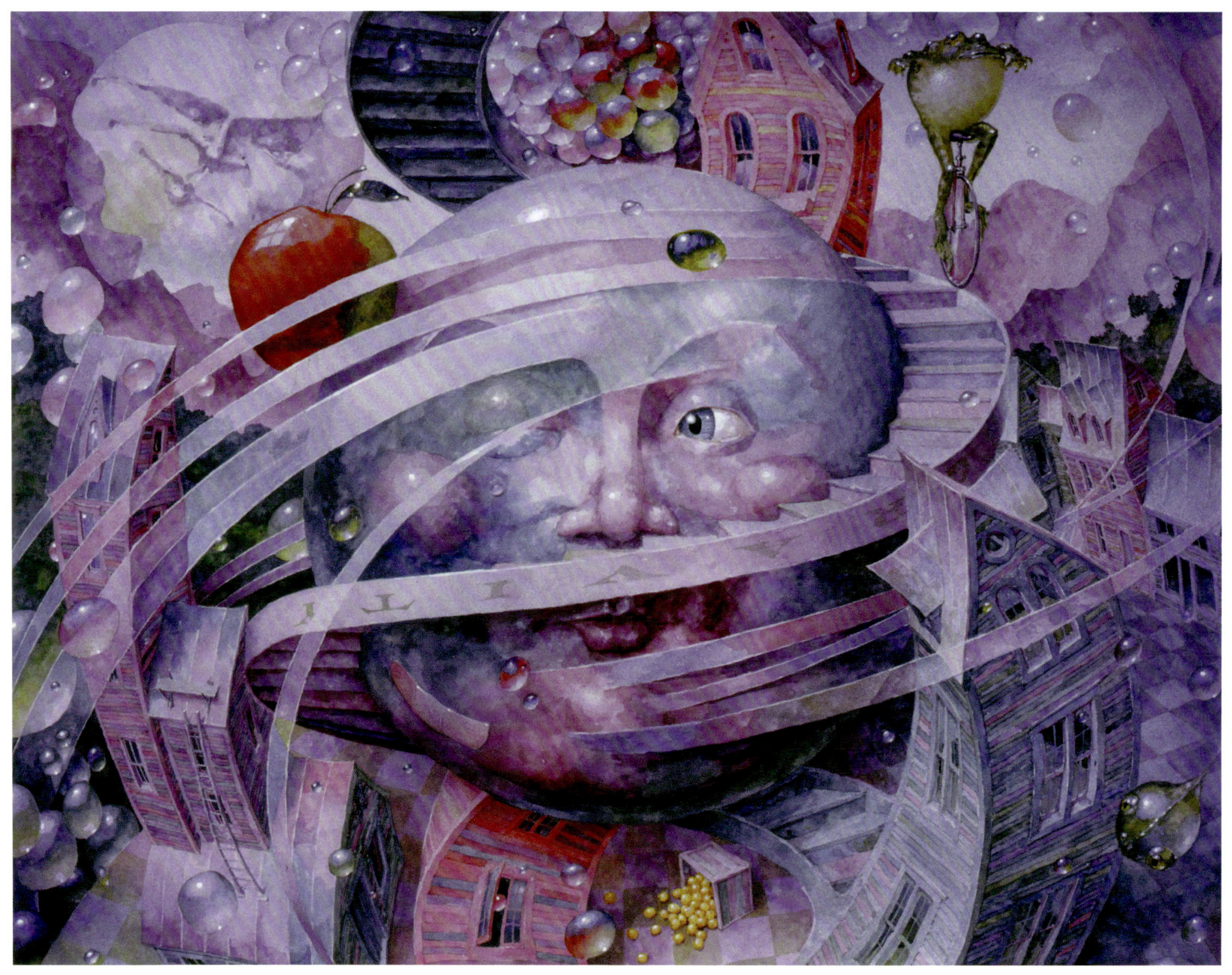

GRAVITY
1991, WATERCOLOR ON PAPER
18.5" X 24"

When I was twenty-three I moved to the harbor city of Portland, Maine. Working for an art gallery, I was able to arrange a rent/trade agreement for the vacant basement below. It was dark and musty, and the furnace seemed to use up most of the oxygen. The walls were made of crumbling brick and fieldstone. The mortar had turned to dust, and calcium deposits lined the cracks. I found some old French doors, built them into partitions, and hung drop lights from the ceiling. It was home for a while, but eventually the furnace exploded and the basement was flooded with black, sooty water. I found myself out on the street on a cold winter night walking through a snowstorm, too proud to go home to my parents and needing a floor on which to sleep.

There were times when I felt like giving up, but eventually I turned things around by perfecting my artistic talent. If it had not been for my weaknesses, I never would have discovered my strengths. As my body of work grew, so did my place in the art community.

There are people in our society who believe in the artist's place in the world. I am fortunate to know some of those people, and they have never stopped believing in me. They have shared their thoughts and feelings and given me support and encouragement. They have shown me that what I do is important. Through my art I have learned the importance of following my heart.

DANIEL B. MERRIAM

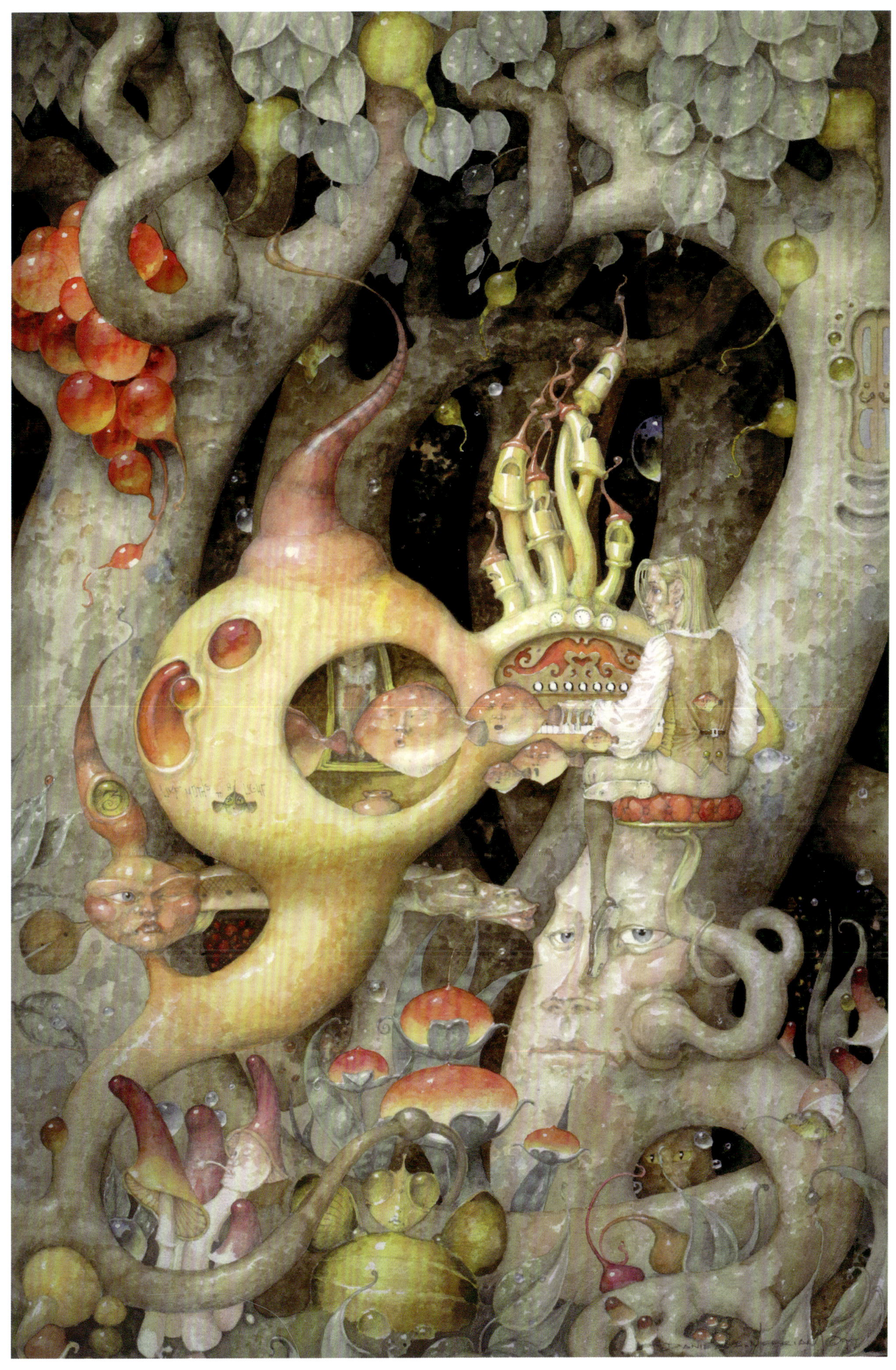

INTERMISSION
1997, WATERCOLOR ON PAPER
18.25" X 12.25"

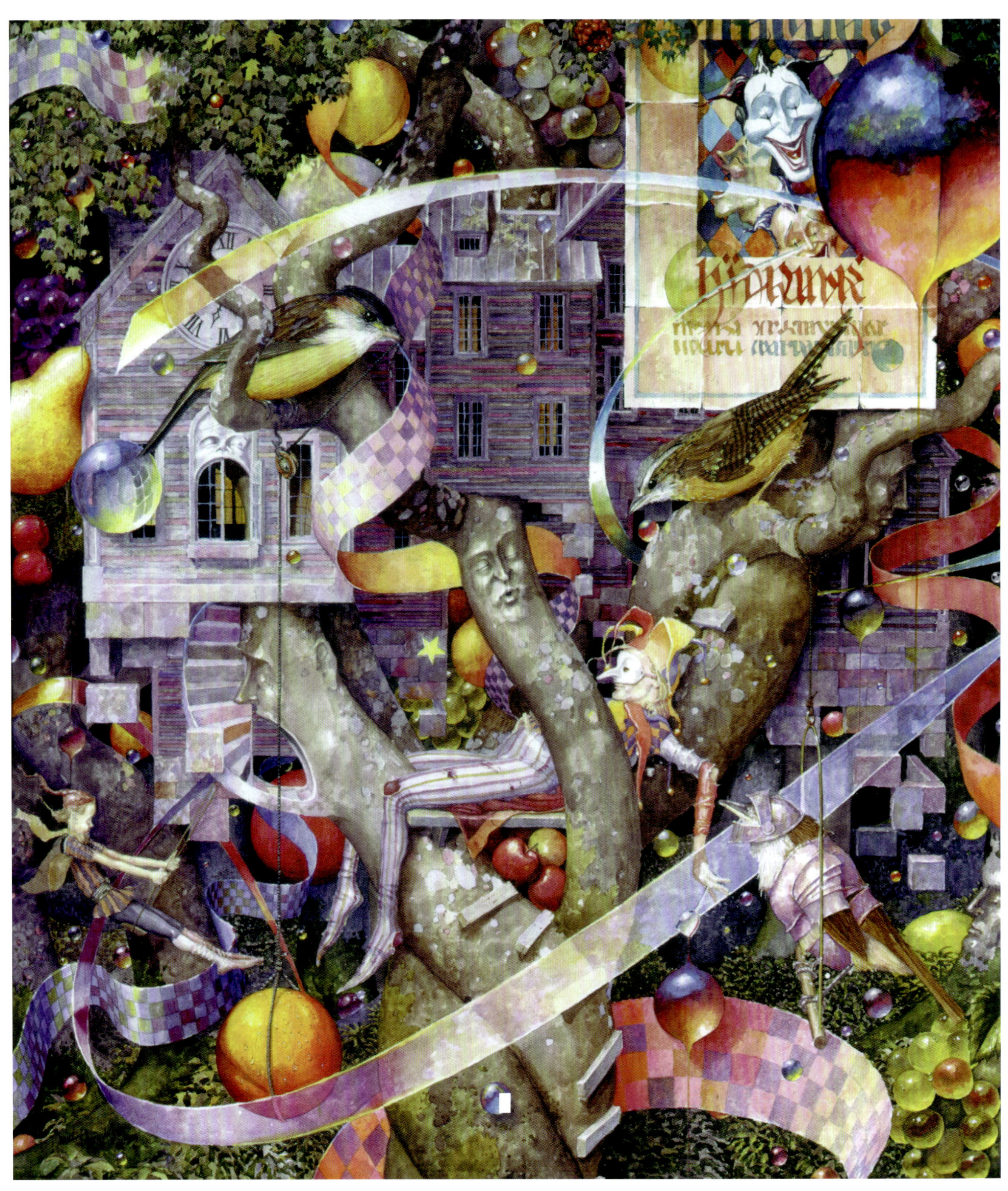

THE ALL NIGHT TREEHOUSE
1989, WATERCOLOR ON PAPER
A. 20" X 16"

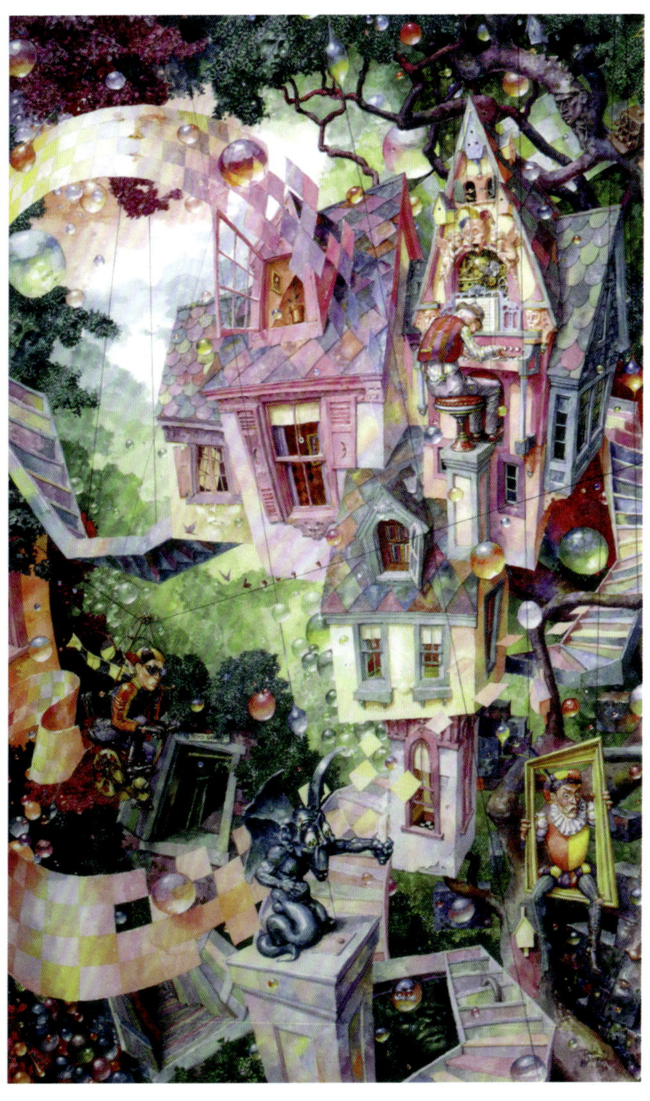

GRANDPA'S WALK
1993, WATERCOLOR ON PAPER
50" X 36"

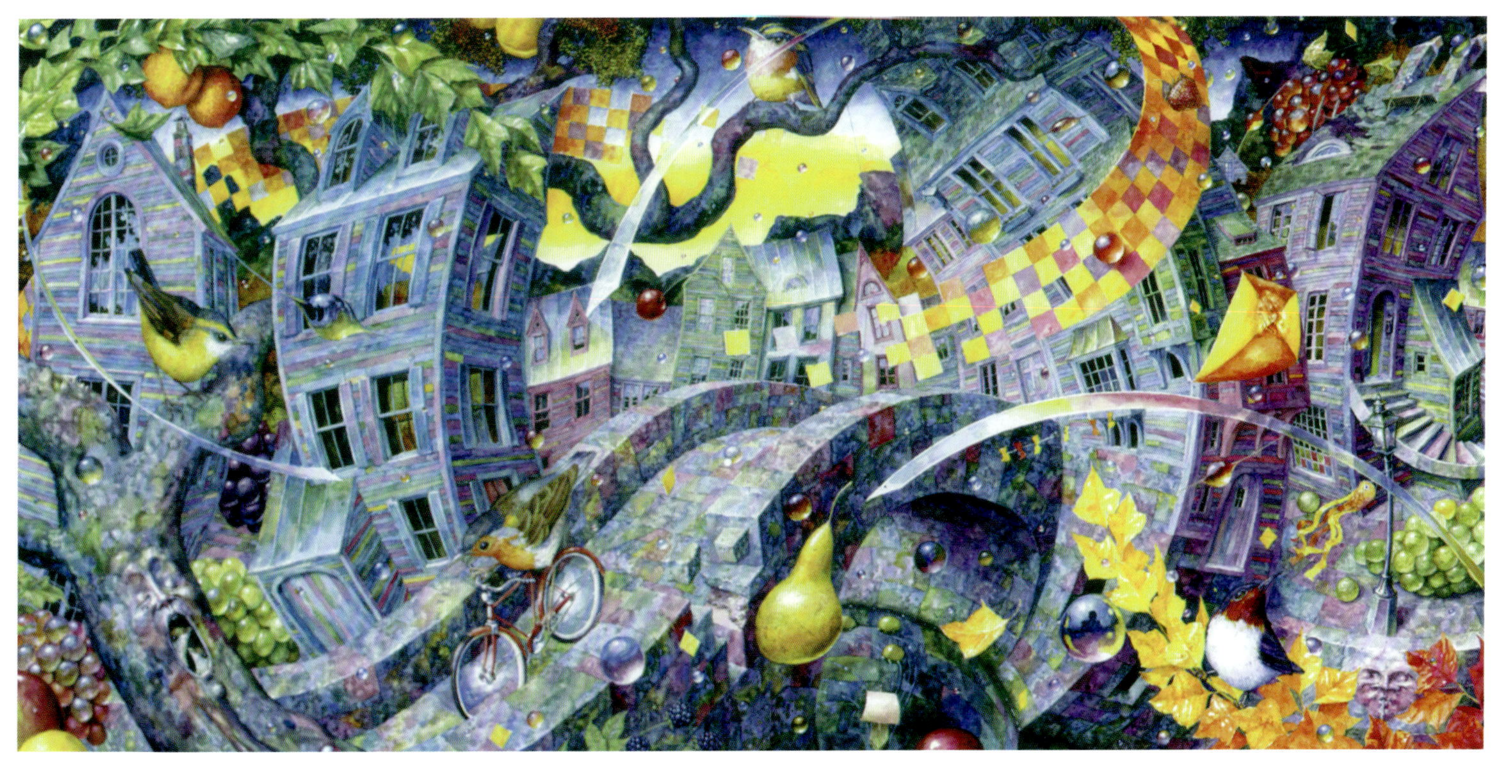

SEPTEMBER WIND
1993, WATERCOLOR ON PAPER
39" X 19"

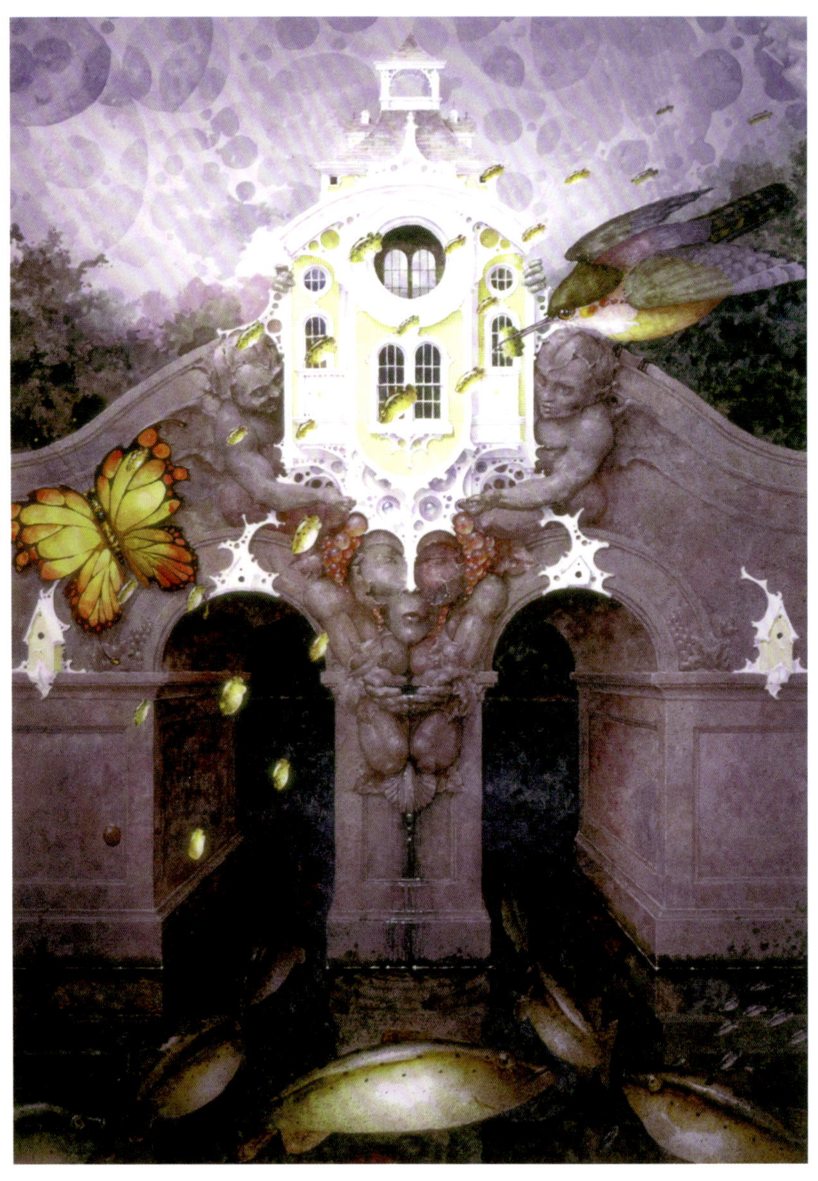

Under The Bridge
1993, watercolor on paper
28" x 22"

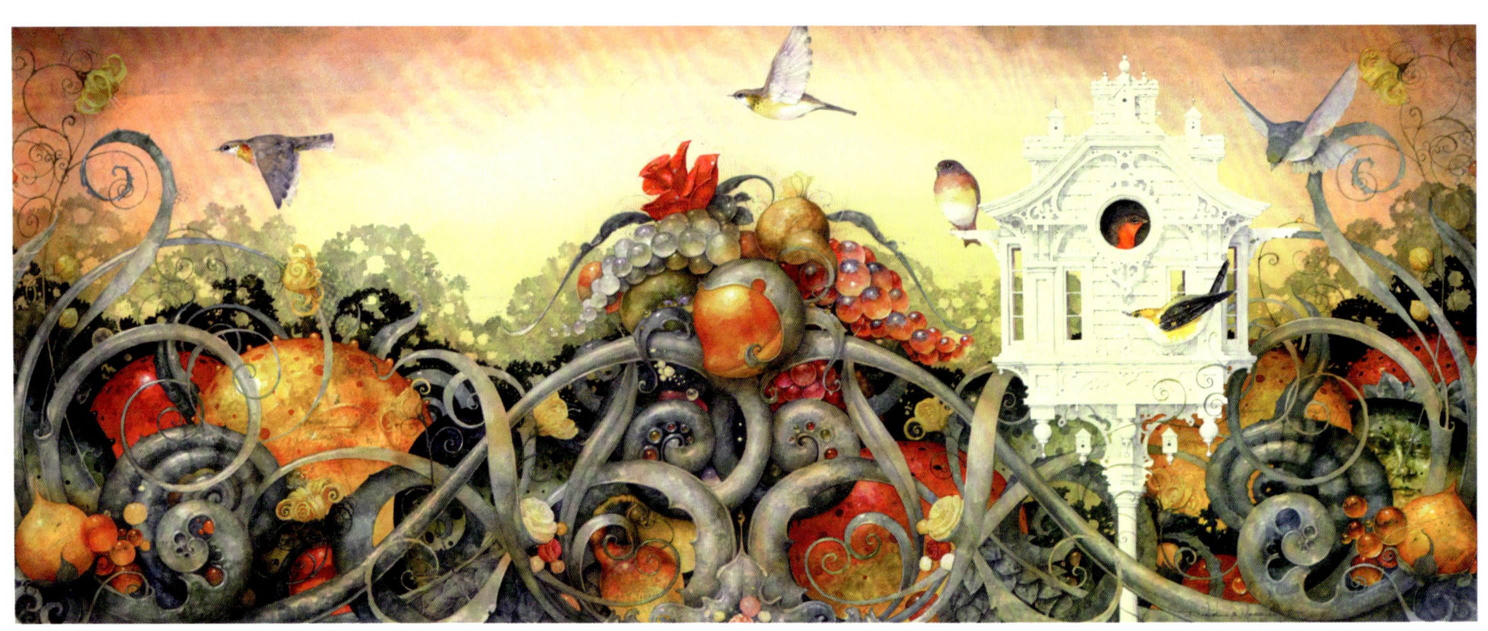

Garden of Earthly Delights
1997, watercolor on paper
18" x 39"

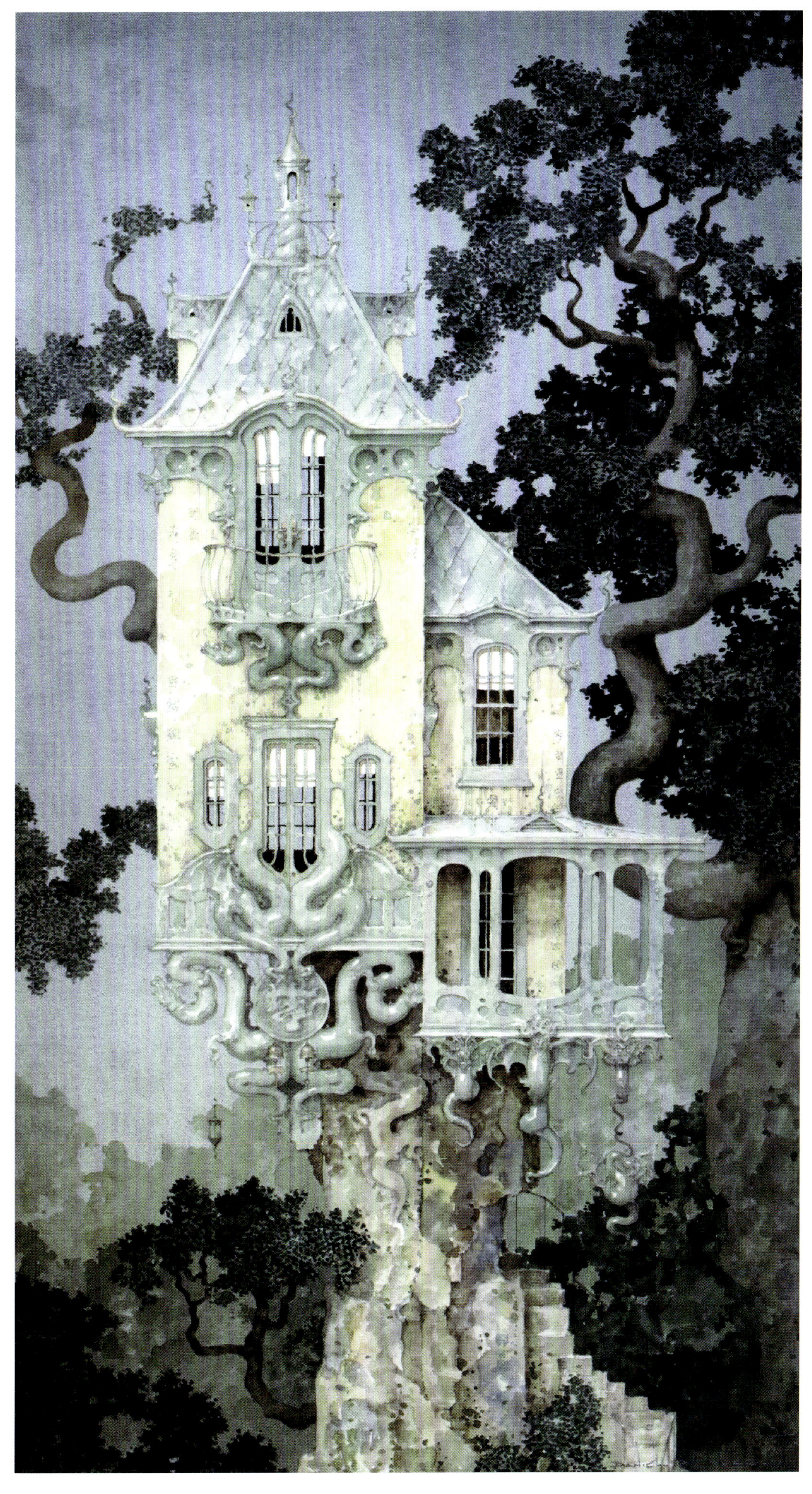

Jade
1997, watercolor on paper
16.75" x 9"

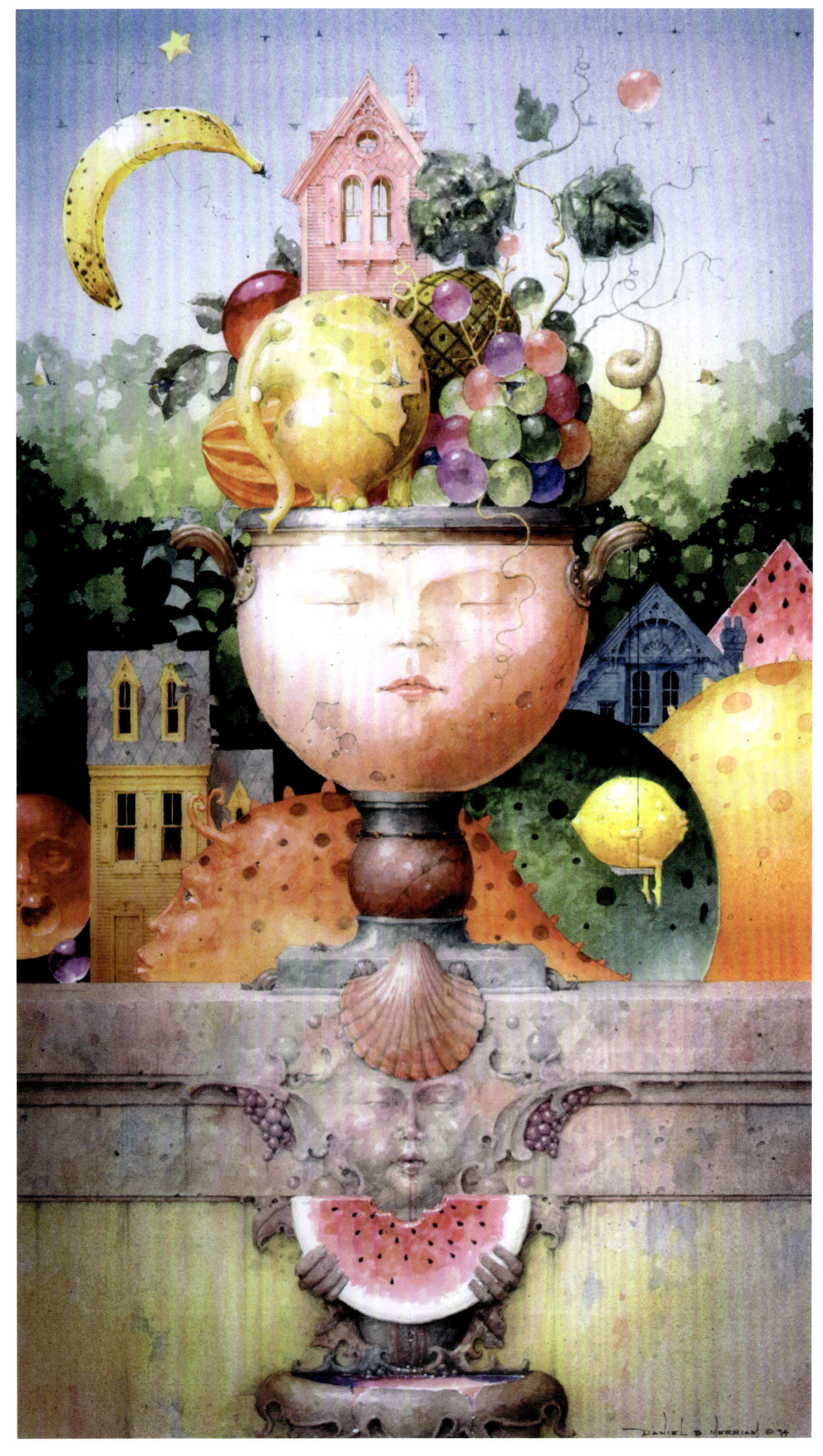

Mental Fruit
1994, watercolor on paper
A. 22" x 13"

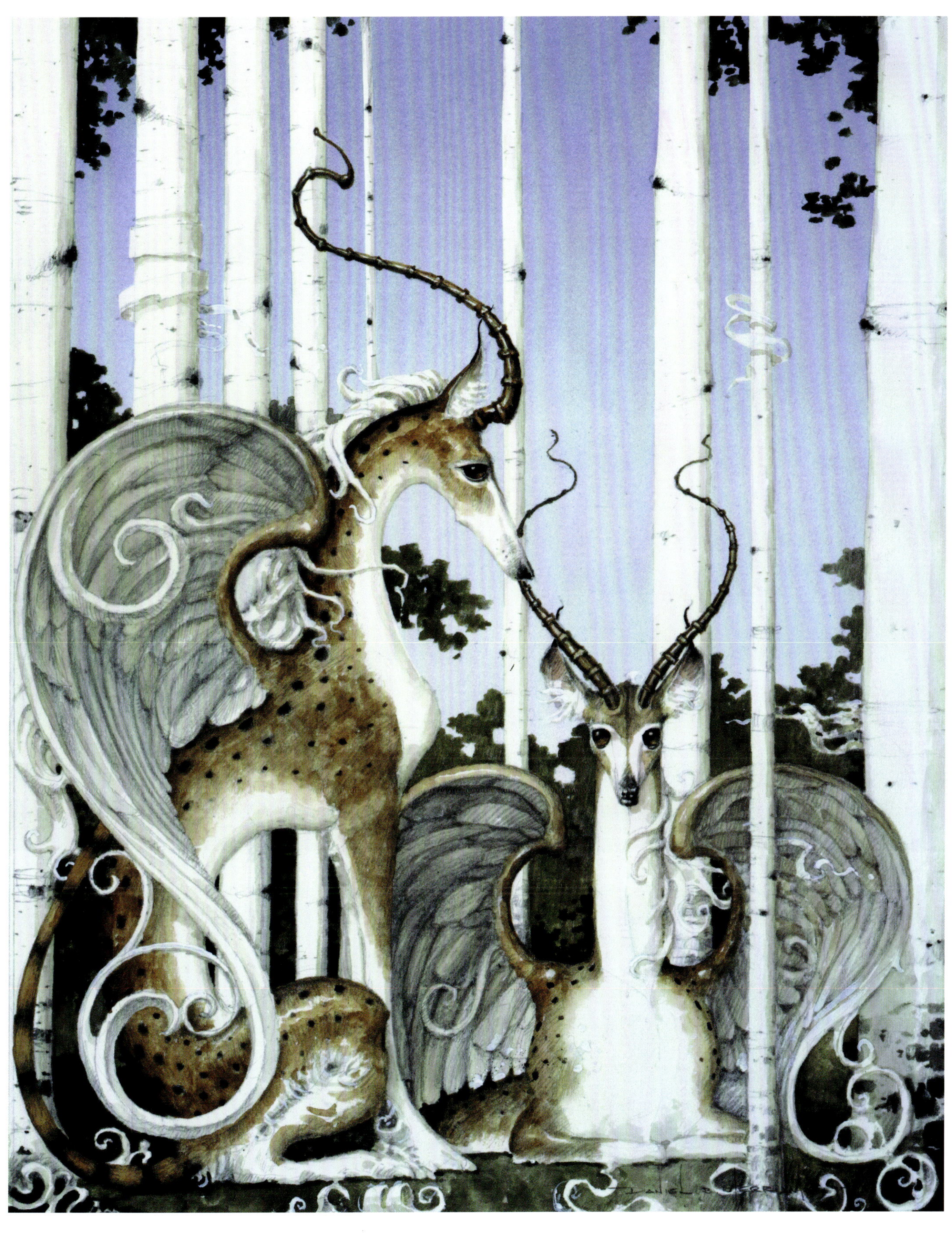

Two of a Kind
1997, watercolor on paper
11.5" x 9.25"

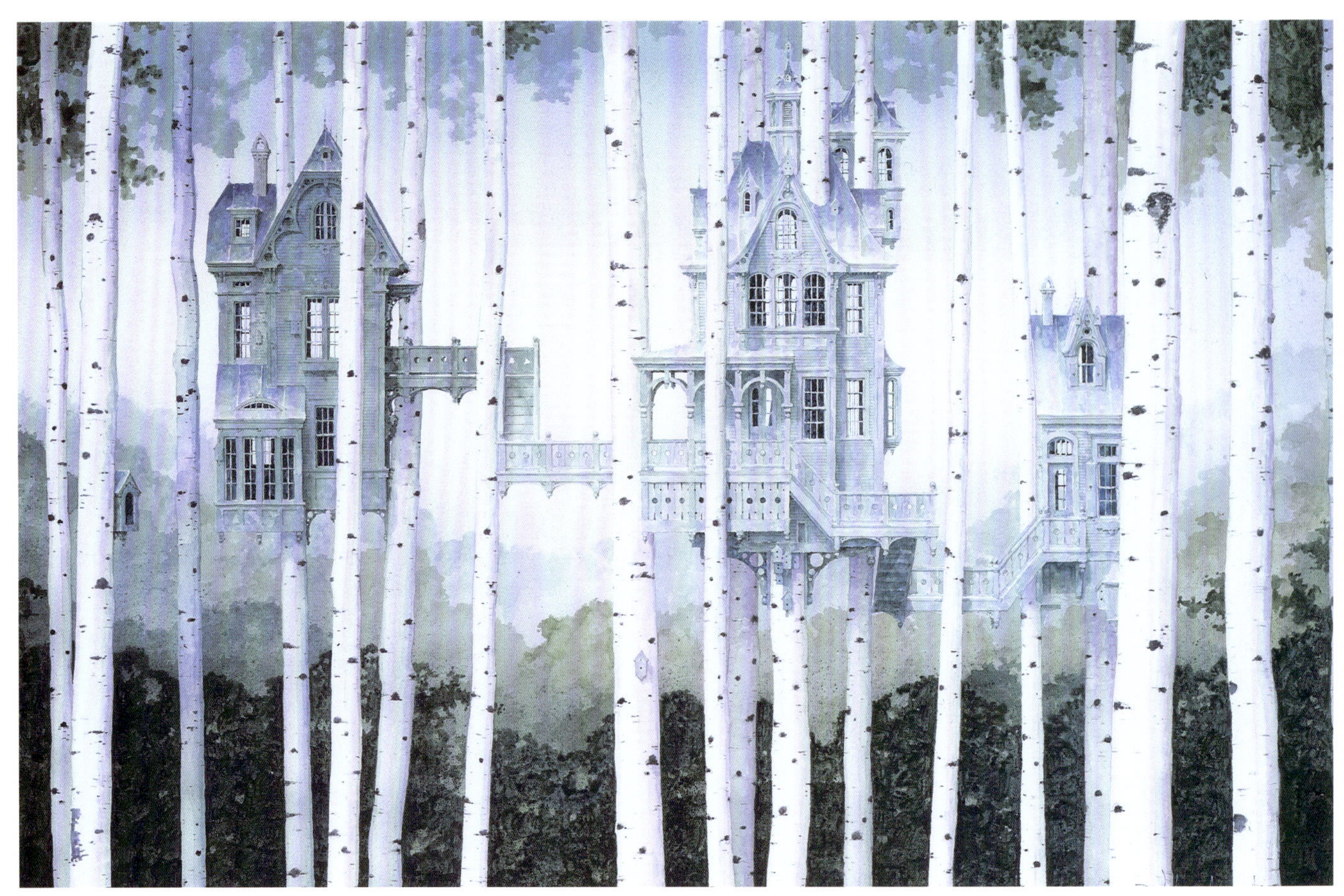

Forest for the Trees
1994, watercolor on paper
A. 15" x 30"

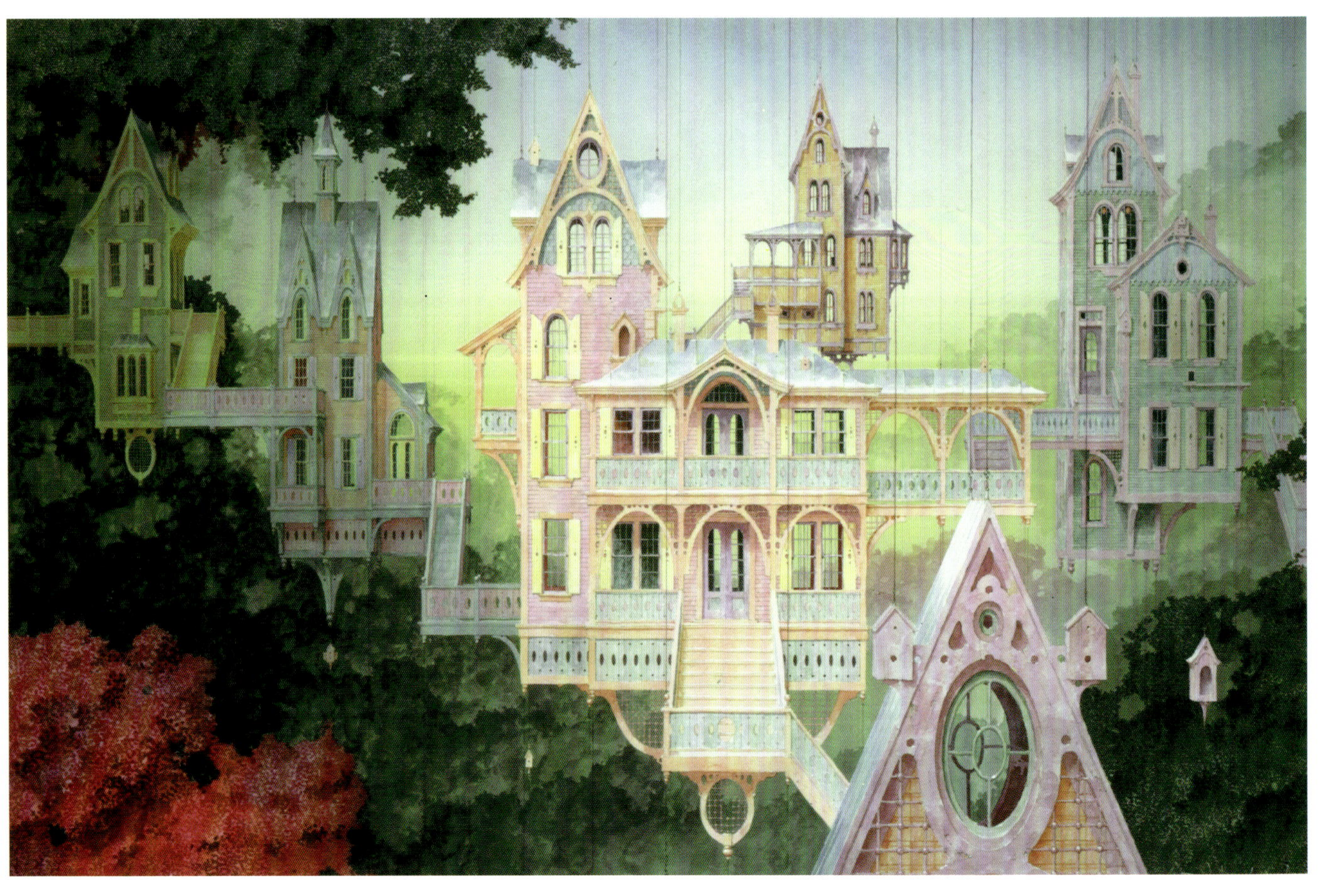

Catwalk
1994, watercolor on paper
18" x 28"

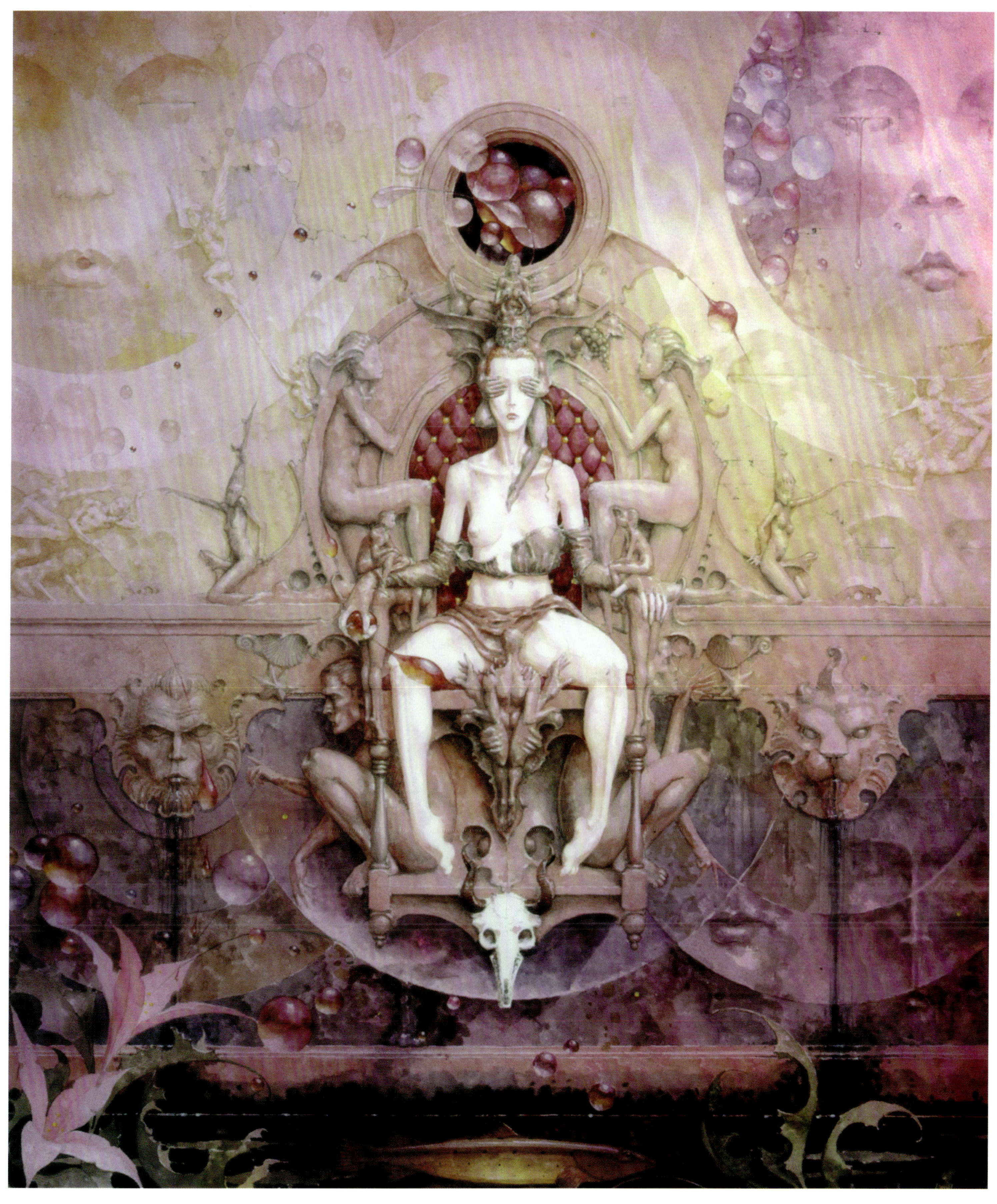

Everything She Wants
1993, watercolor on paper
a. 20" x 18"

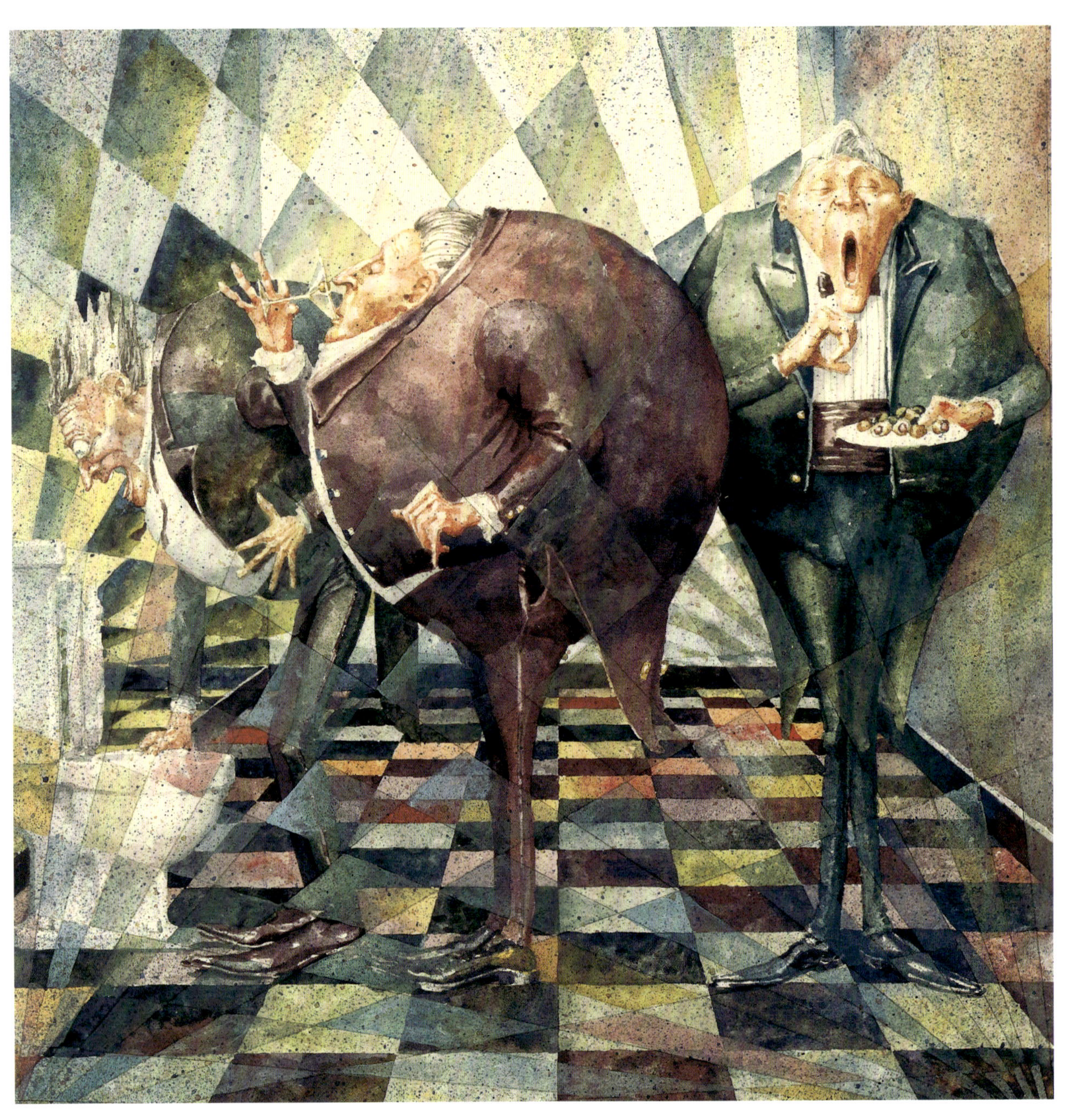

Black Tie
1991, watercolor on paper
a. 12" x 12"

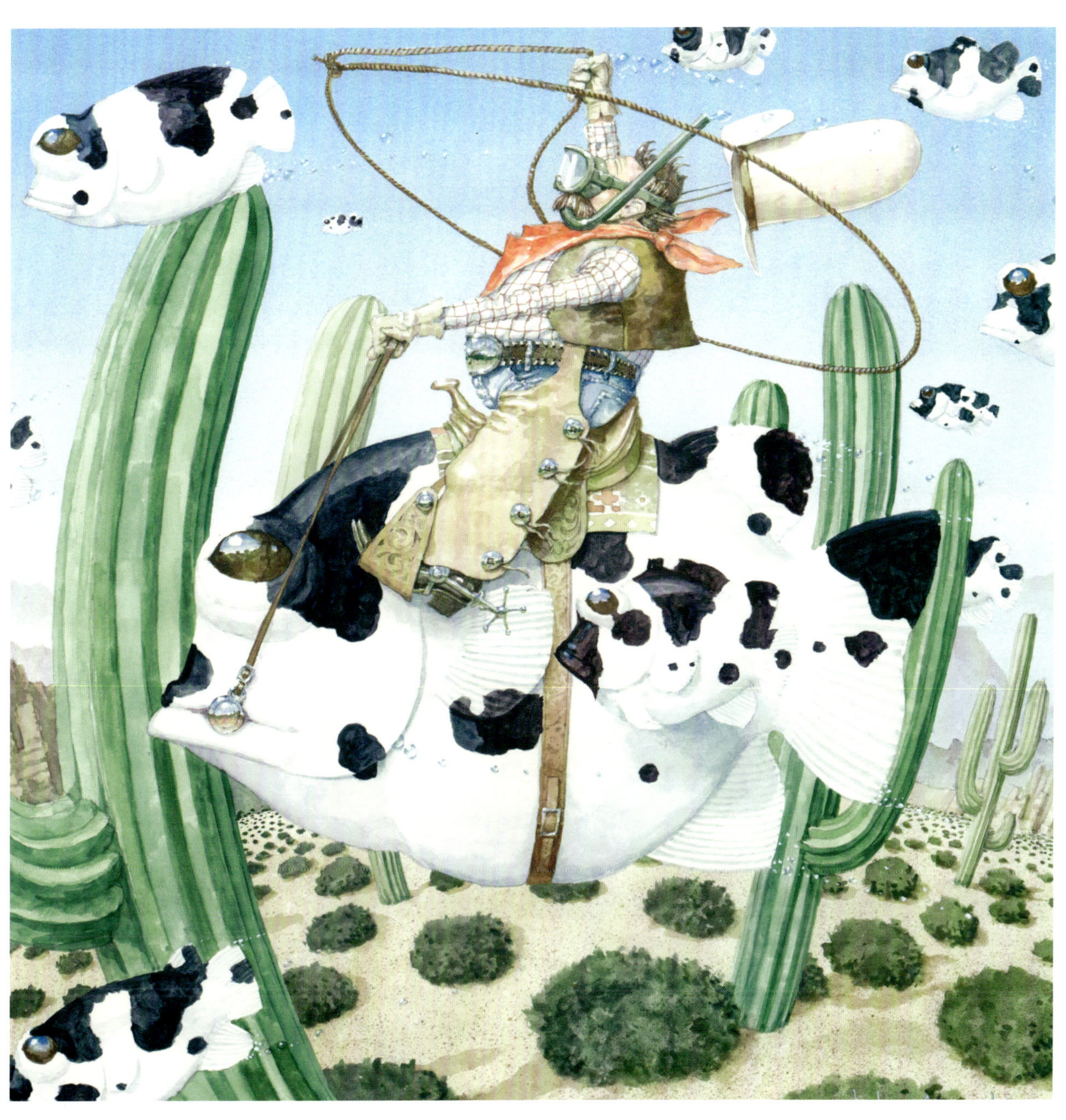

Holstein Fish
1993, watercolor on paper
15.5" x 15.5"

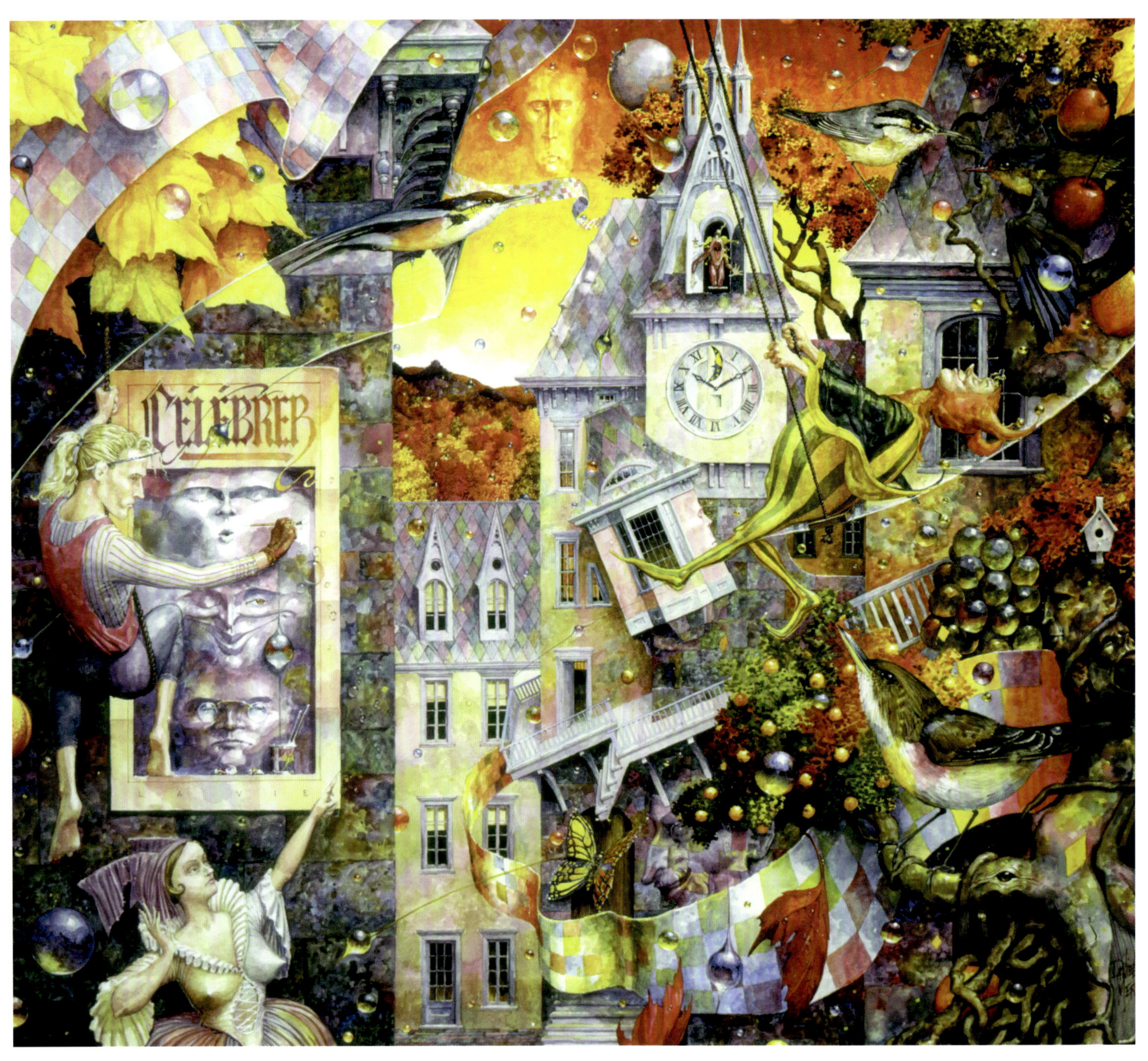

CELEBRATE LIFE
1990, WATERCOLOR ON PAPER
A. 20" X 24"

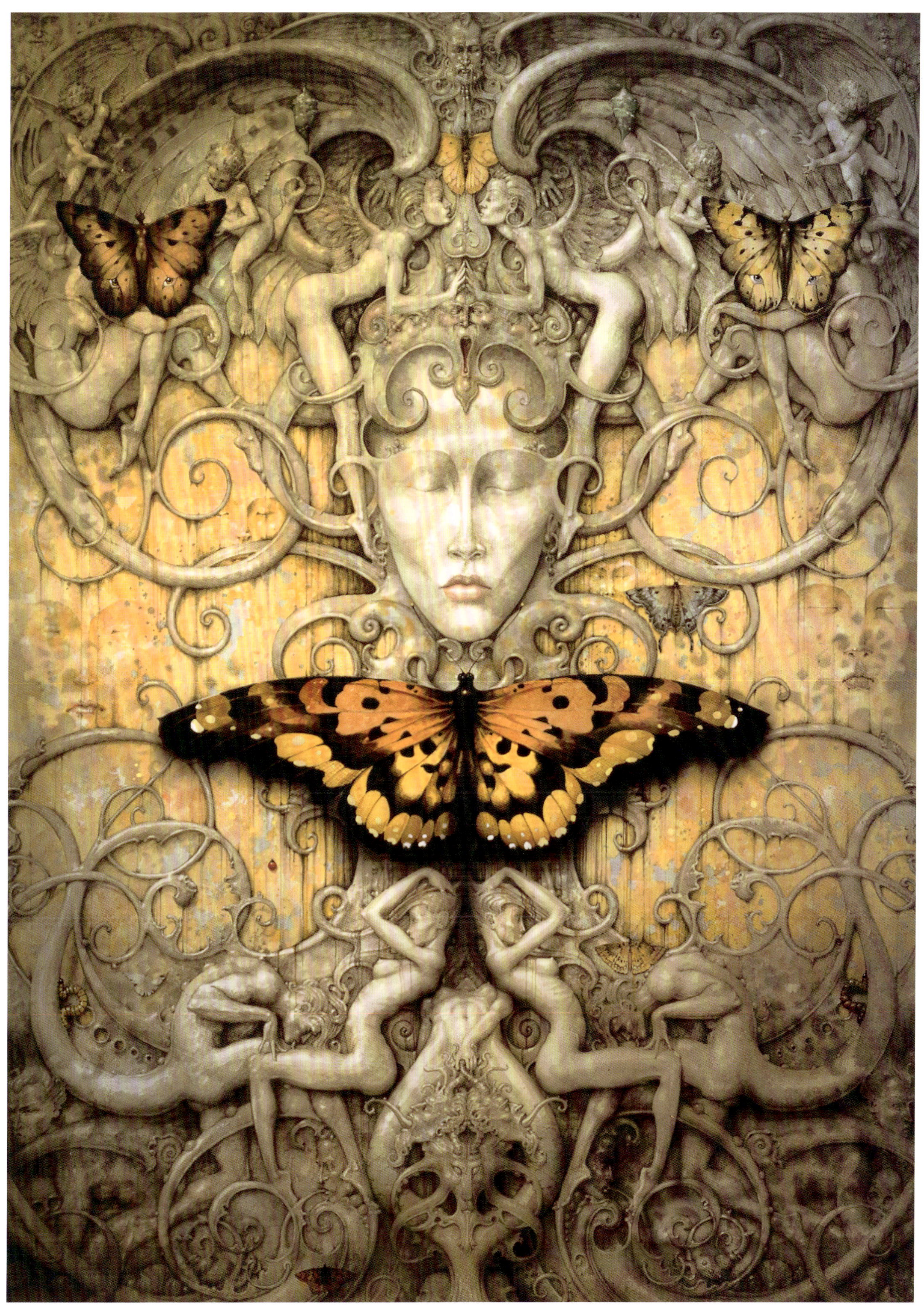

BEYOND BELIEF
1995, WATERCOLOR ON PAPER
49" X 36"

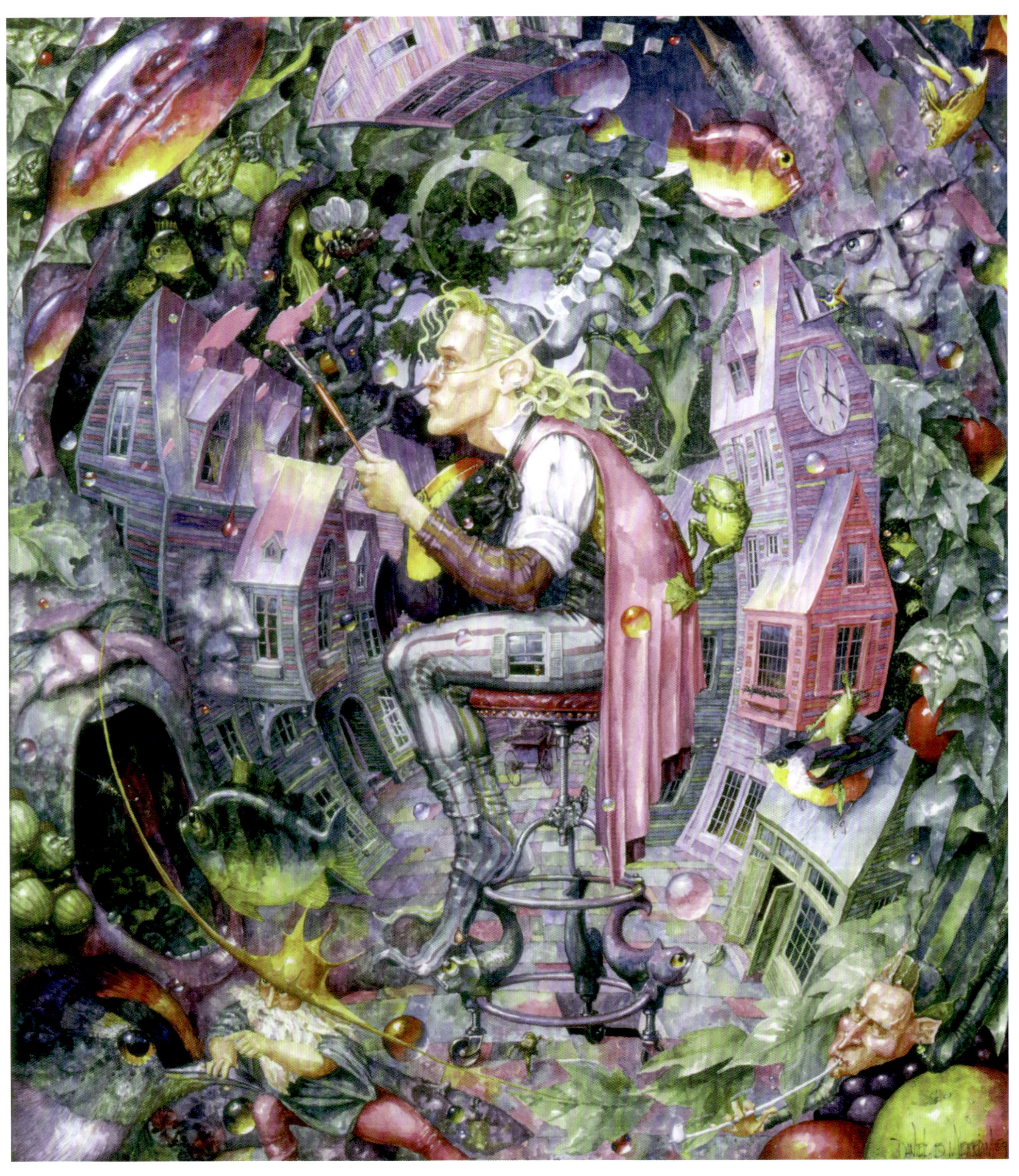

Once Around
1990, watercolor on paper
26" x 22"

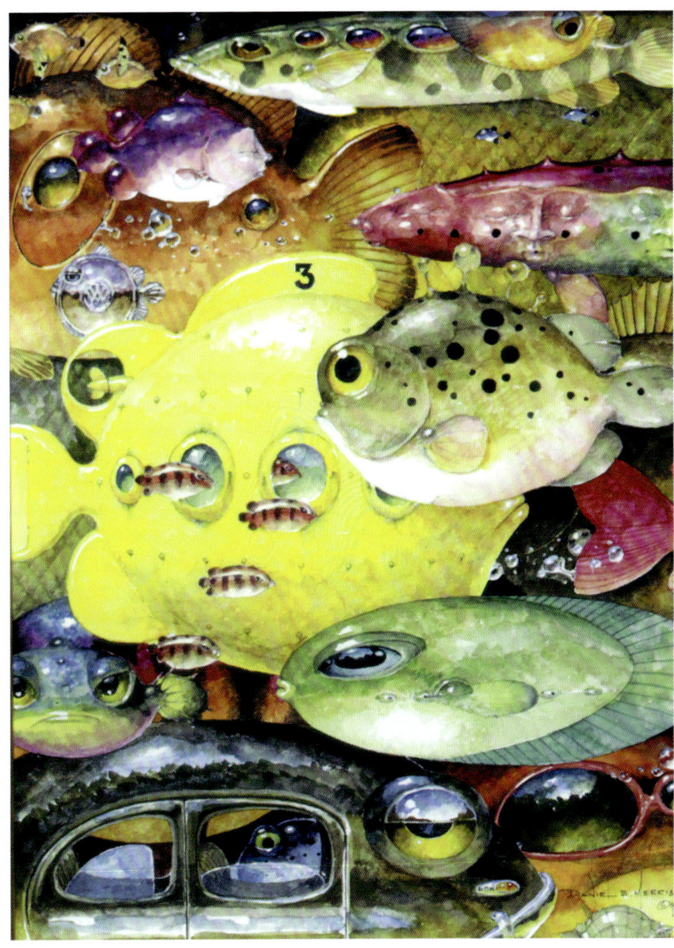

TRAFFIC JAM
1996, WATERCOLOR ON PAPER
12" x 9"

FOCUS

I work on one image at a time. I picture each painting completely in my mind before I begin it. Working on multiple paintings at once would cause me to lose the original inspiration for each, as the image in my mind would begin to change. Rather than draw multiple studies for any given painting, I cultivate the original sketch into the final piece. Each painting is its own unique experience, and other studies would be other paintings.

As I work through a painting, I complete certain areas in full detail before moving on. When watercolor is laid down, it cannot be removed or covered up. Getting the effect you want on the first attempt is critical because with this medium there is little going back to fix mistakes.

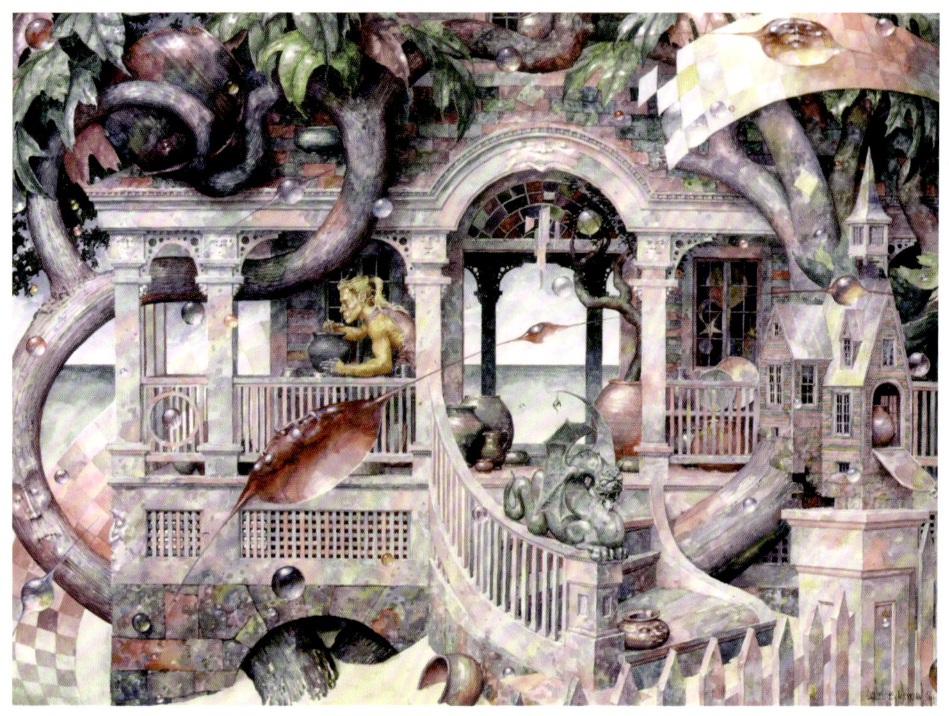

Discovery of the Wheel
1991, watercolor on paper
a. 20" x 28"

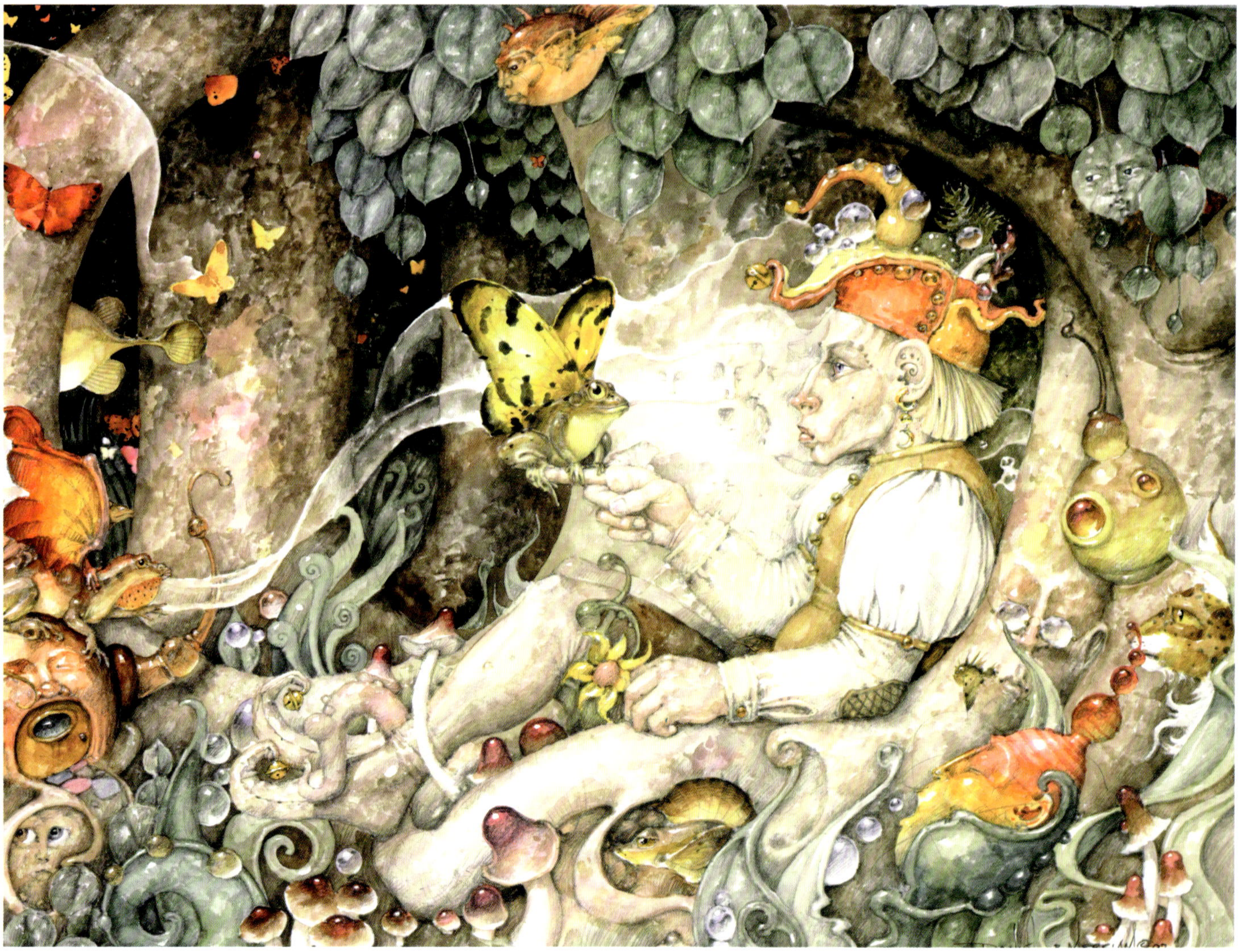

Fiddlehead Grove
1997, watercolor on paper
12" x 18"

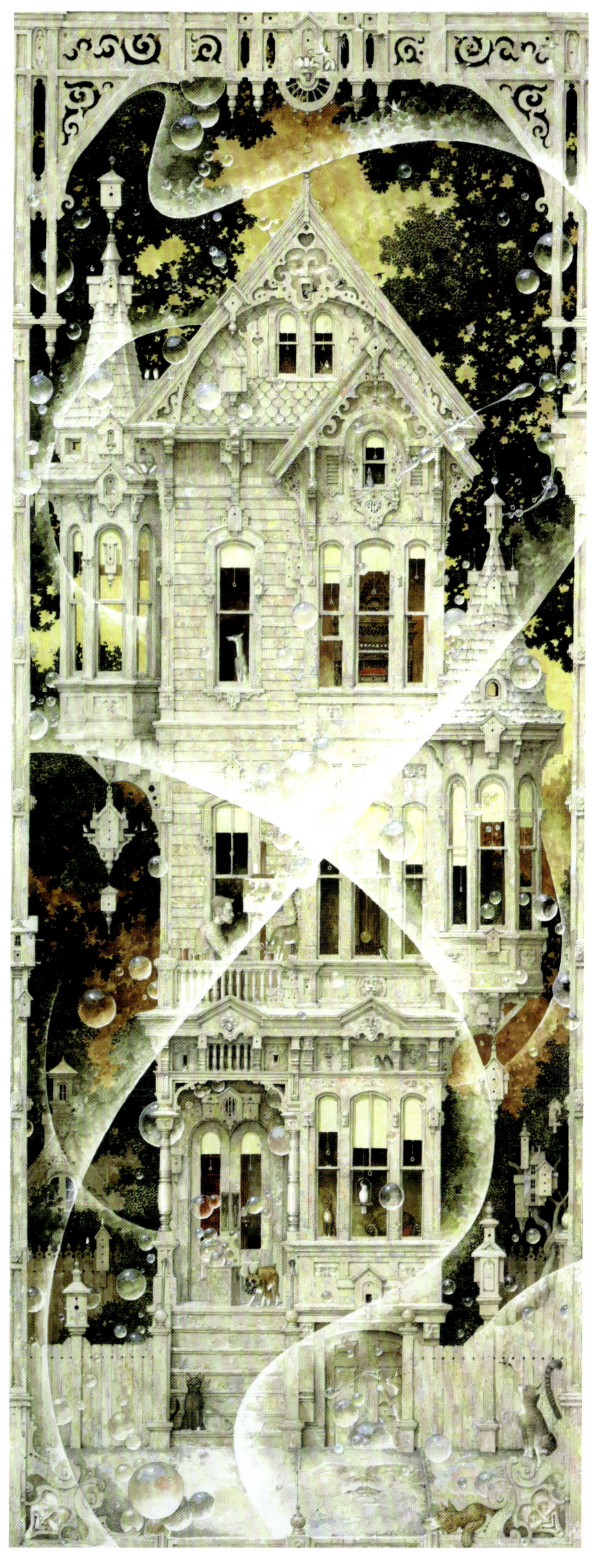

Dish Soap
1997, watercolor on paper
37.1" x 14.5"

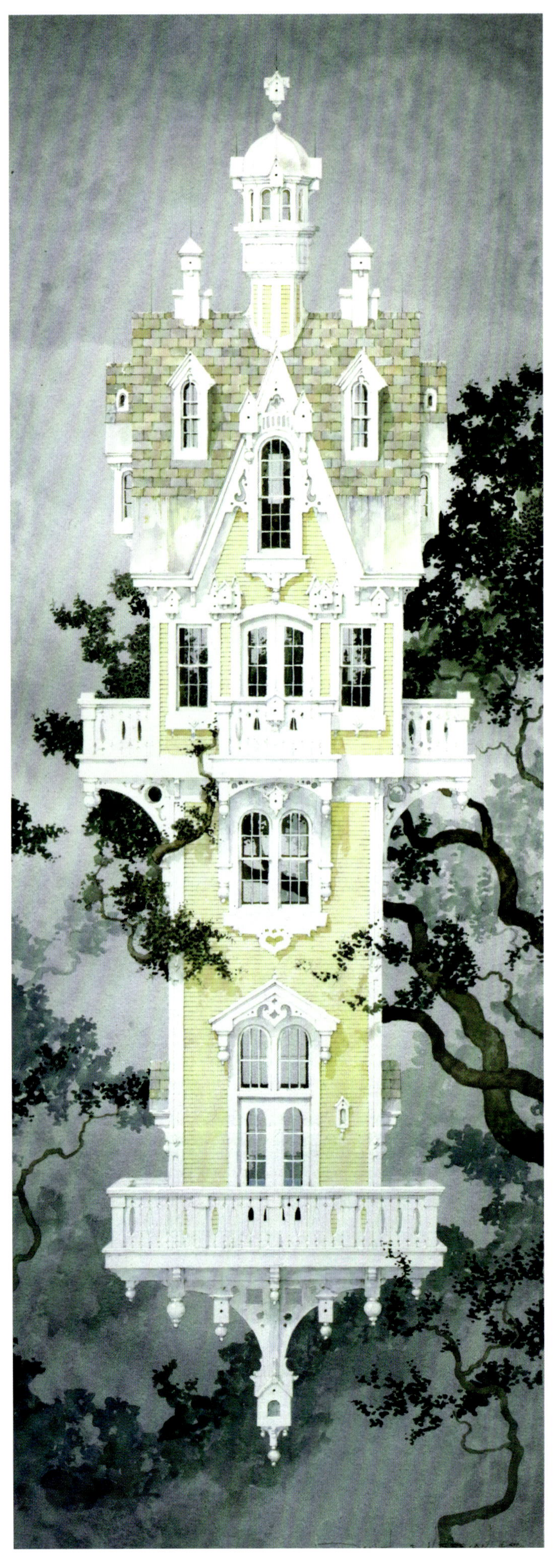

Out on a Limb
1996, watercolor on paper
21" x 7.5"

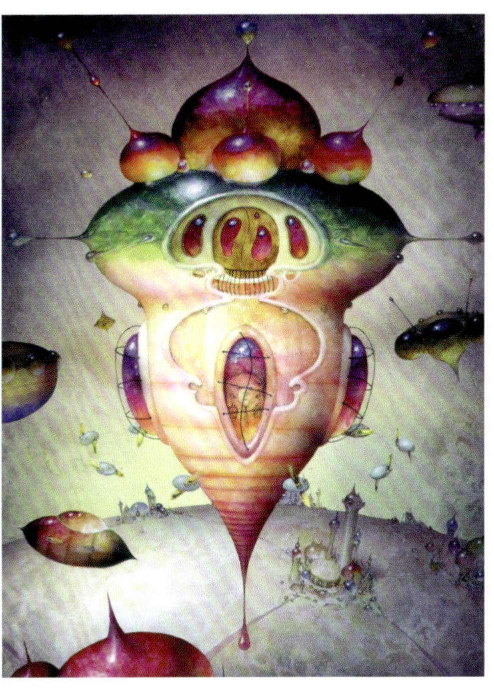

Satellite
1996, watercolor on paper
15.5" x 12"

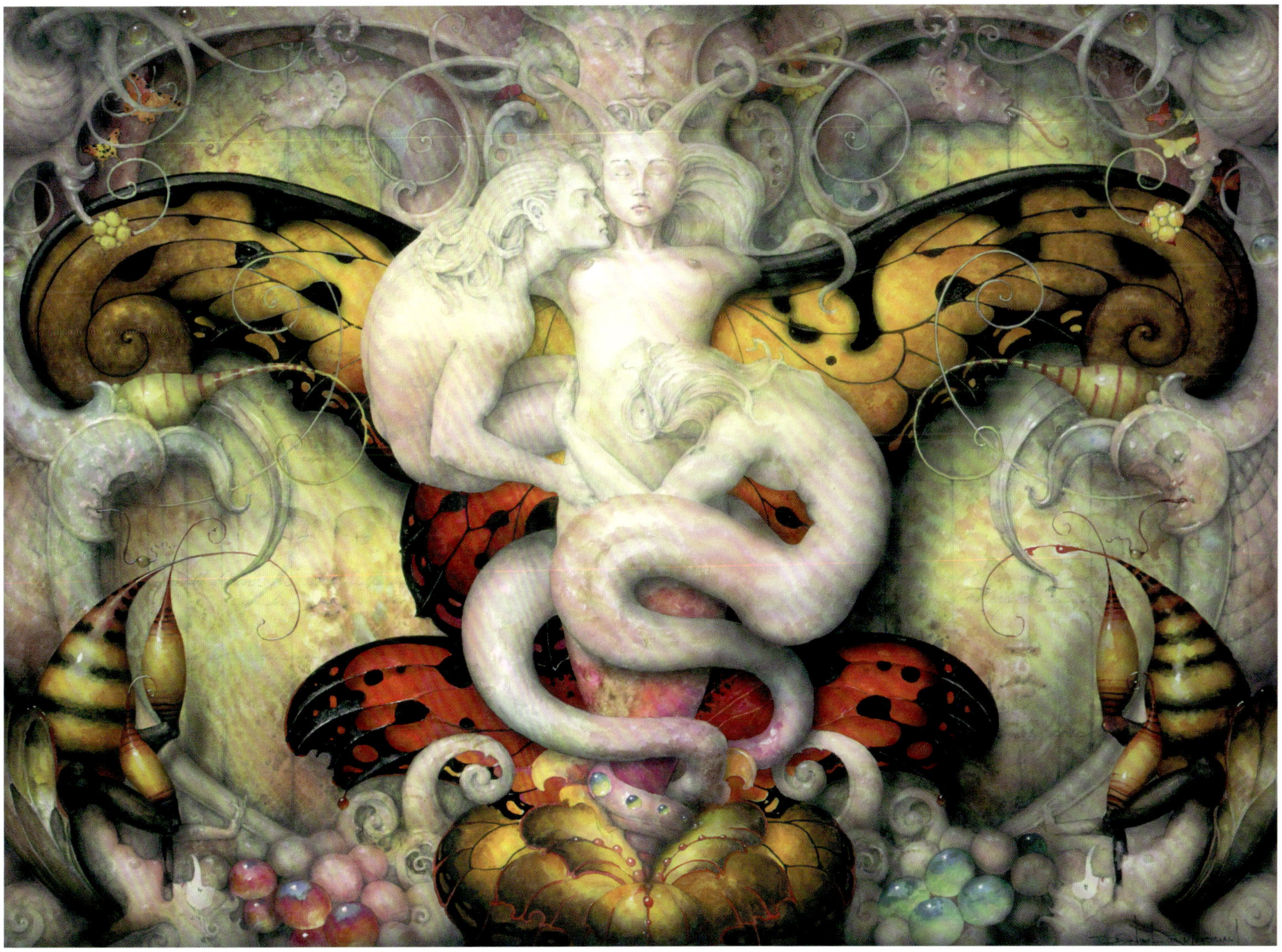

The Embrace
1996, watercolor on paper
28" x 36"

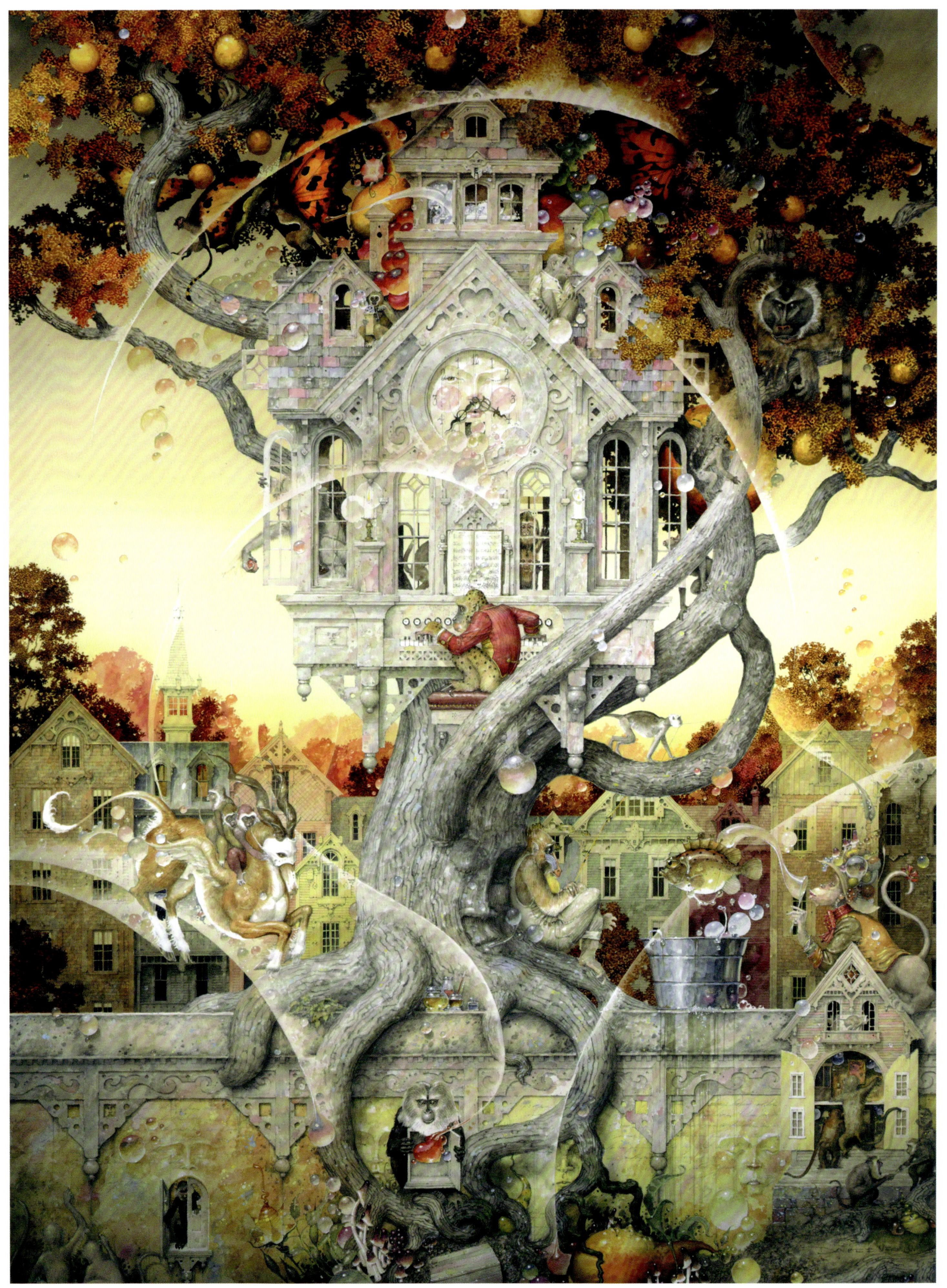

Tail Spin
1996, watercolor on paper
46" x 34.5"

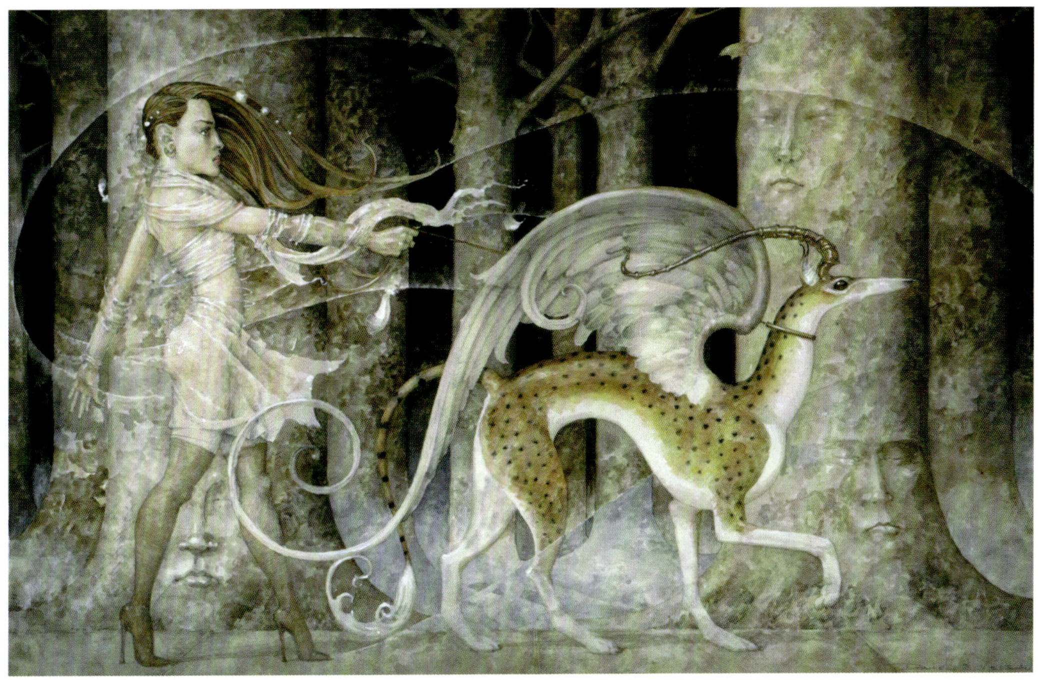

A WALK IN THE WILD
1997, WATERCOLOR ON PAPER
12.5" X 20.9"

INSPIRATION

I find inspiration in the work of many artists. I am enthralled by the paintings of Hieronymus Bosch, who thought the impossible and blatantly, yet subliminally, taught us its lessons. His images are saturated with obscure, profound messages that likely eluded many of those who commissioned his works. The art of Salvador Dali, with its vivid and disquieting vision, lead me beyond reasoned thought and into the realm of boundless abstraction. Through paintings that were hallucinogenic daydreams, Dali depicted the movement of disinhibited imagery. Perhaps they are footprints of a path less traveled. Maybe they are the longings for something much more than this world can offer. Or perhaps these puzzling views are the reflections of human ideas inverted so that we can see their secrets.

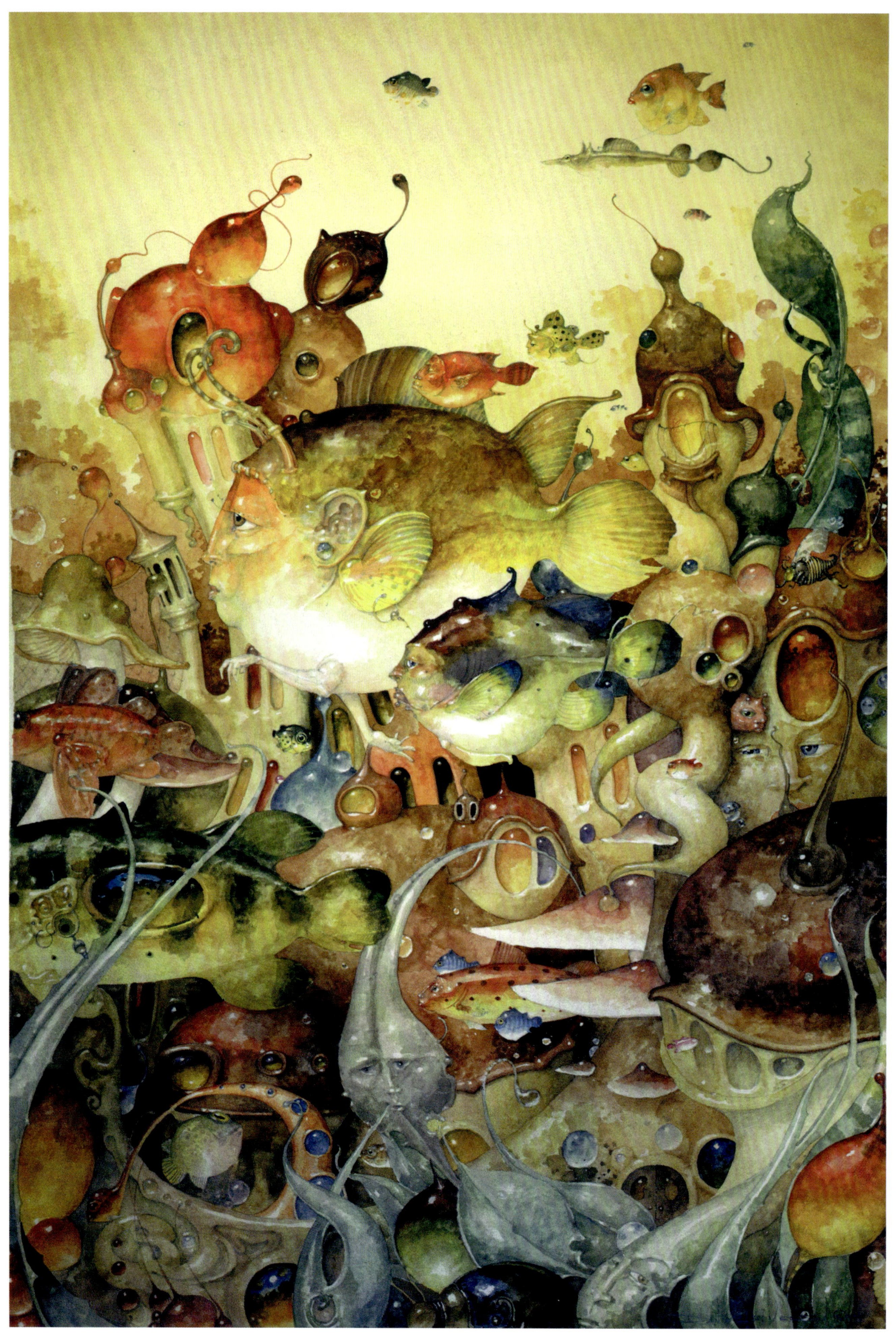

Undertow
1997, watercolor on paper
19.75" x 13.75"

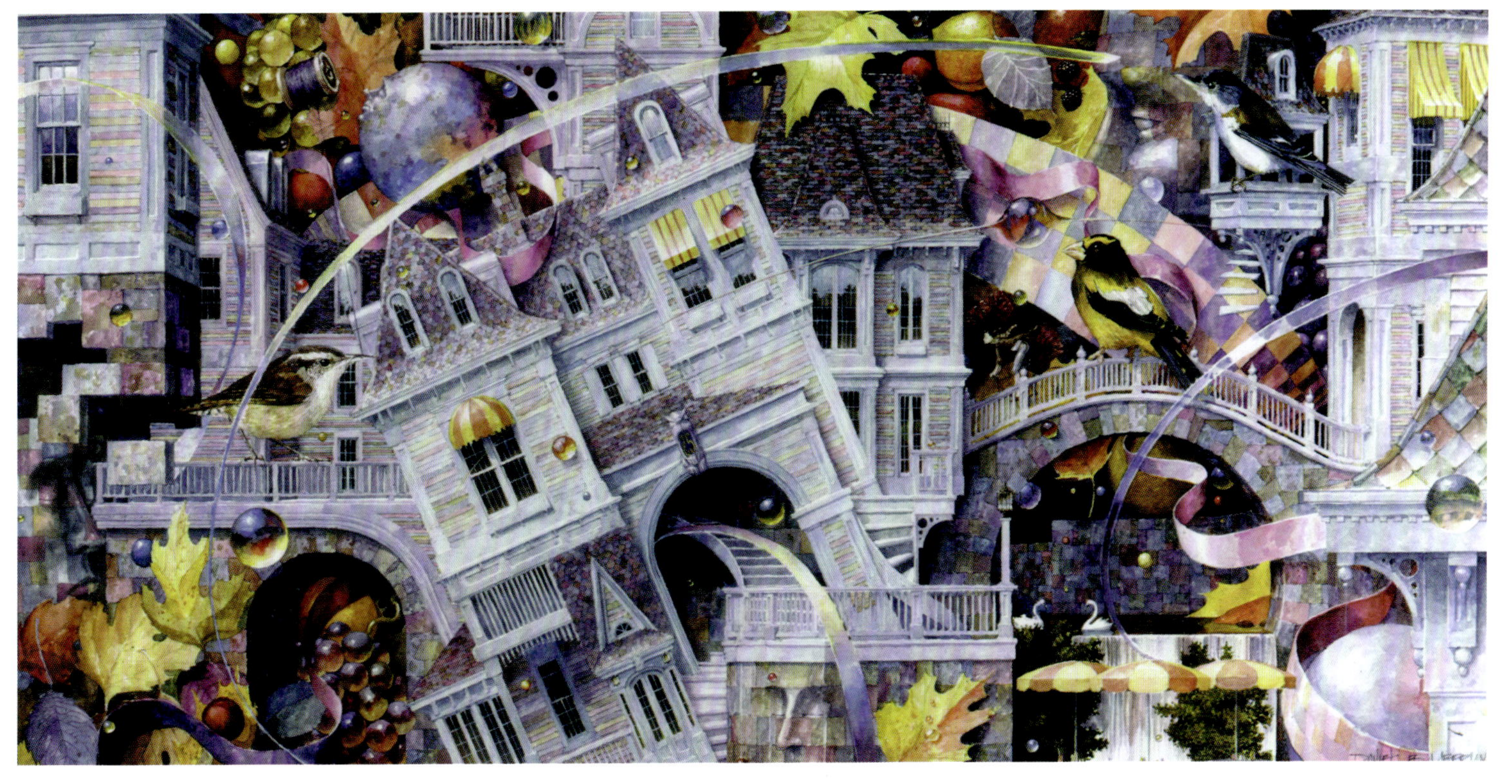

25 Blue Street
1990, watercolor on paper
a. 30" x 14"

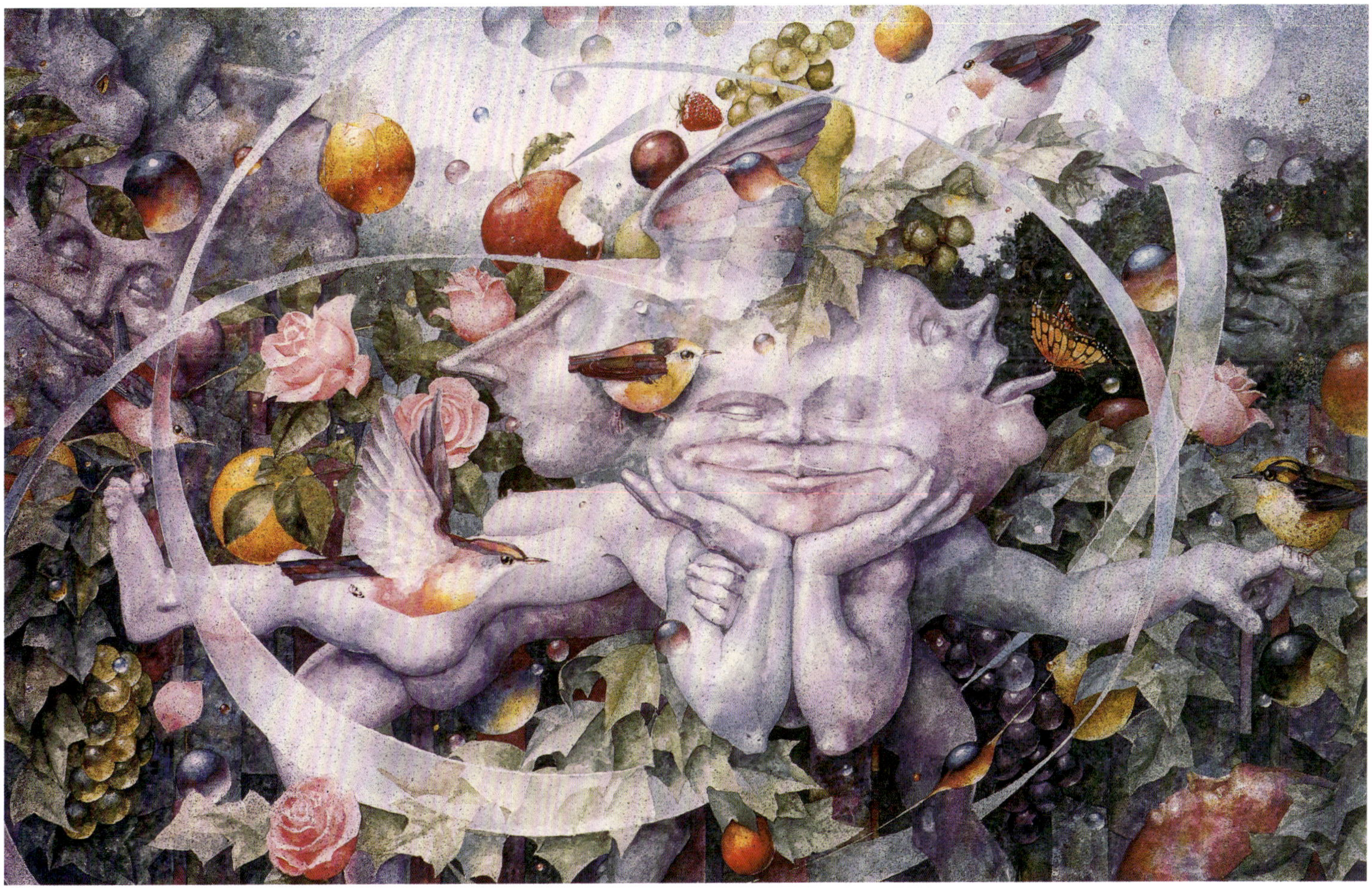

A Tranquil Note
1992, watercolor on paper
a. 22" x 14"

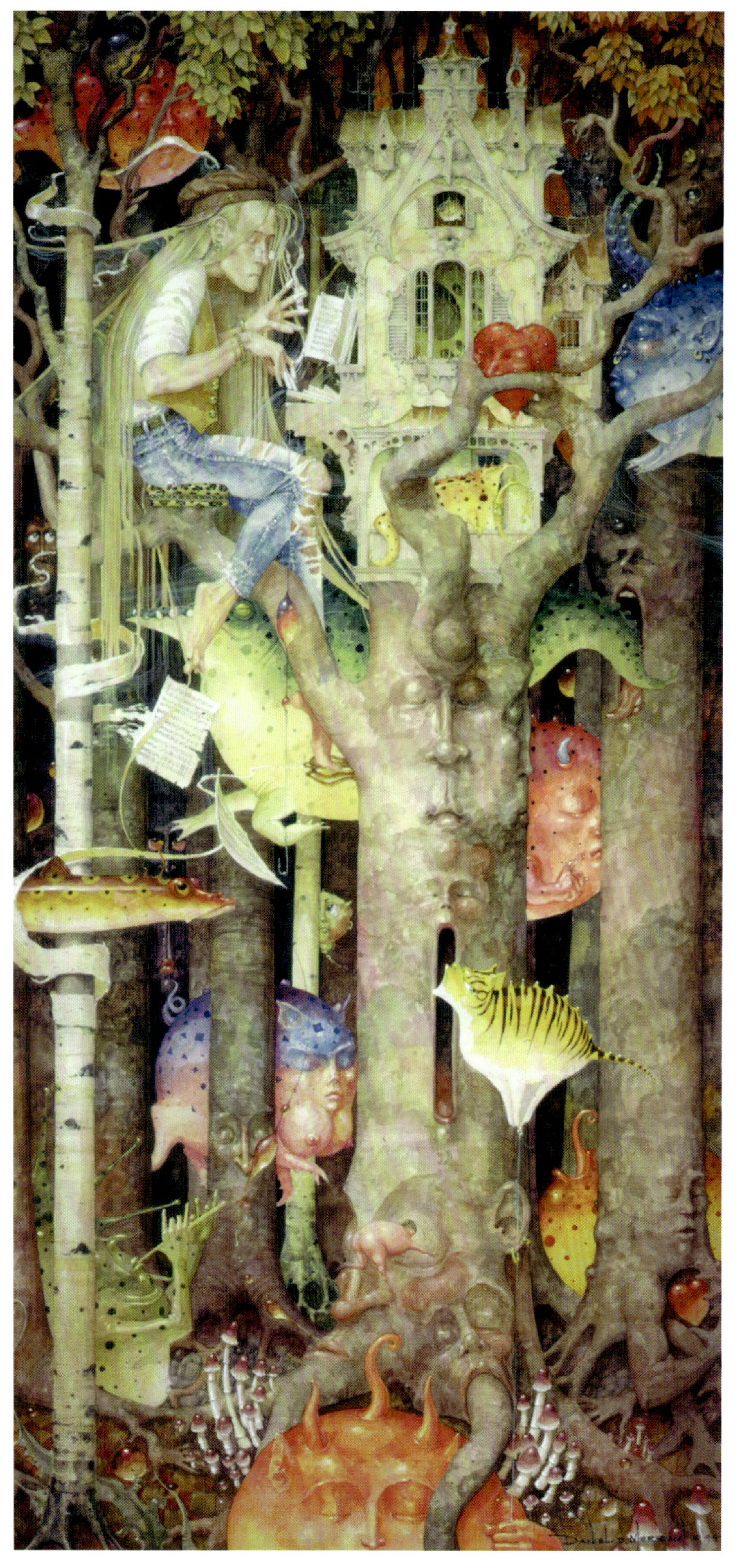

Triano
1994, watercolor on paper
a. 30" x 14"

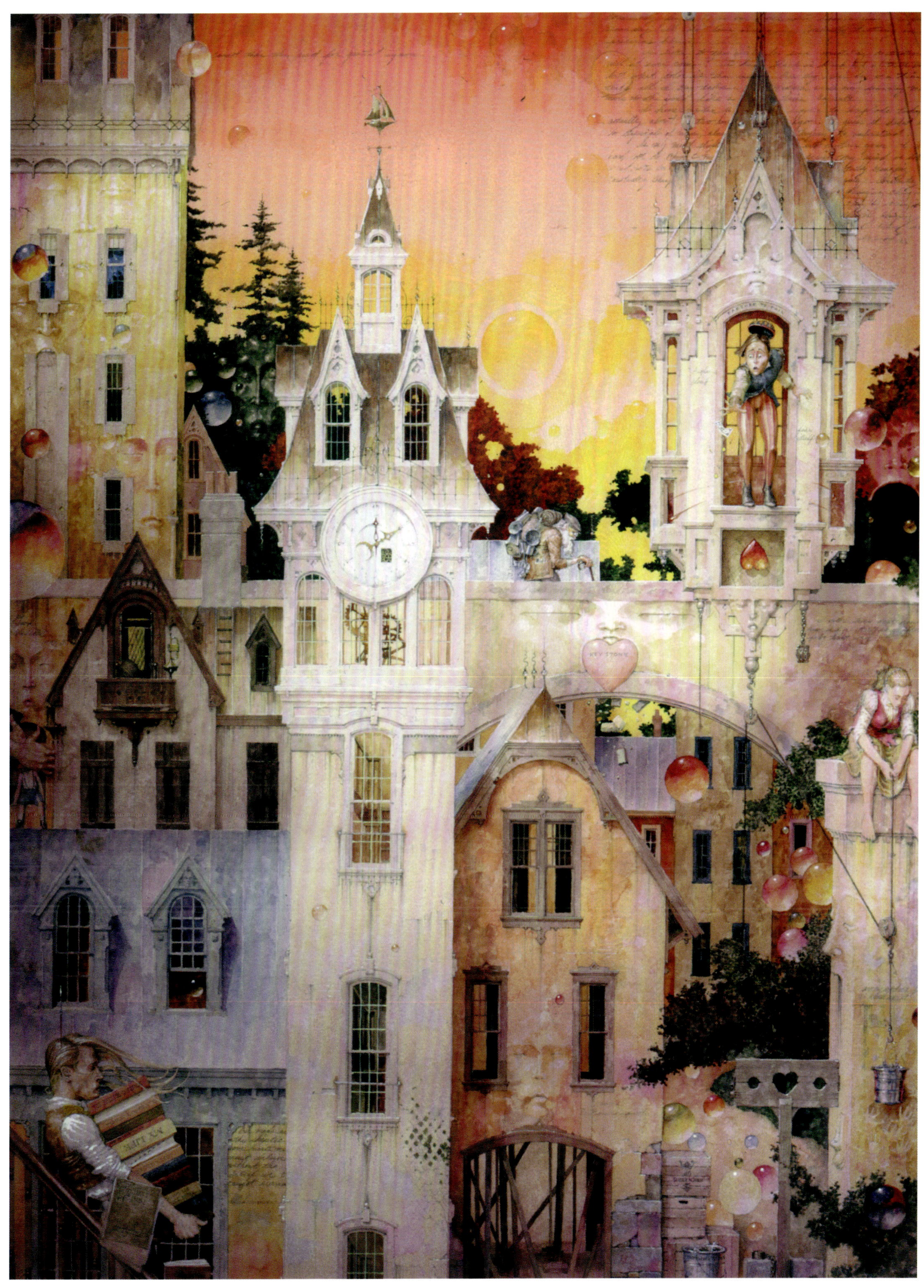

Constant Climb
1994, watercolor on paper
a. 30" x 22"

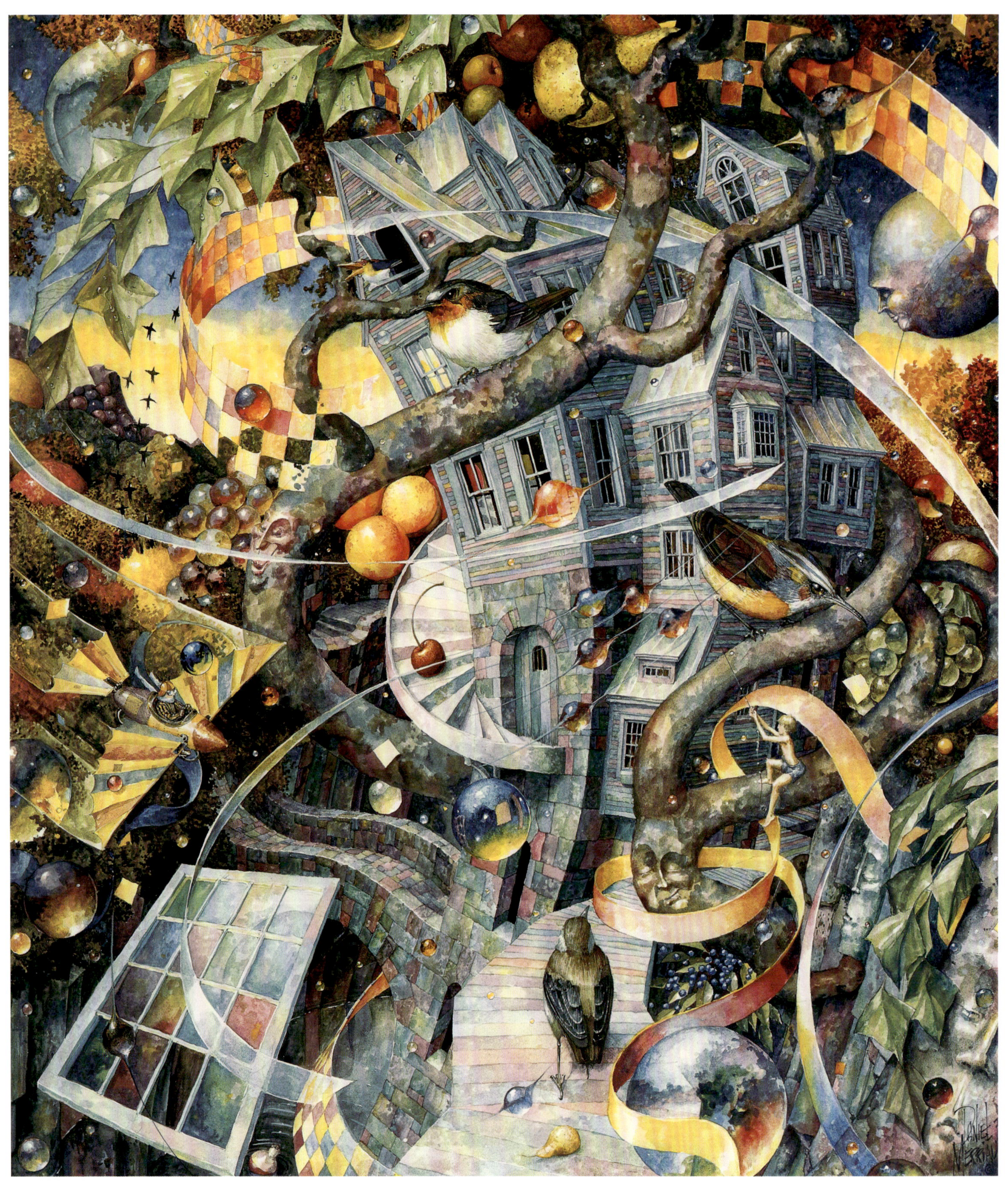

Autumn Breeze

1992, watercolor on paper

a. 20" x 18"

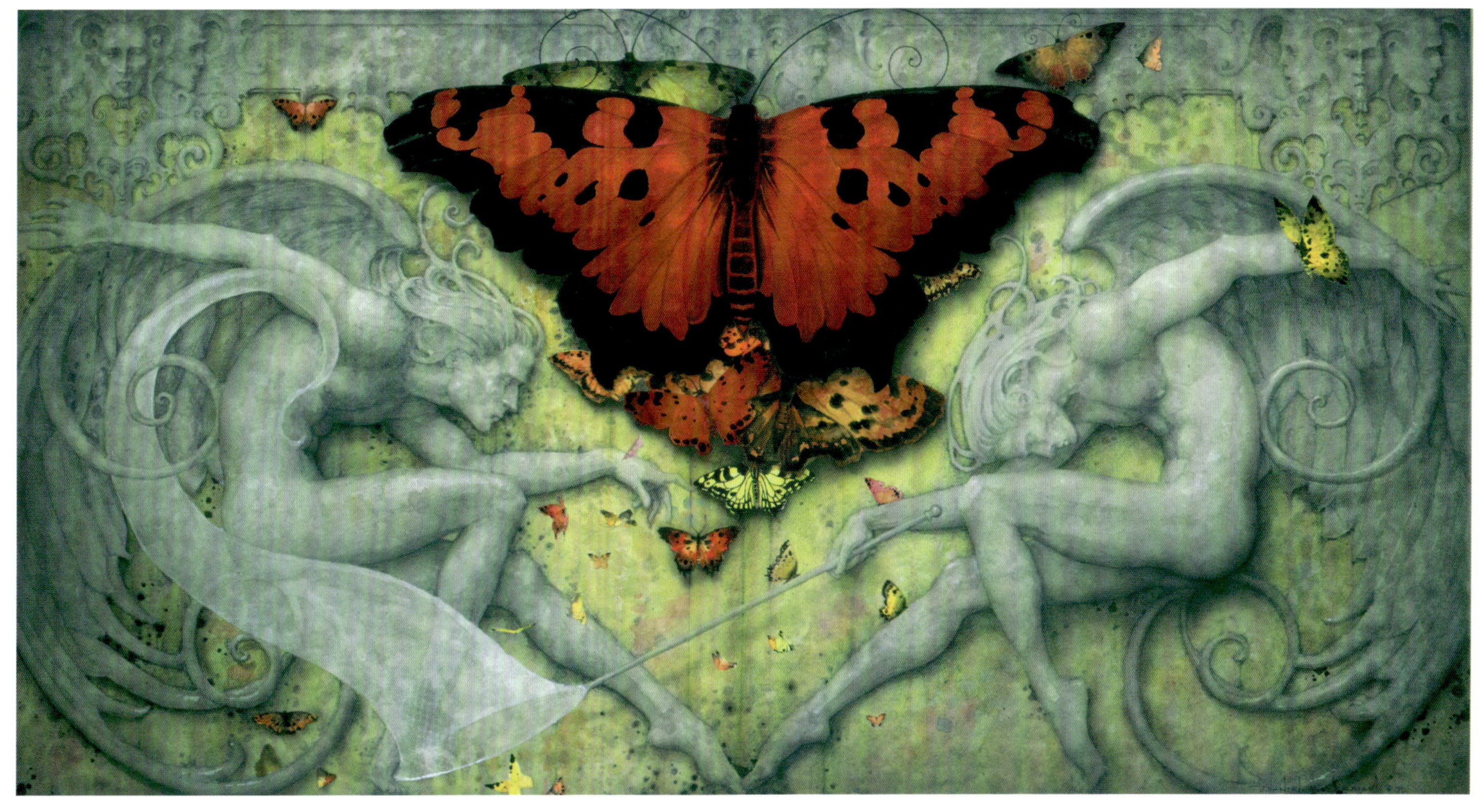

ALLURE
1995, WATERCOLOR ON PAPER
A. 14" X 30"

VISION

At a very young age, I began experimenting with watercolors. I found the translucent qualities of this medium to reveal the values of light, thus creating depth. The continual changes in tonalities allowed me endless possibilities as I layered strokes of pigment, creating limitless variations in color. The challenge to control the medium required a discipline that brought with it a natural sense of timing, rhythm, and fluidity. It required cycles of carefully timed fusions of paint and a subtle wiping of the brush to maintain the perfect moistness for the desired effects. As a subtractive sculptor carves at his stone, I combined the images in my mind with the sweep of my brush.

From dawn till dusk, I always make good use of daylight, painting to the rhythm of multiple styles of music as the hours slip away. I work in a trancelike meditative state, where unfiltered, raw, chaotic images flow from the essence of what's beneath my conscious facade. Within this hidden world spins the gateway to infinity. I sometimes stop to find I have not even been aware of the passage of time.

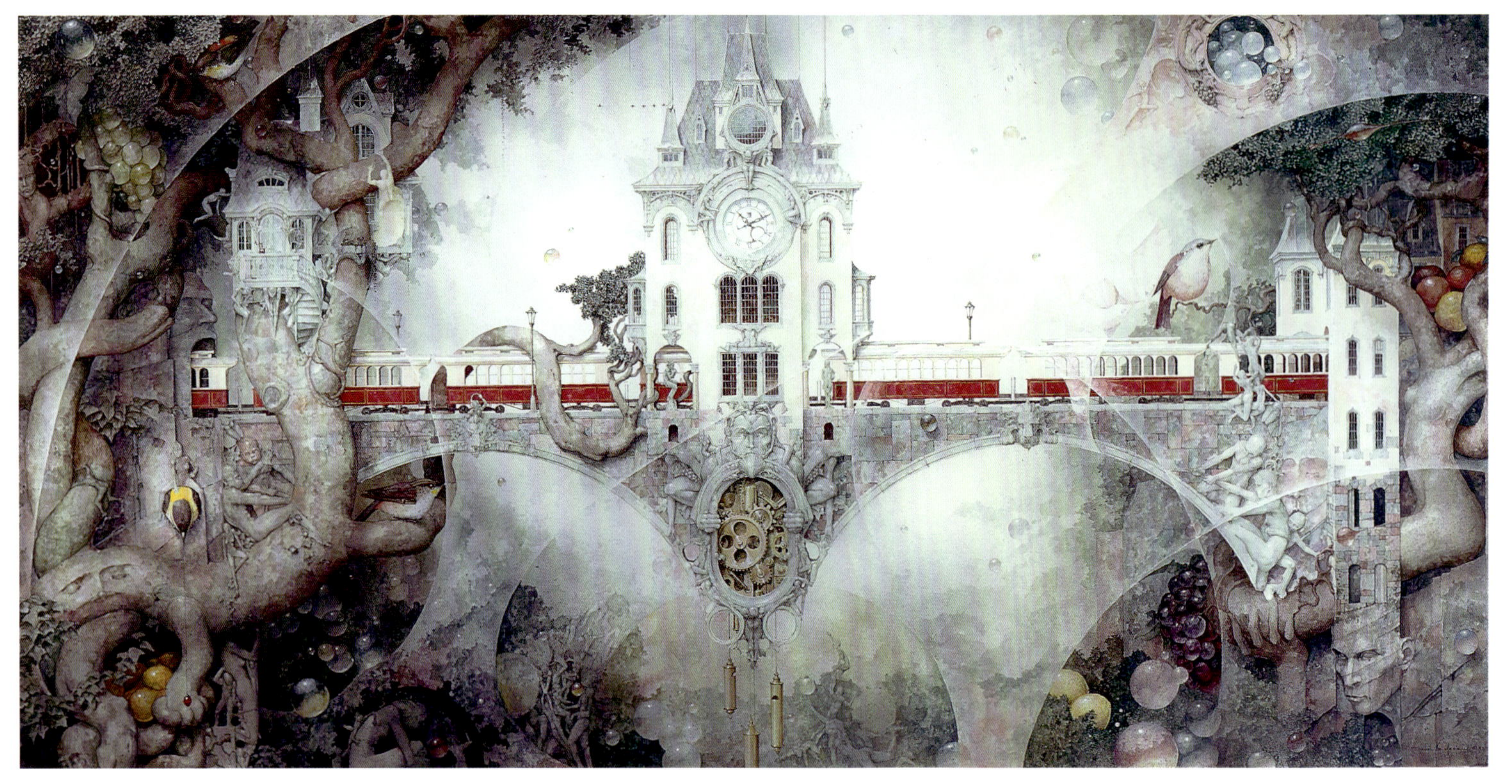

Bridging the Distance
1993, watercolor on paper
a. 30" x 60"

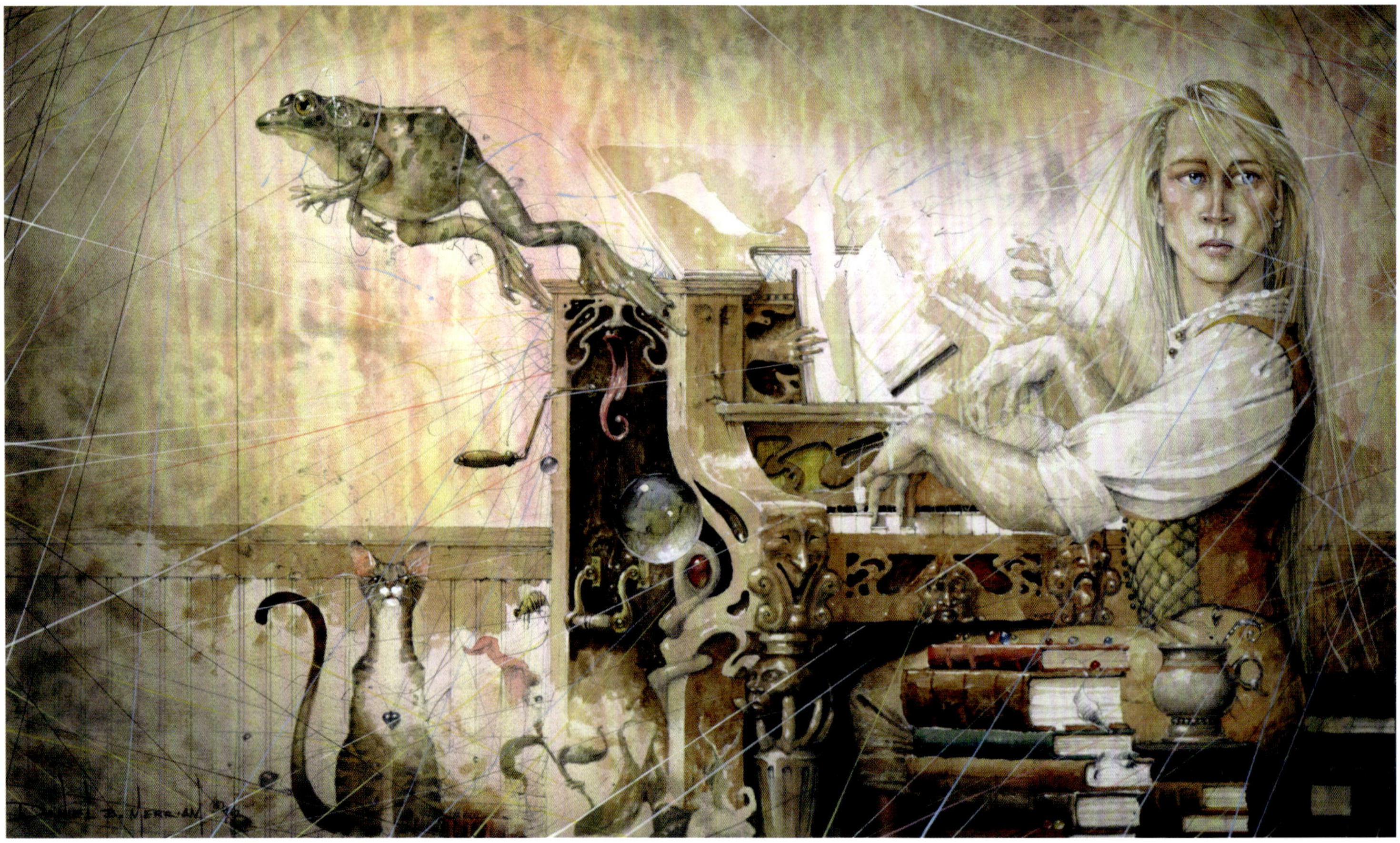

Higher Octave
1995, watercolor on paper
a. 11" x 22"

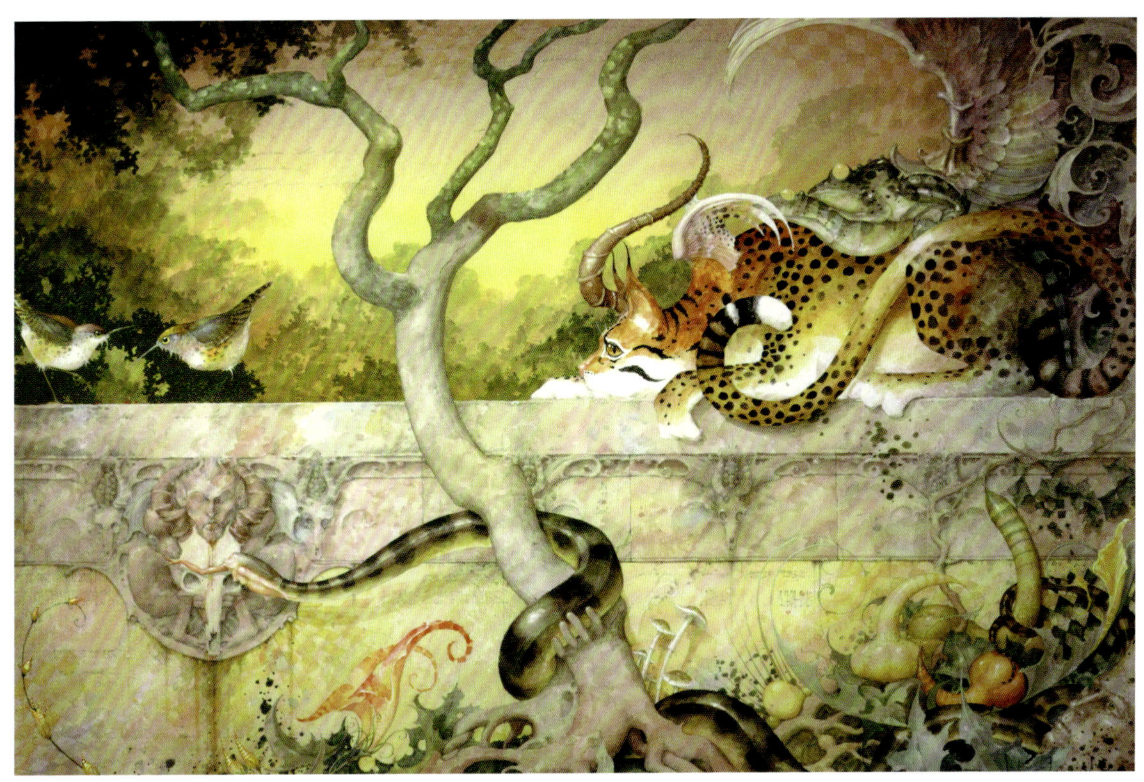

EDEN
1994, WATERCOLOR ON PAPER
A. 18" X 30"

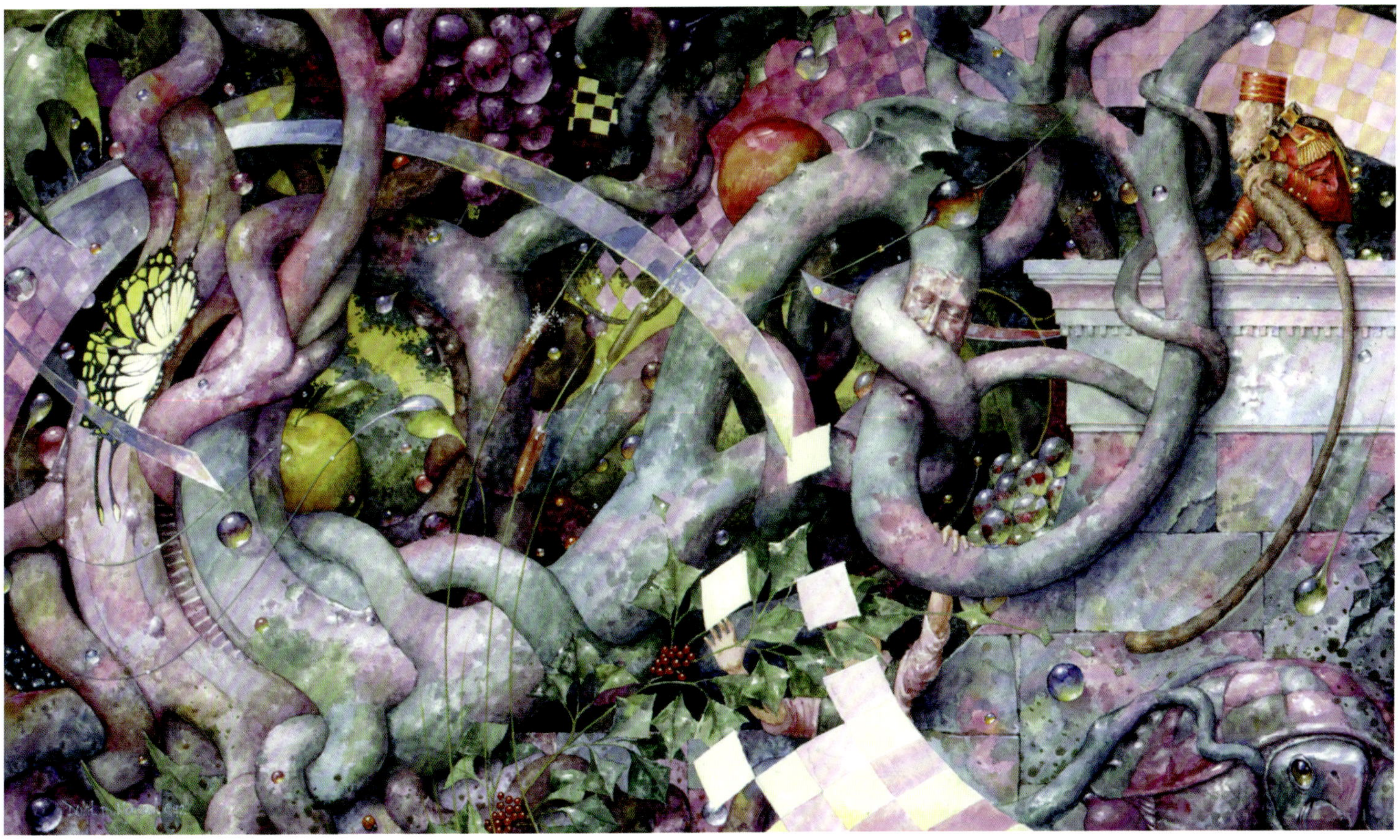

ESCAPE TO FREEDOM
1992, WATERCOLOR ON PAPER
16" X 28"

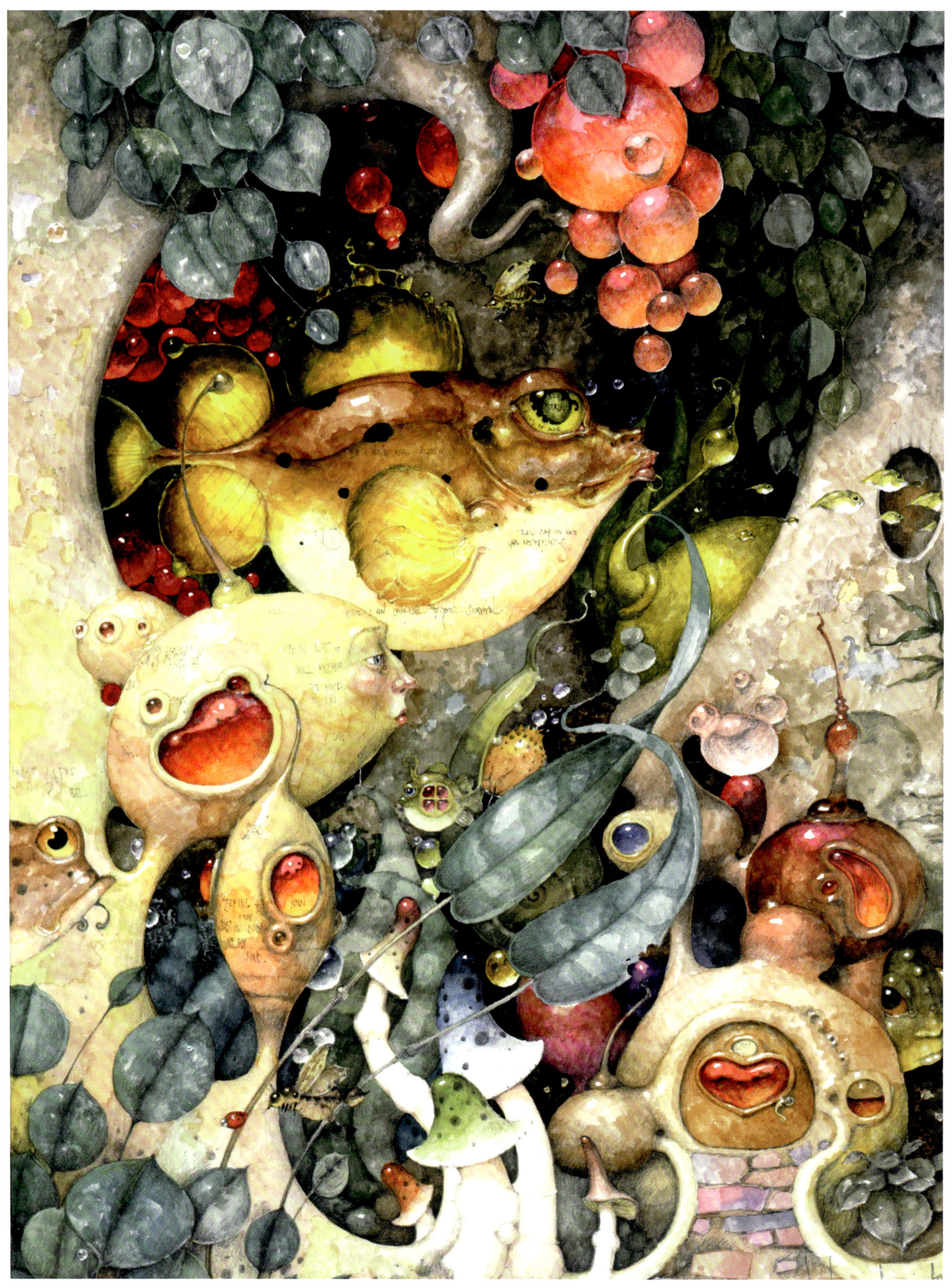

EYES OF AGE
1997, WATERCOLOR ON PAPER
16" X 12"

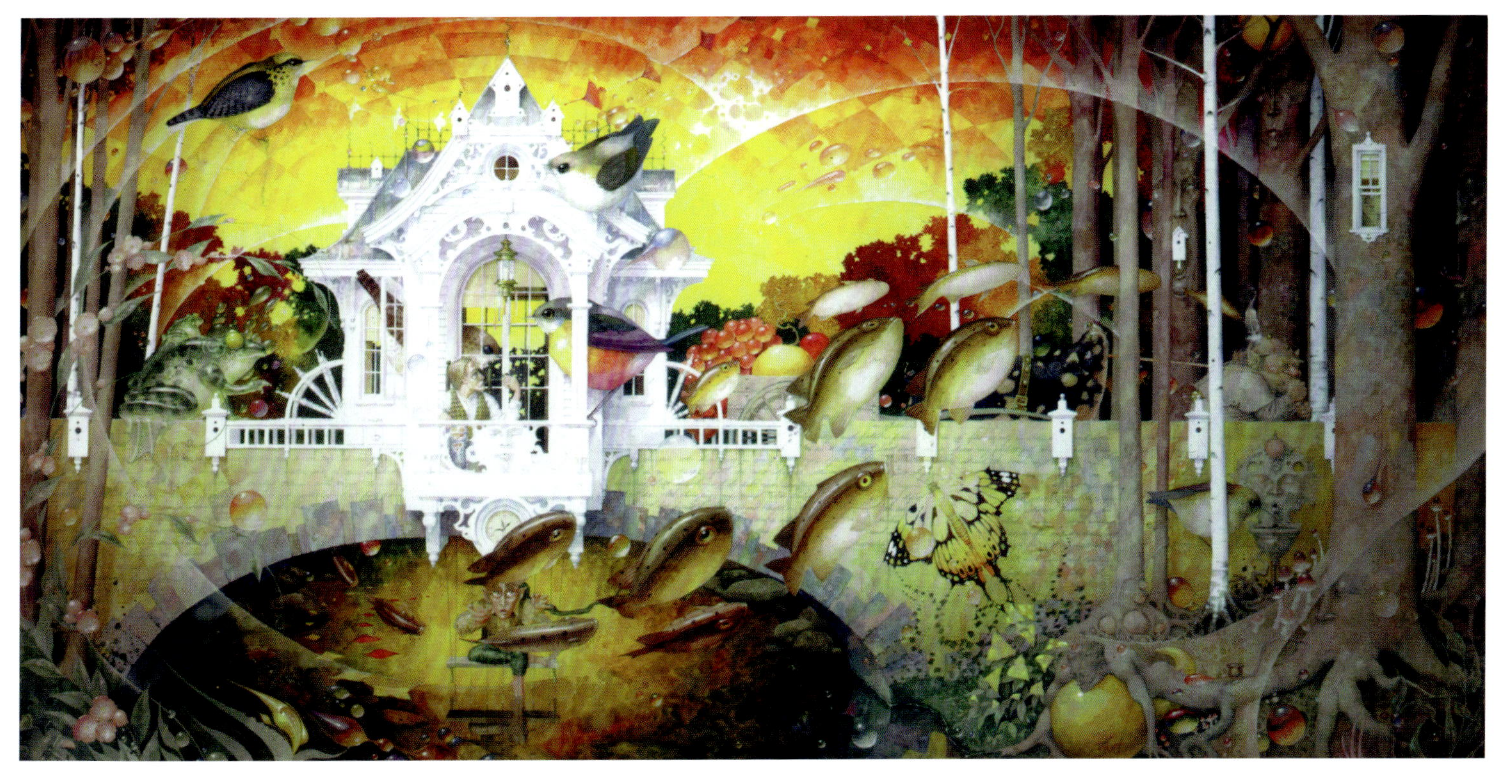

Indian Summer
1995, watercolor on paper
a. 24" x 50"

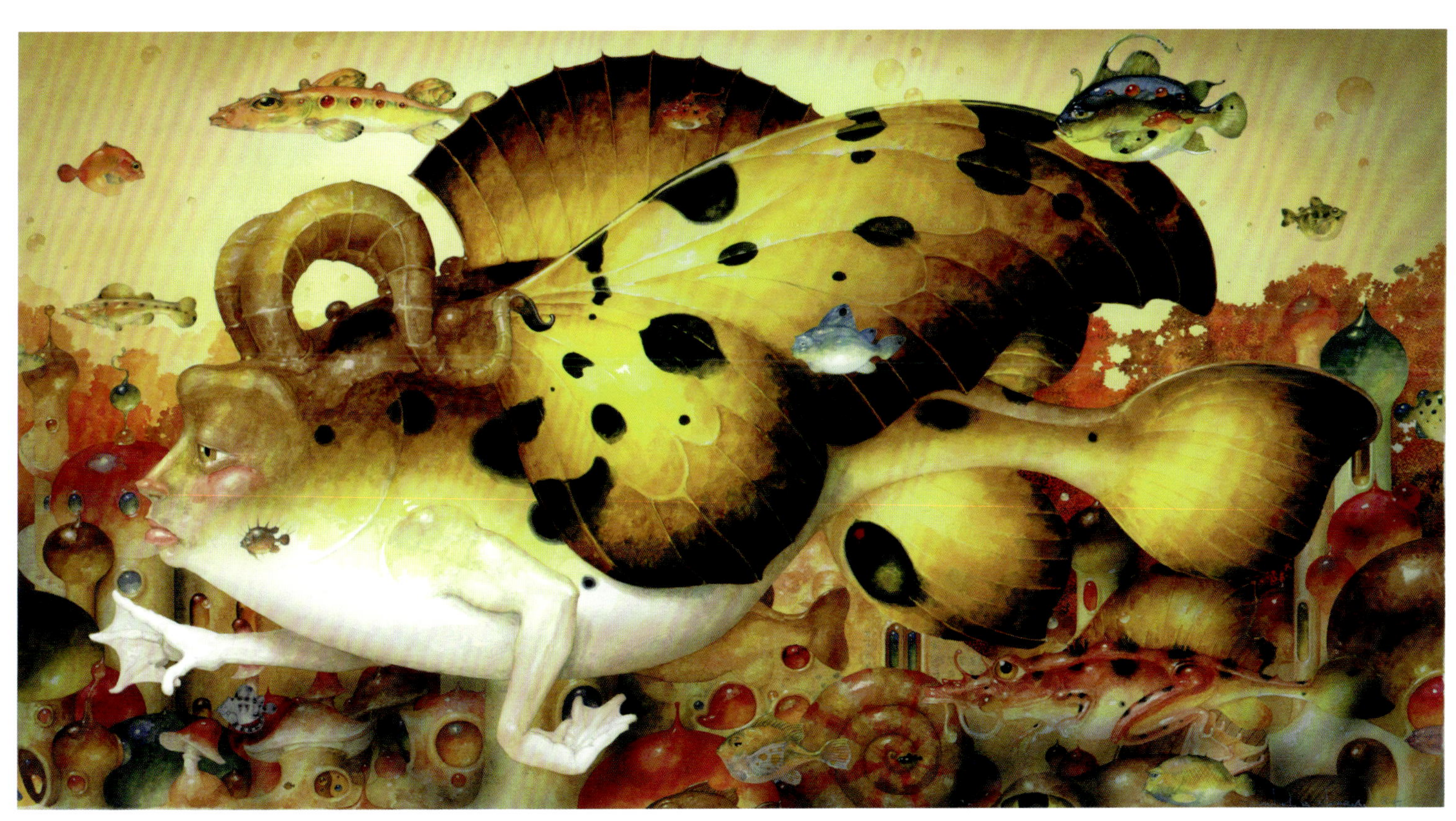

Destination Unknown
1997, watercolor on paper
18.25" x 34"

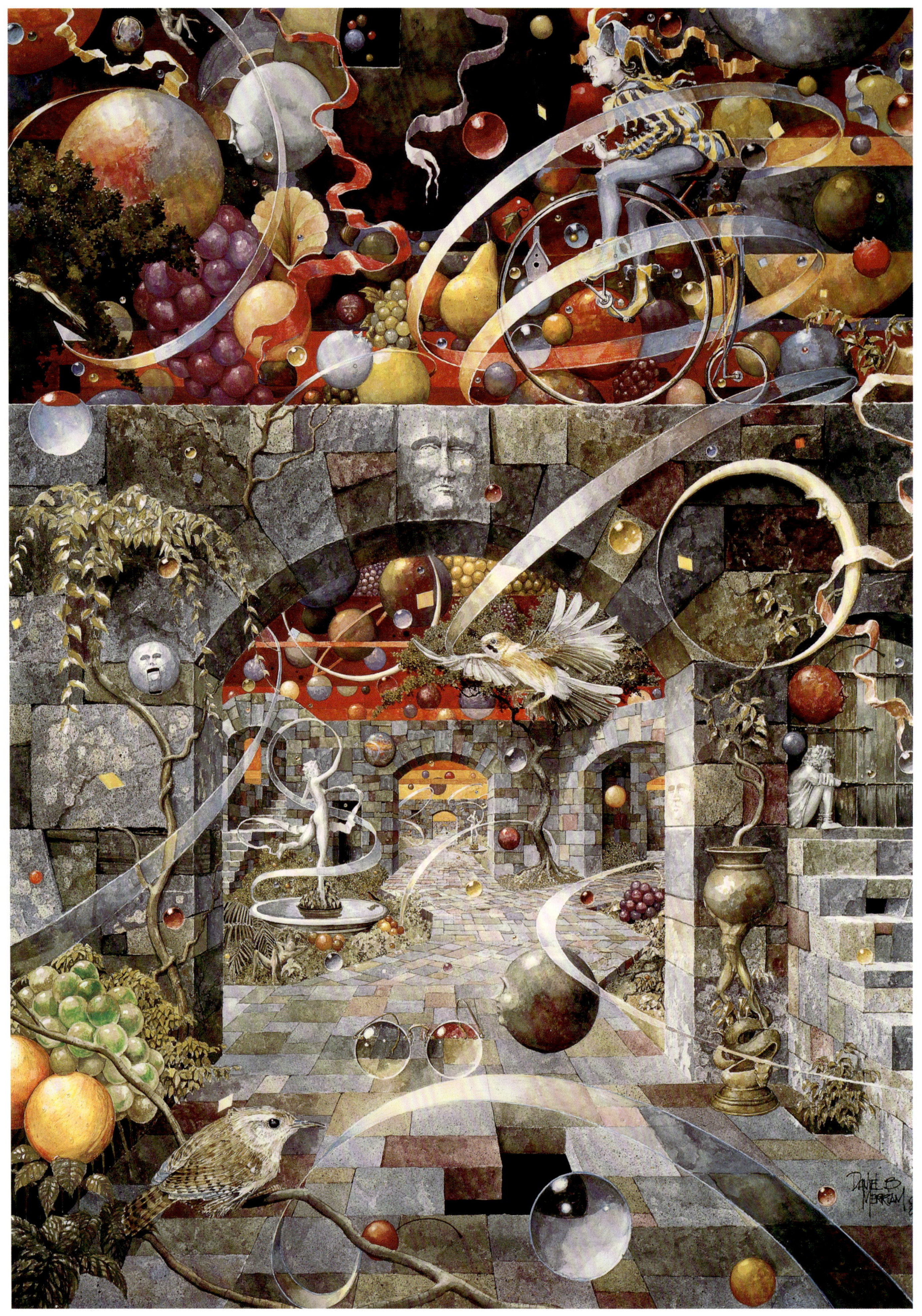

Eternity

1988, watercolor on paper

a. 30" x 20"

Expression

In my paintings, there appear various objects that are abstract only to the conscious mind. Symbols involving food, sexuality, and familiar ornamentations are cursors driven from primitive desires; they keep the eye moving through the painting with a perpetual energy. The bubbles, the faces, the queer and ever-changing surfaces all echo this blissful world, which dances to the edge of frightfulness. Houses are built on precarious cliffs and truth-defying fish fly past. In my art, I choose to enter dreamscapes I might not otherwise take the time to enjoy.

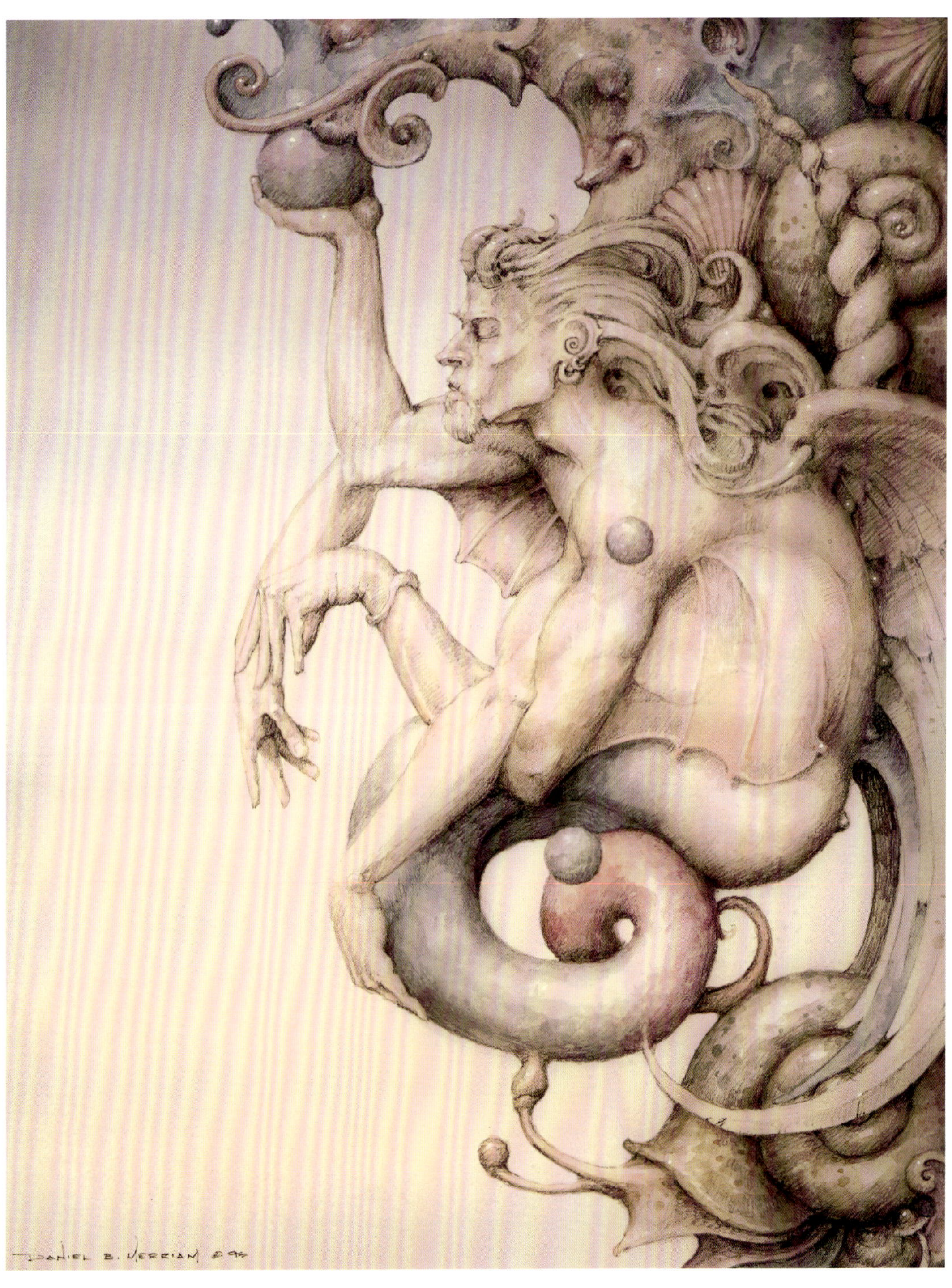

TWILIGHT
1995, WATERCOLOR ON PAPER
A. 11.25" X 9"

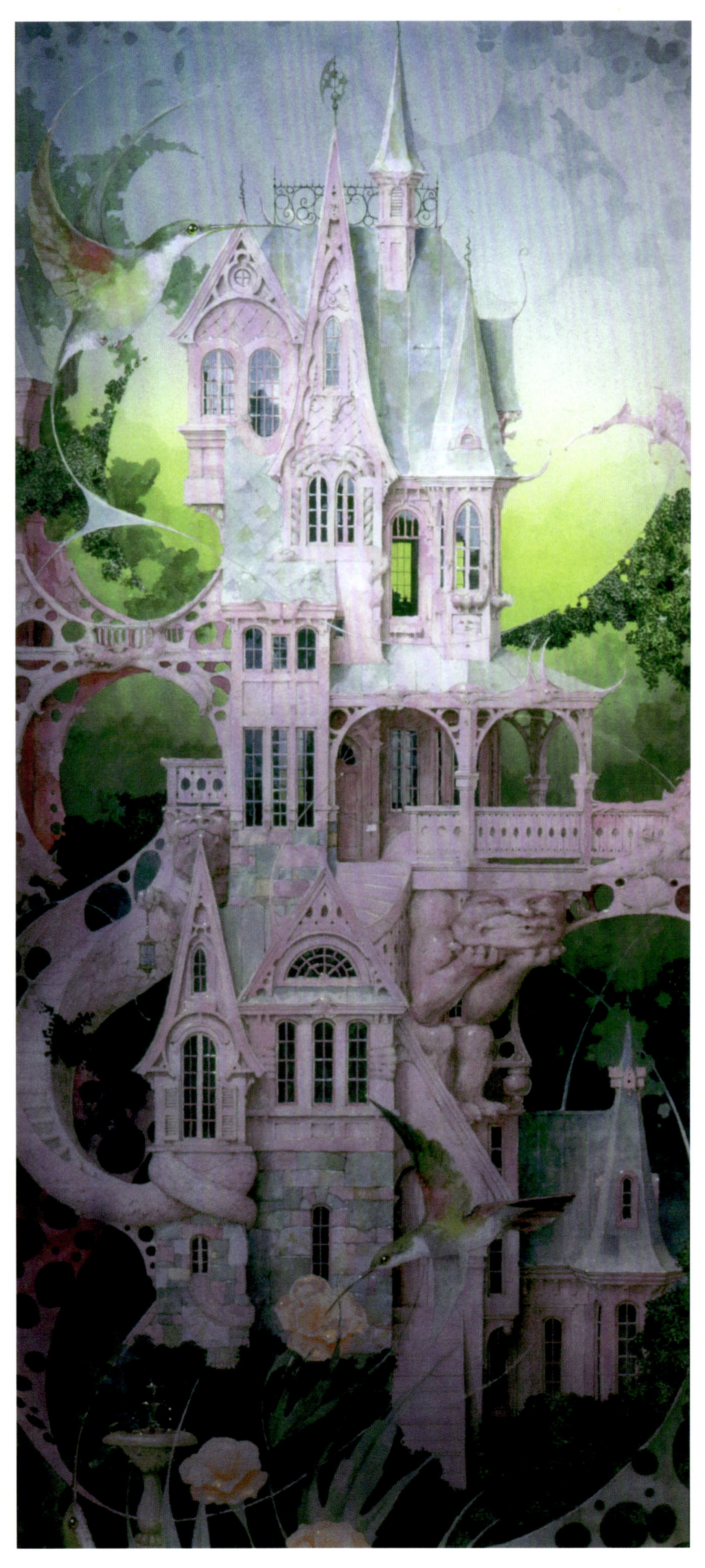

MYSTIC LACE
1992, WATERCOLOR ON PAPER
A. 30" X 14"

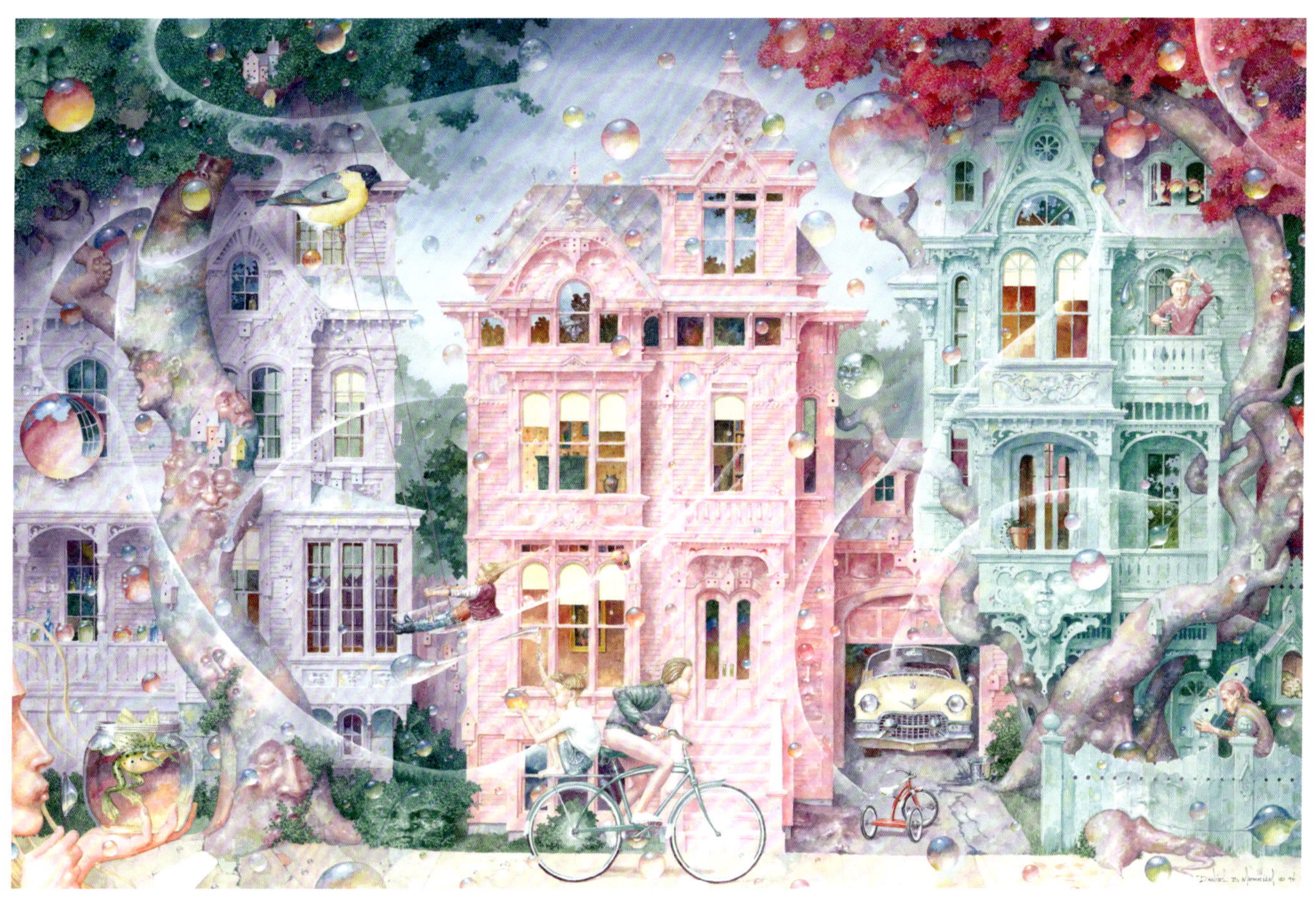

Bubble Street
1994, watercolor on paper
45.5" x 62"

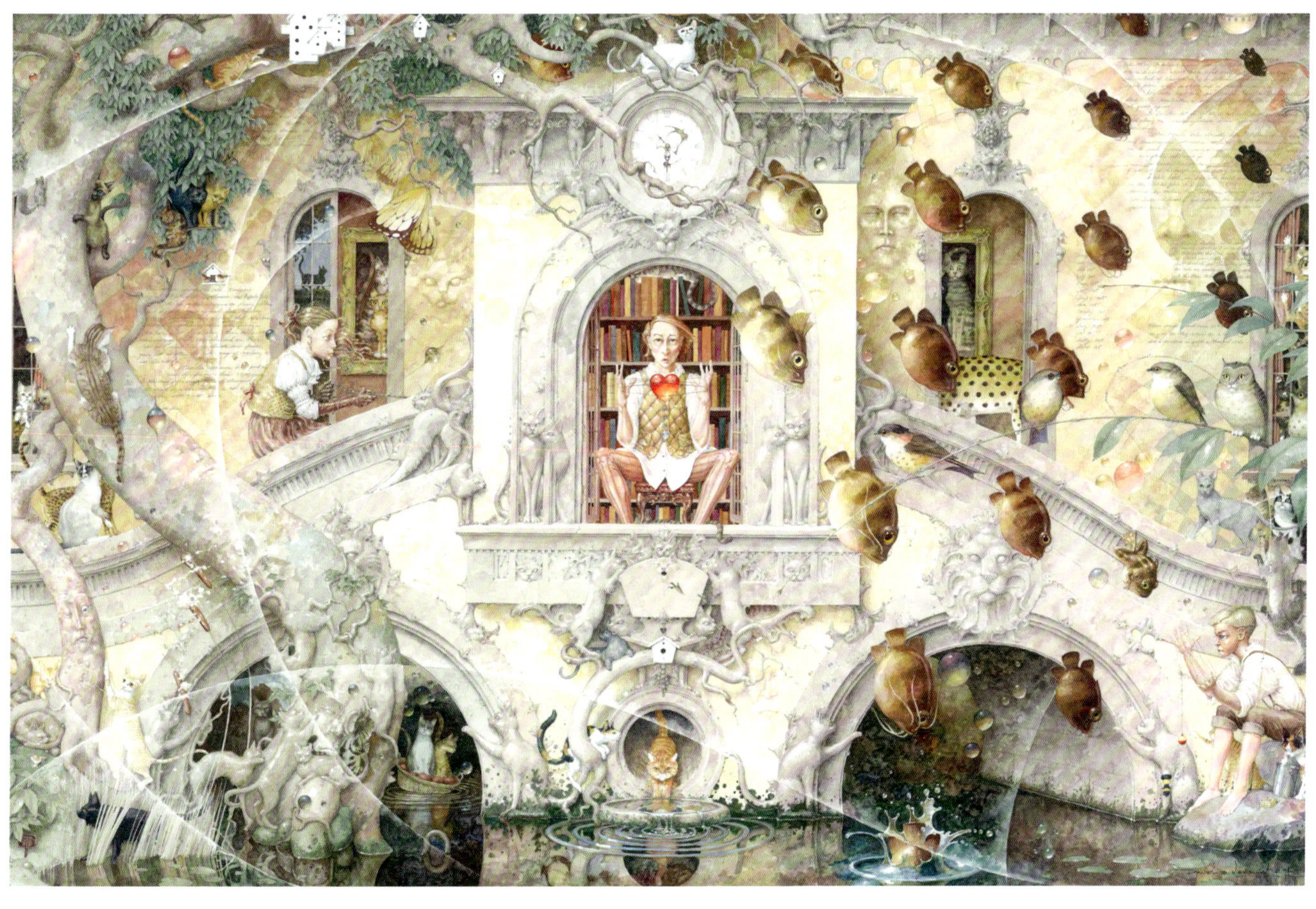

Cat's Cradle
1994, watercolor on paper
a. 30" x 50"

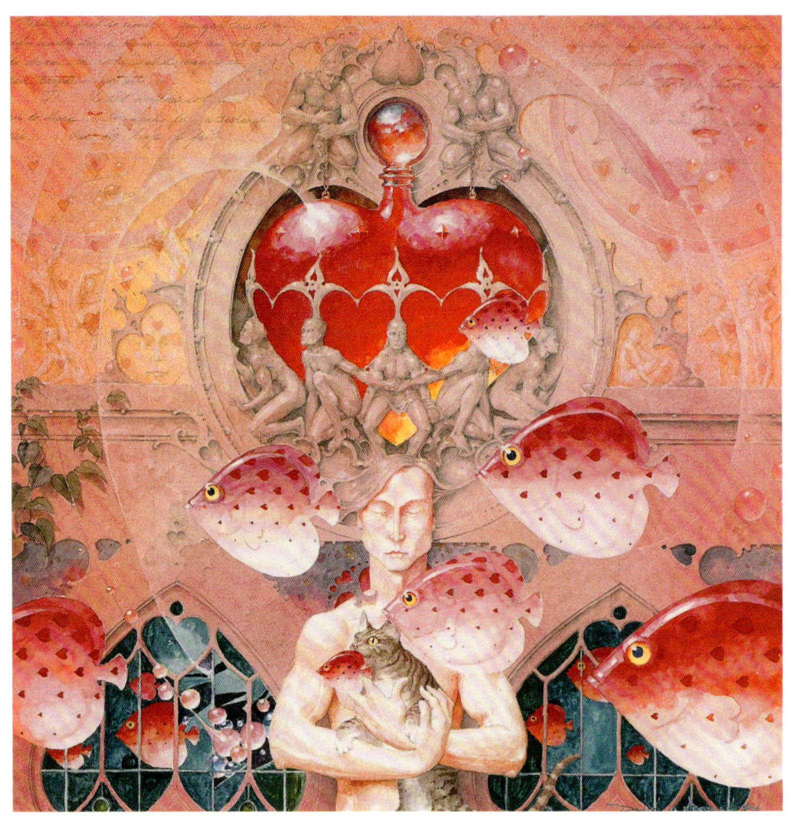

Tell-Tail Heart
1994, watercolor on paper
16" x 16"

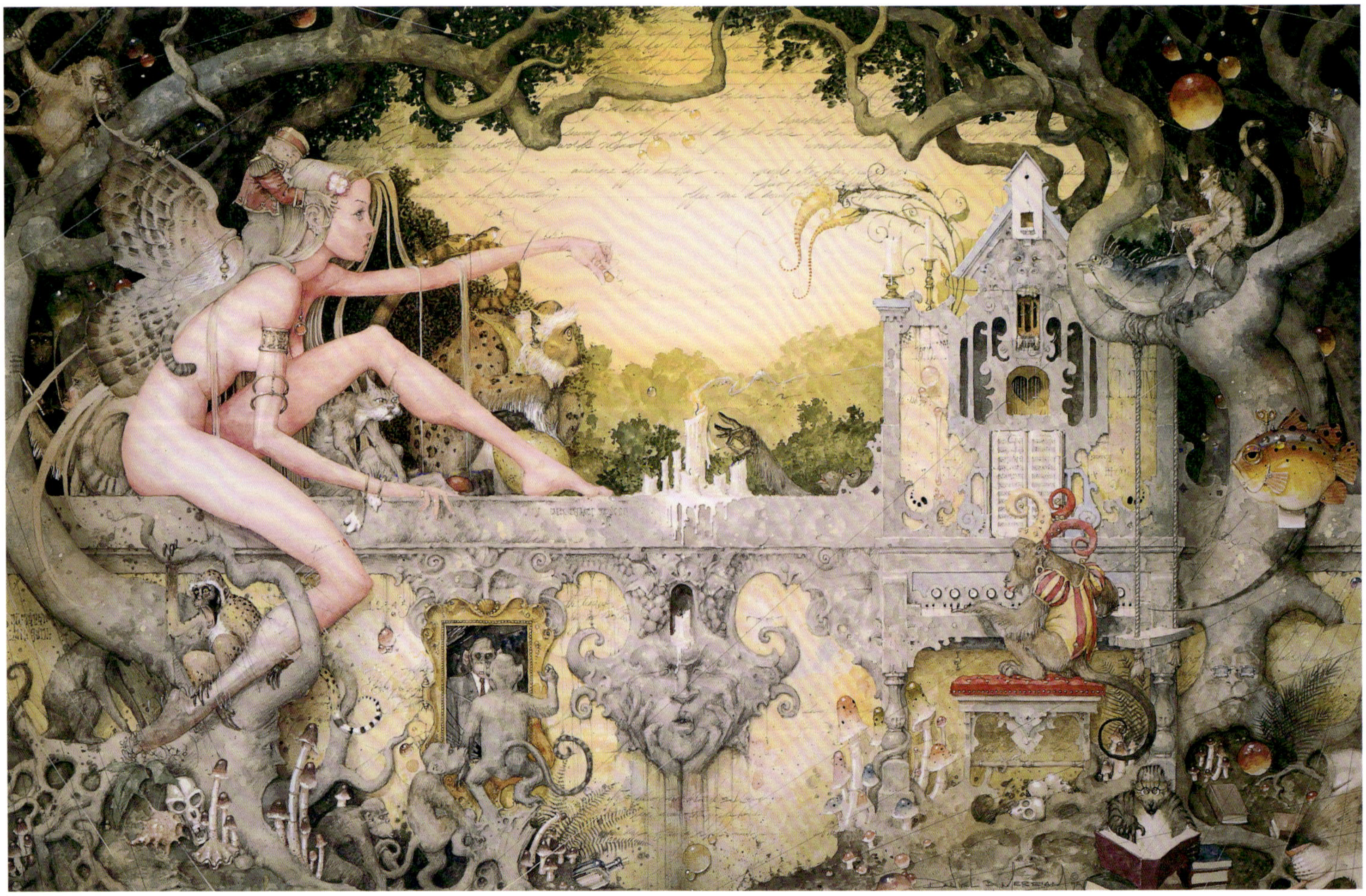

Monkey See
1995, watercolor on paper
a. 16" x 24"

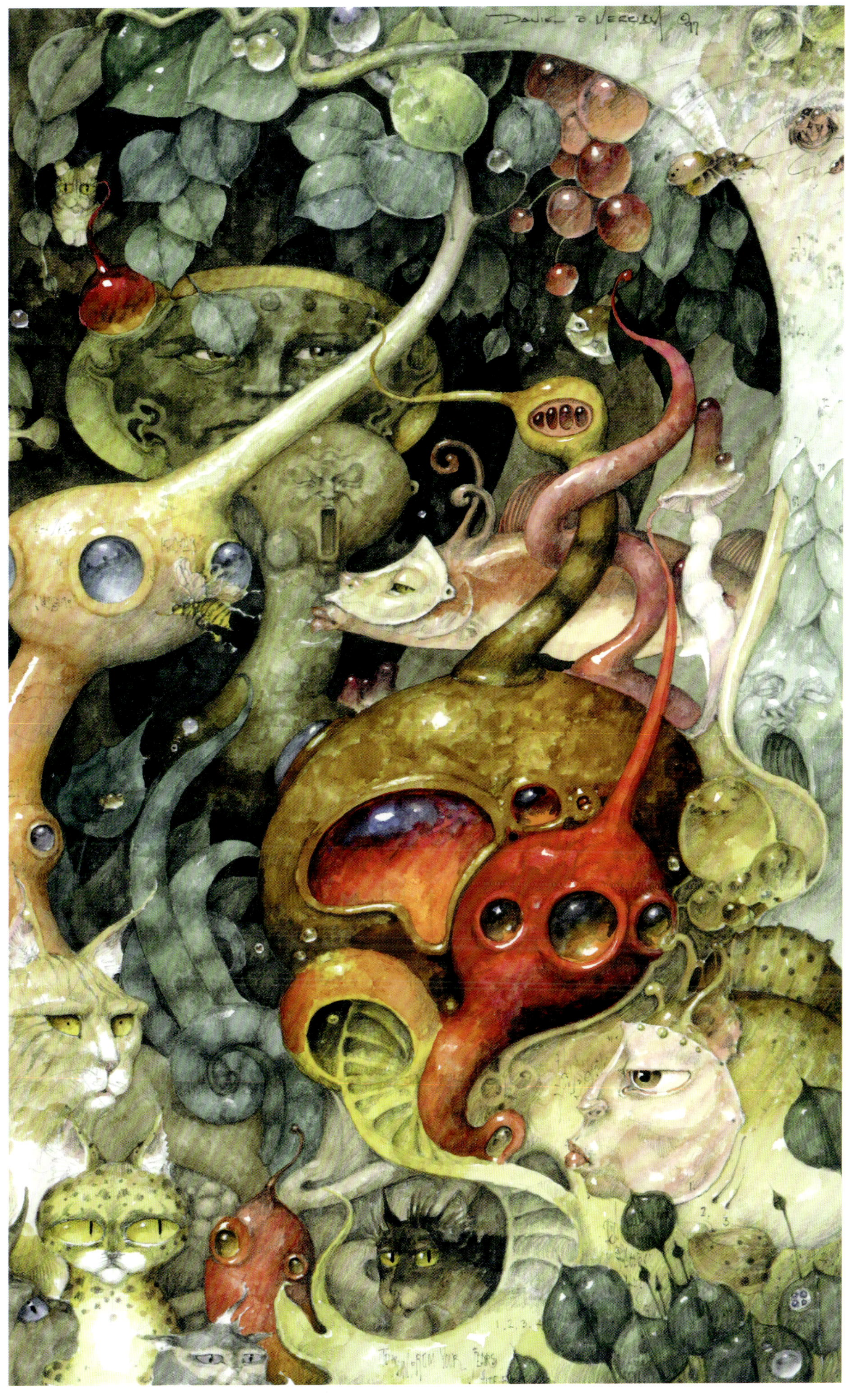

Masquerade
1997, watercolor on paper
14" x 9"

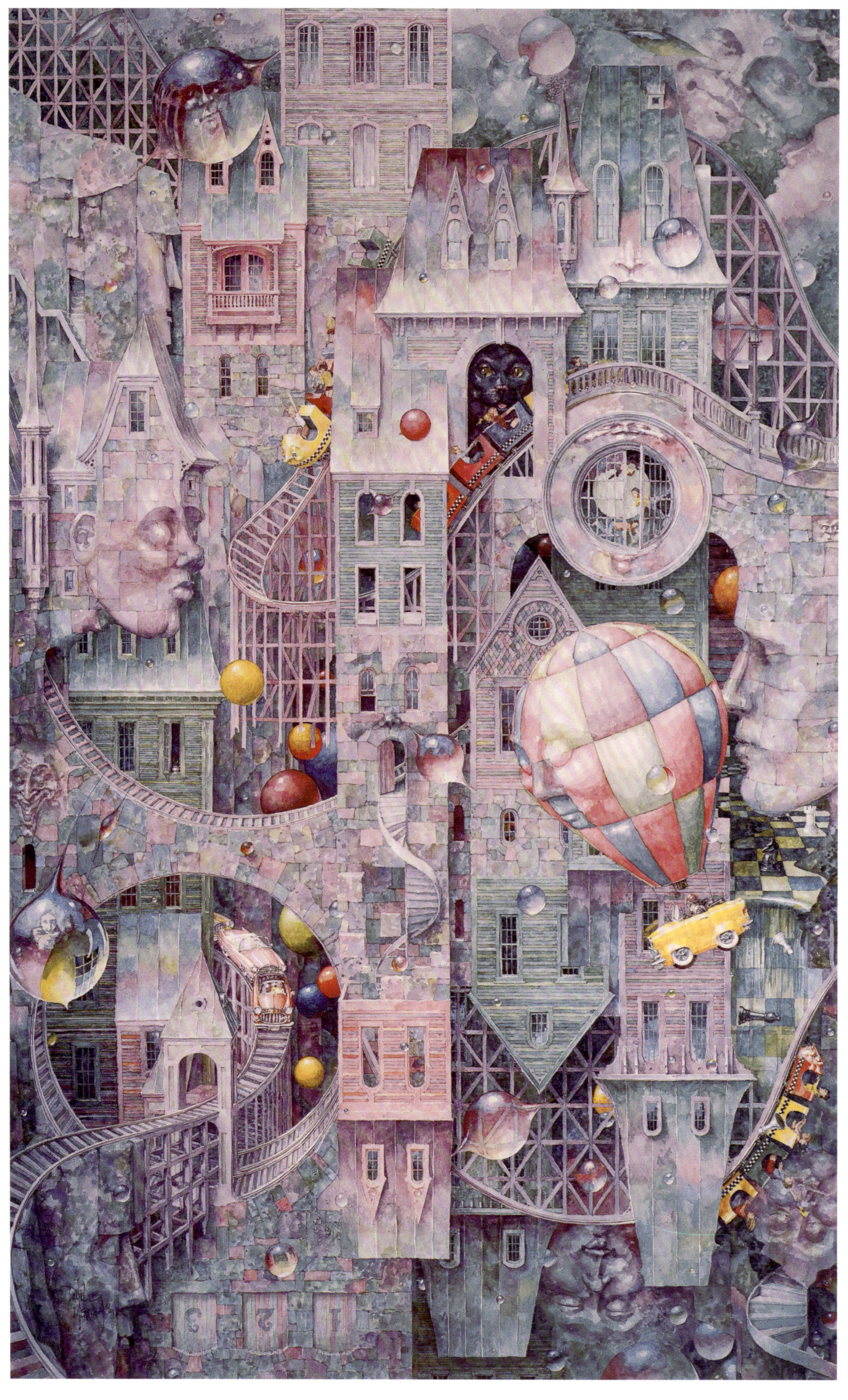

Upside Down
1991, watercolor on paper
a. 40" x 20"

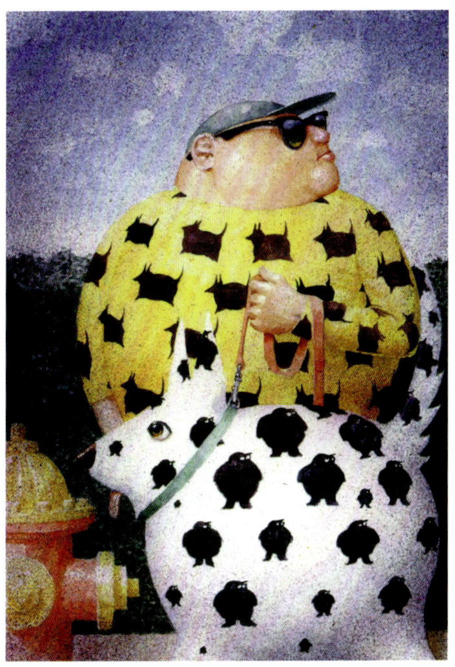

MUTUAL RESPECT
1994, WATERCOLOR ON PAPER
13" X 9"

HARMONICS

It seems to me that modern societies belittle the importance of art. Funding is minimal, and schools and colleges overload their curricula with technical subjects. Our minds are too regimented, and we are losing touch with our passion, our spirit, and our humanity. Art is a gateway to the emotions and intuition. It is a source of our wisdom and a venue to free expression. If more priority were given to the arts, we would see and feel how it enhances our ability to learn.

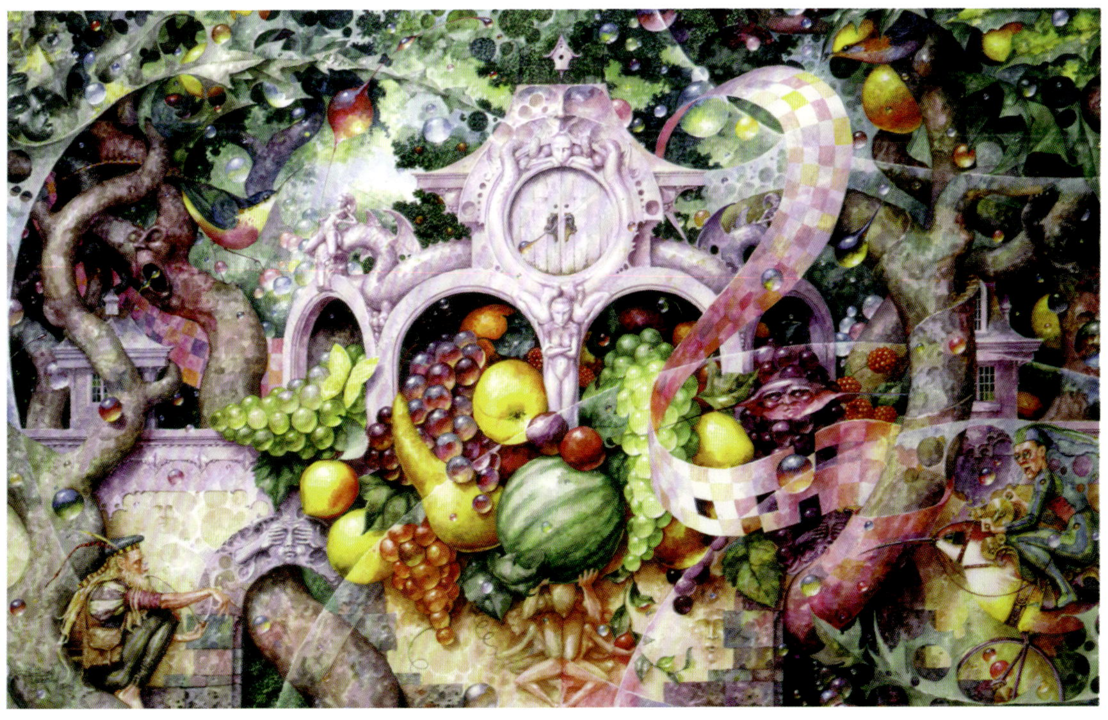

WHERE THE SECRET'S KEPT
1993, WATERCOLOR ON PAPER
A. 24" X 36"

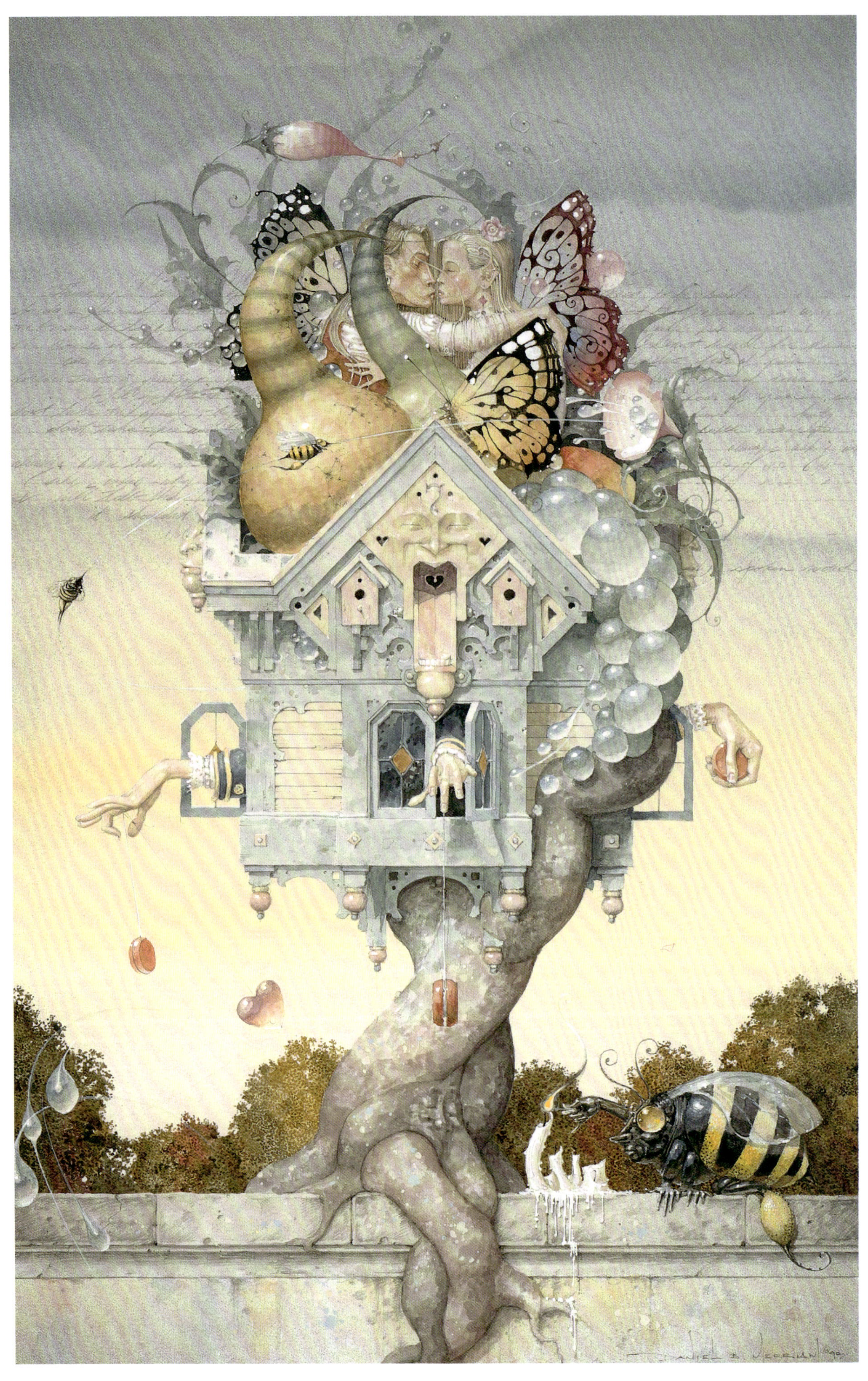

IF IT WERE
1995, WATERCOLOR ON PAPER
DIPTYCH, LEFT PANEL
A. 22" X 12"

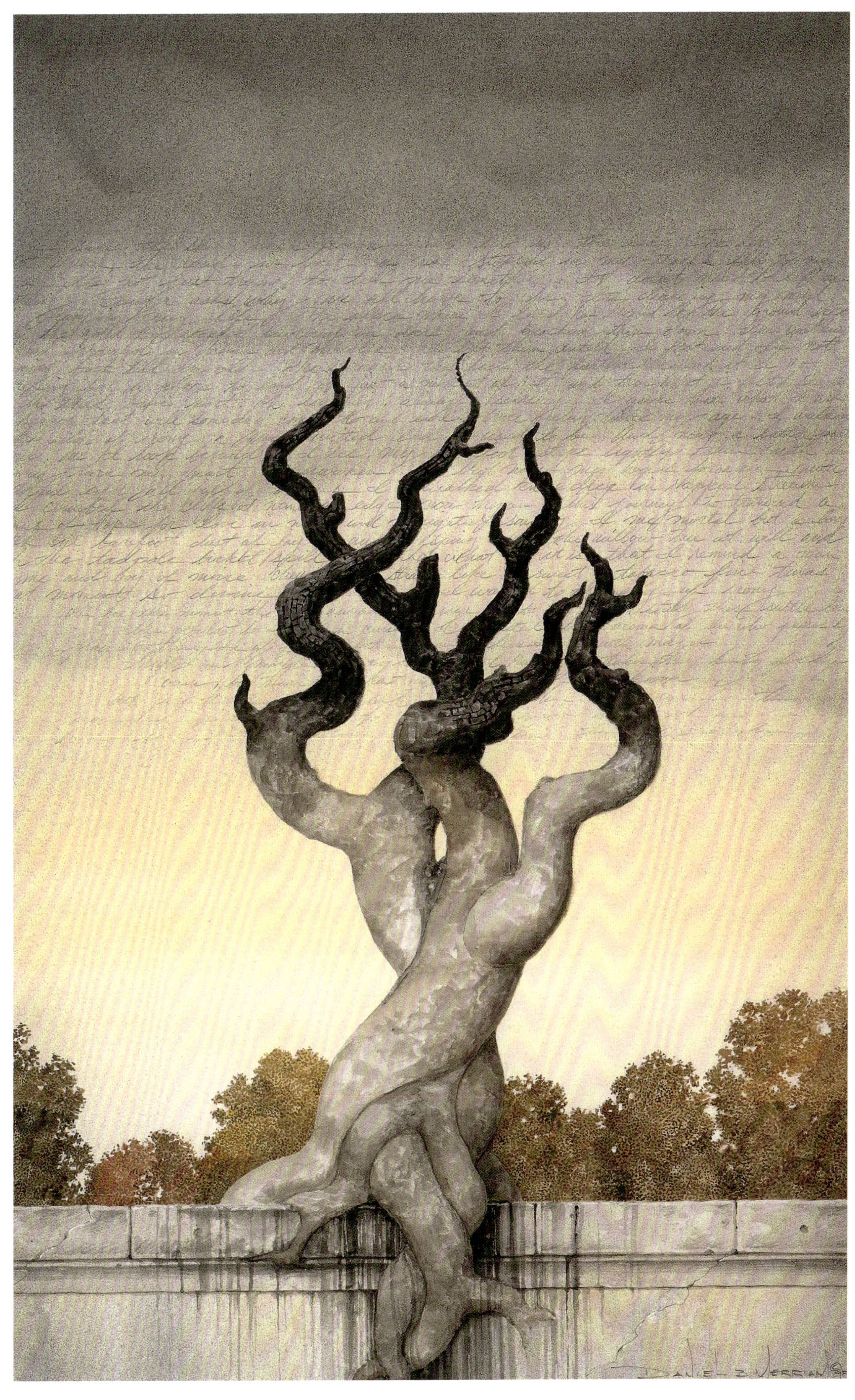

If It Were Not
1995, watercolor on paper
diptych, right panel
a. 22" x 12"

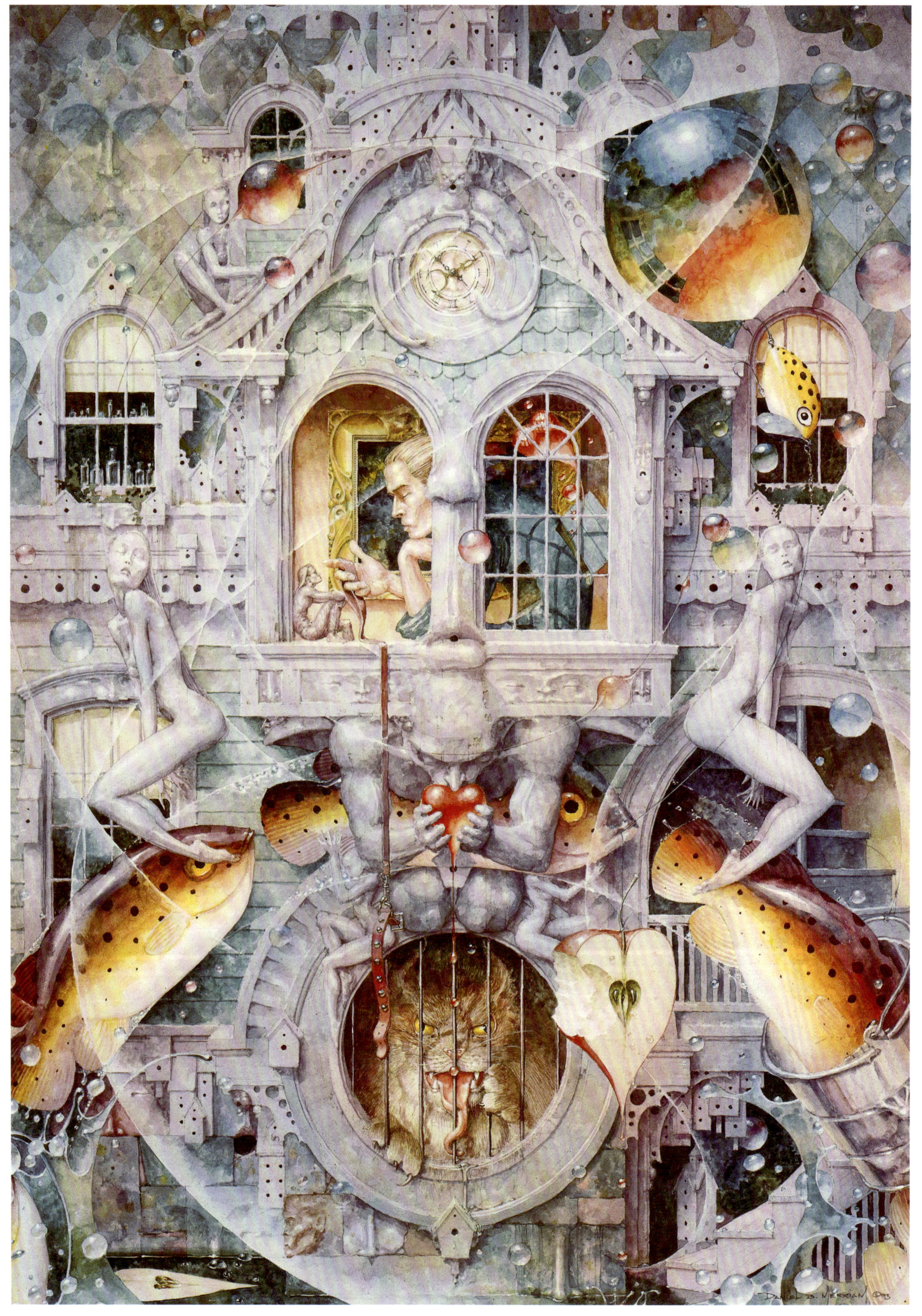

Holding On
1993, watercolor on paper
28" x 20"

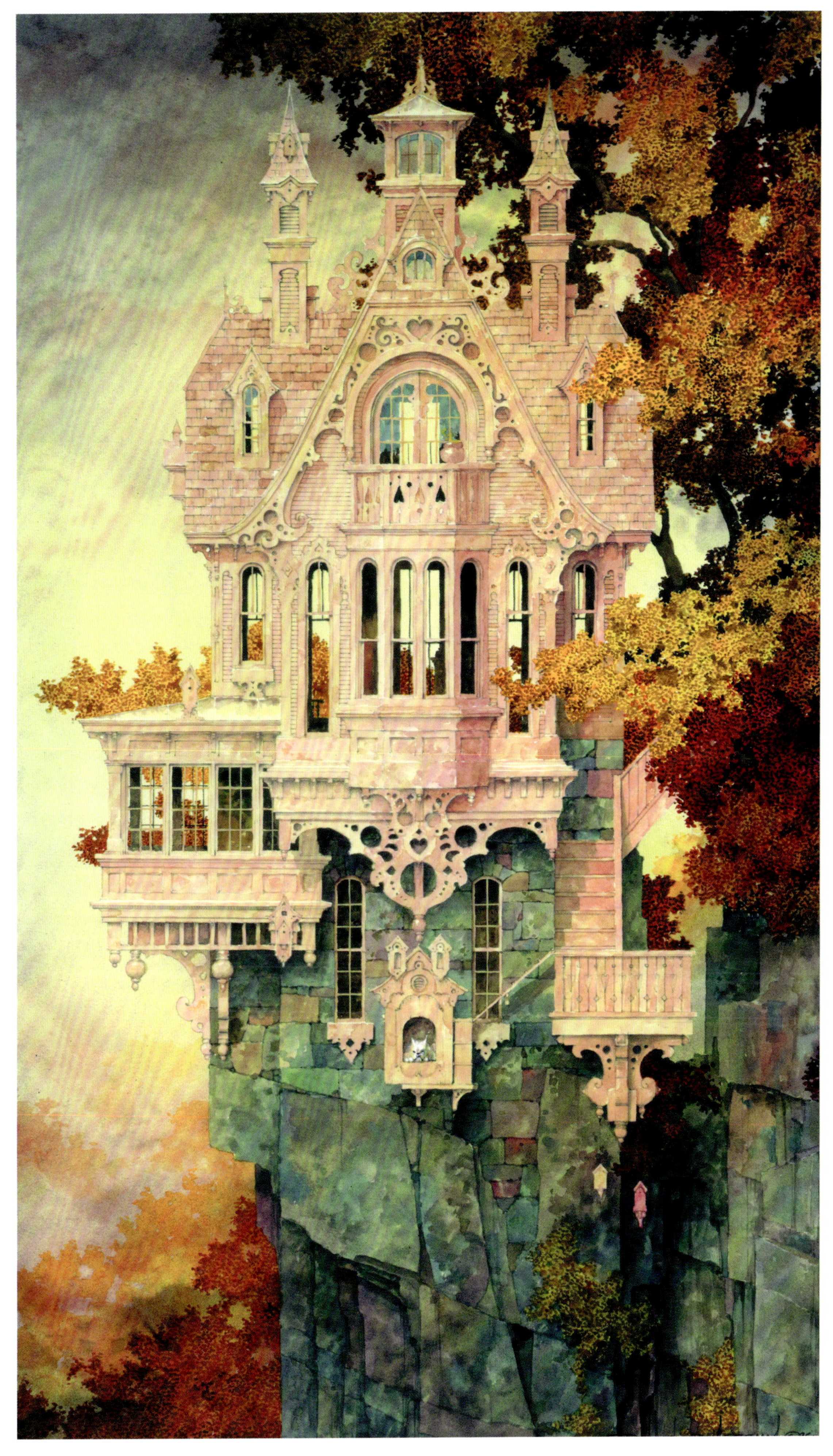

In the Dog House
1996, watercolor on paper
26.25" x 17.8"

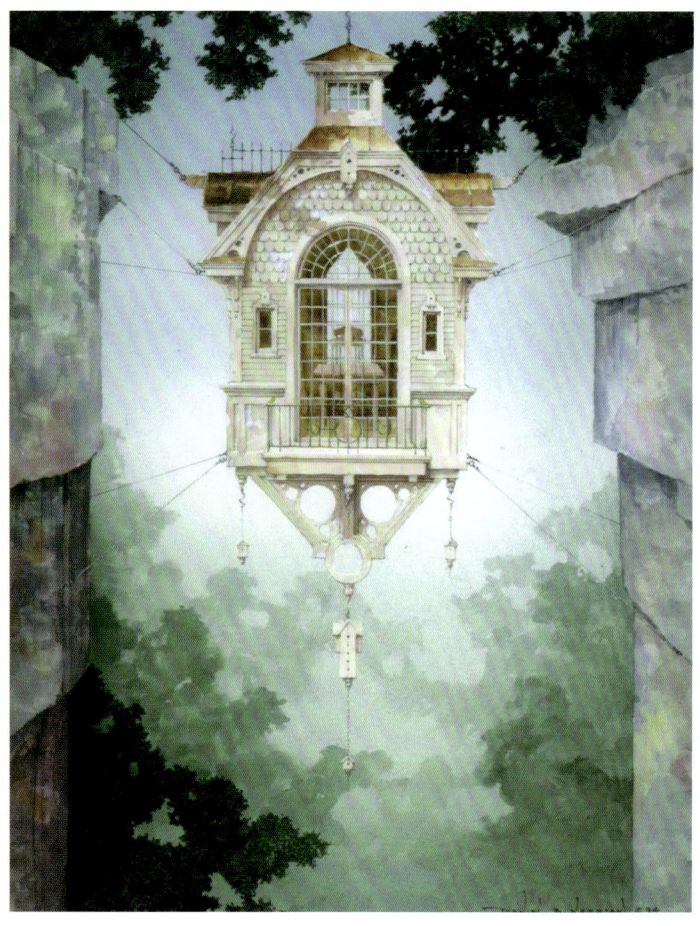

BETWEEN TWO WORLDS
1994, WATERCOLOR ON PAPER
A. 12" X 10"

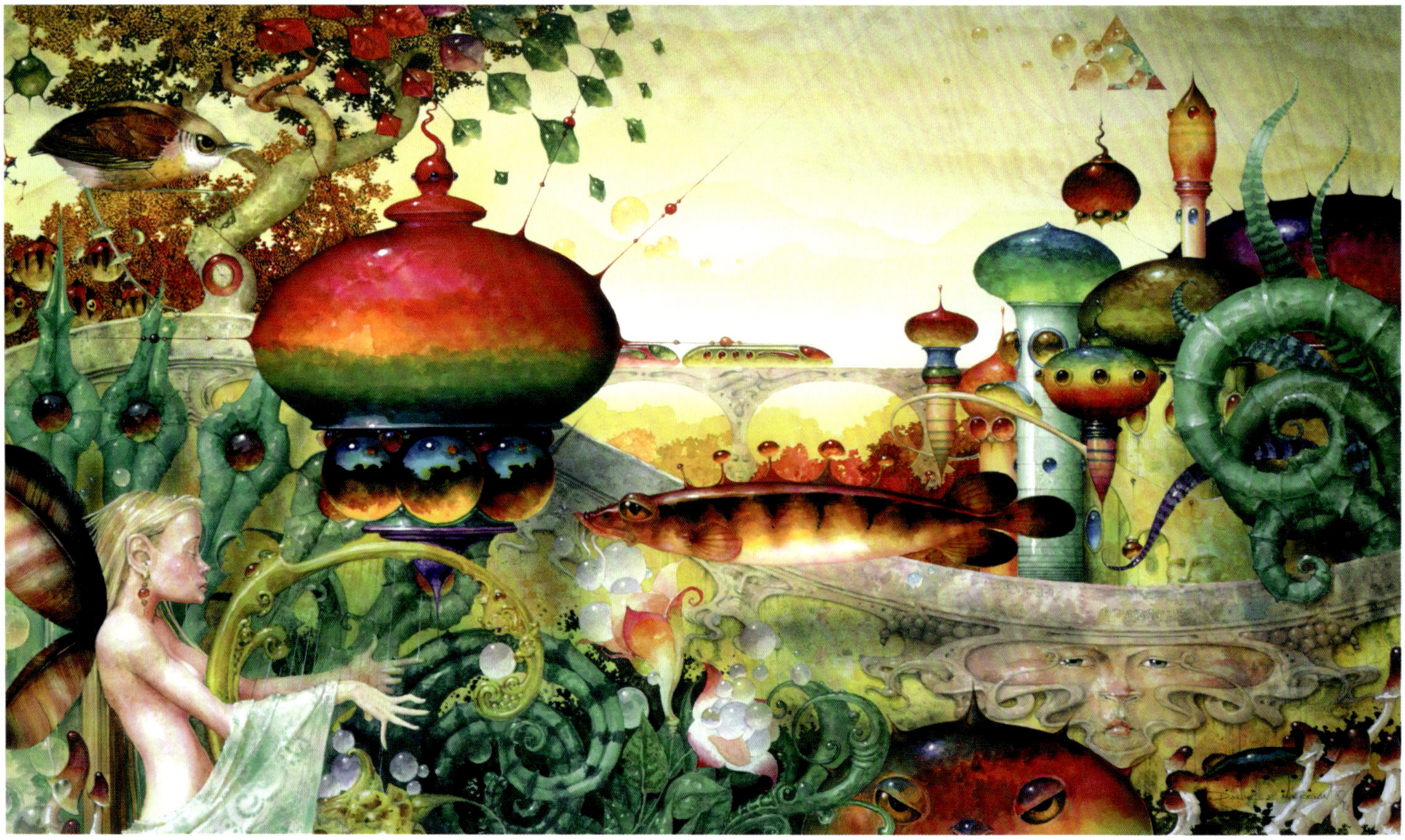

FUTURE PAST
1996, WATERCOLOR ON PAPER
15.5" X 27.5"

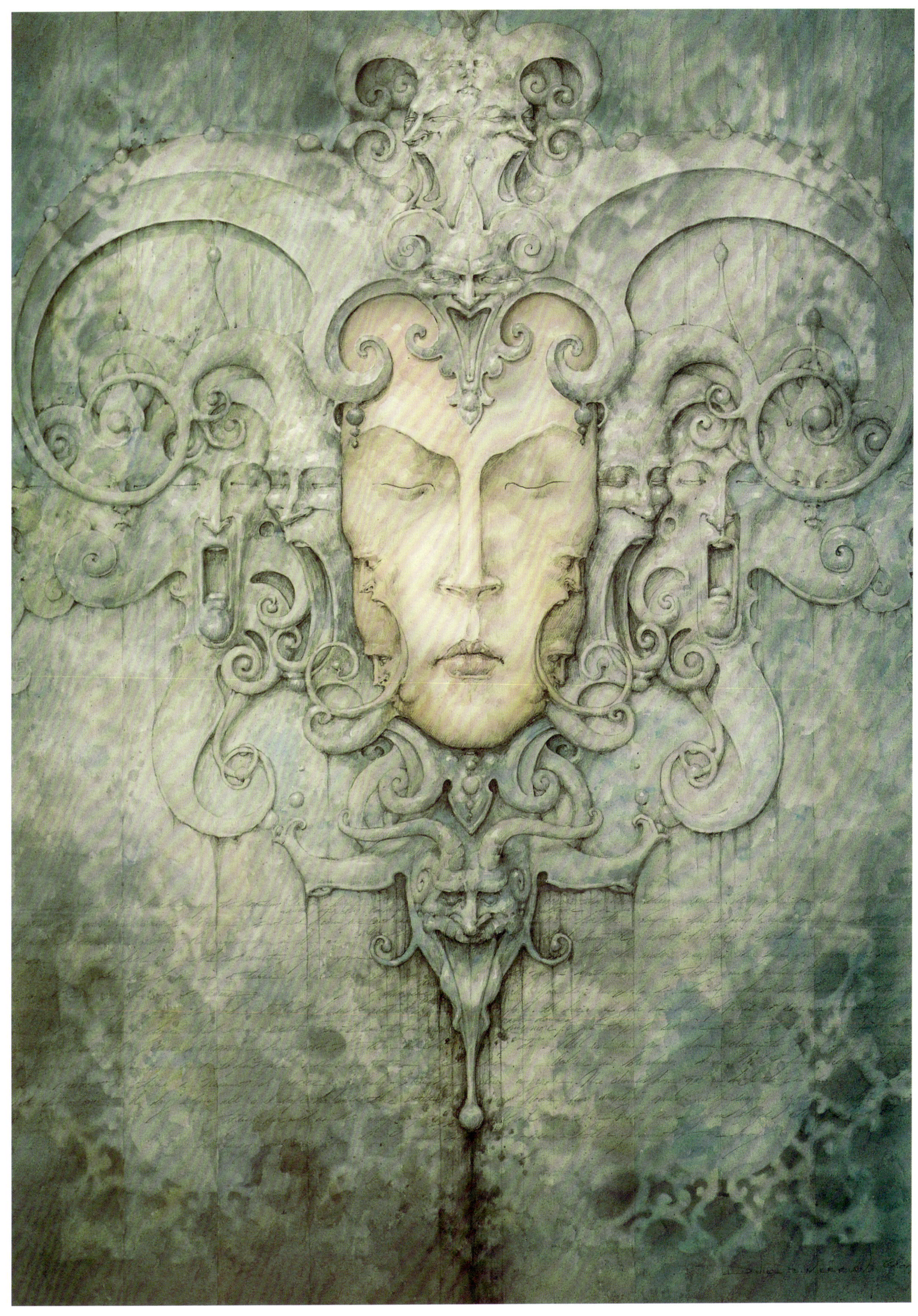

In My Sleep
1995, watercolor on paper
28.5" x 21"

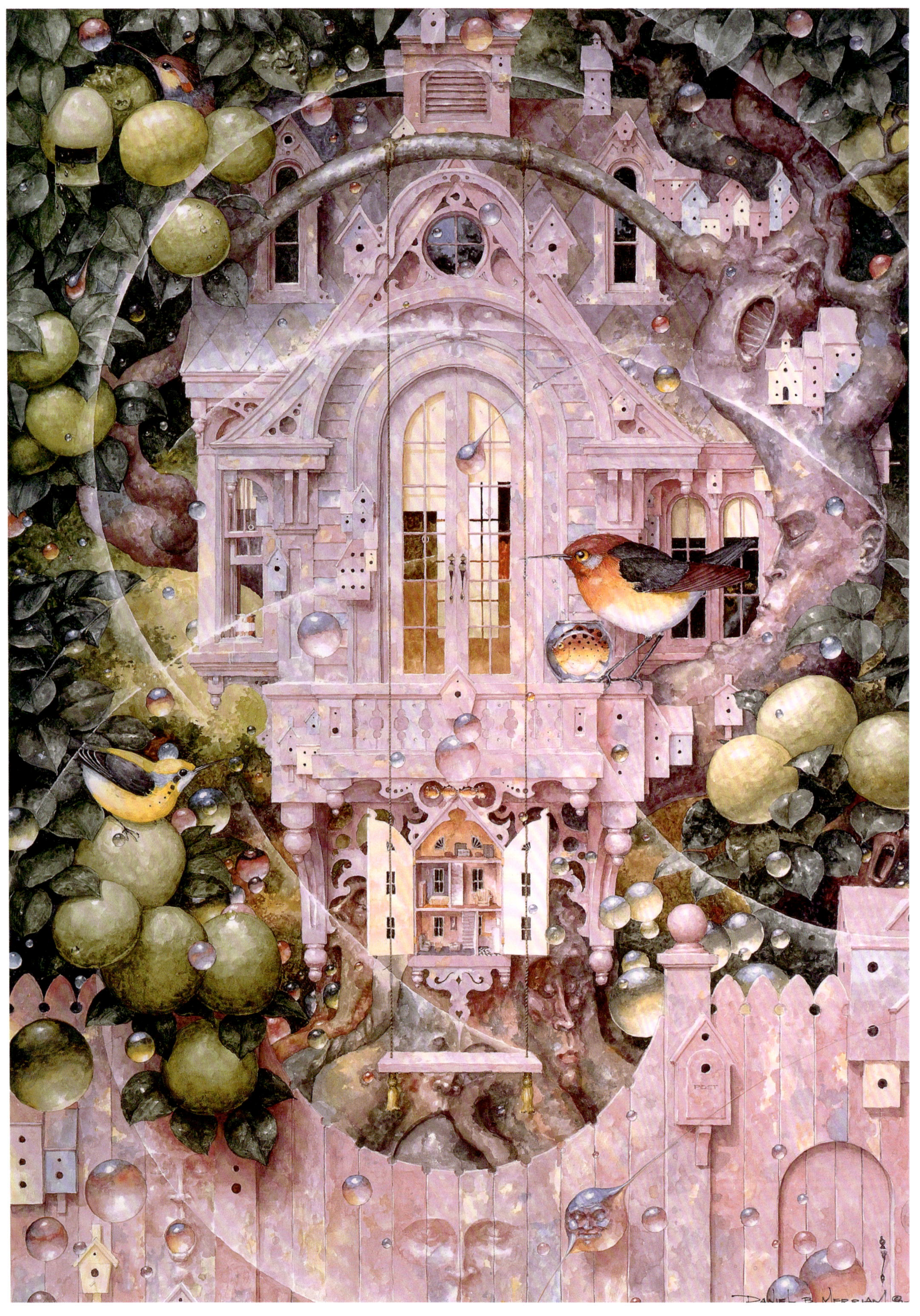

APPLE TREE HOUSE
1993, WATERCOLOR ON PAPER
A. 30" X 22"

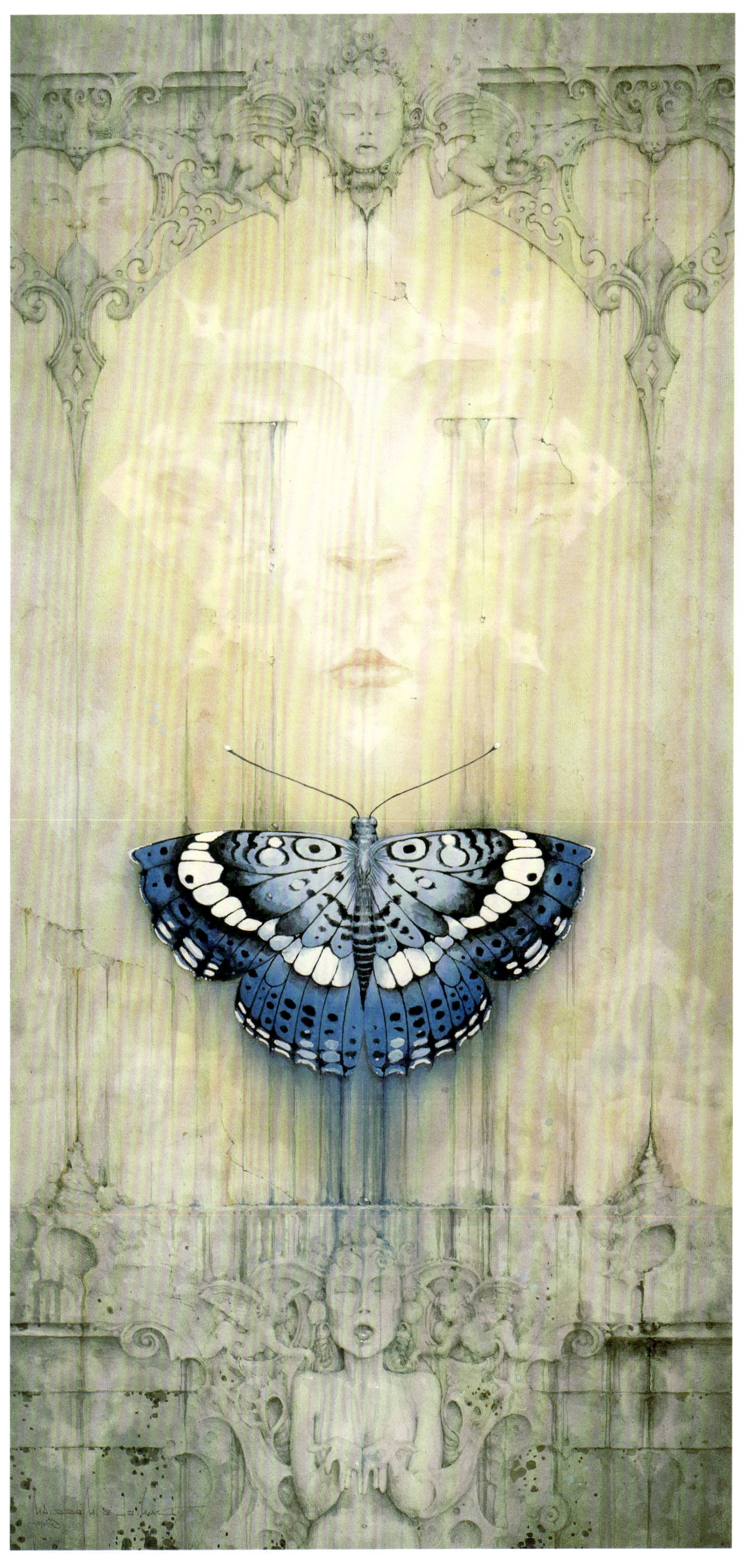

Washing Away
1995, watercolor on paper
a. 30" x 14"

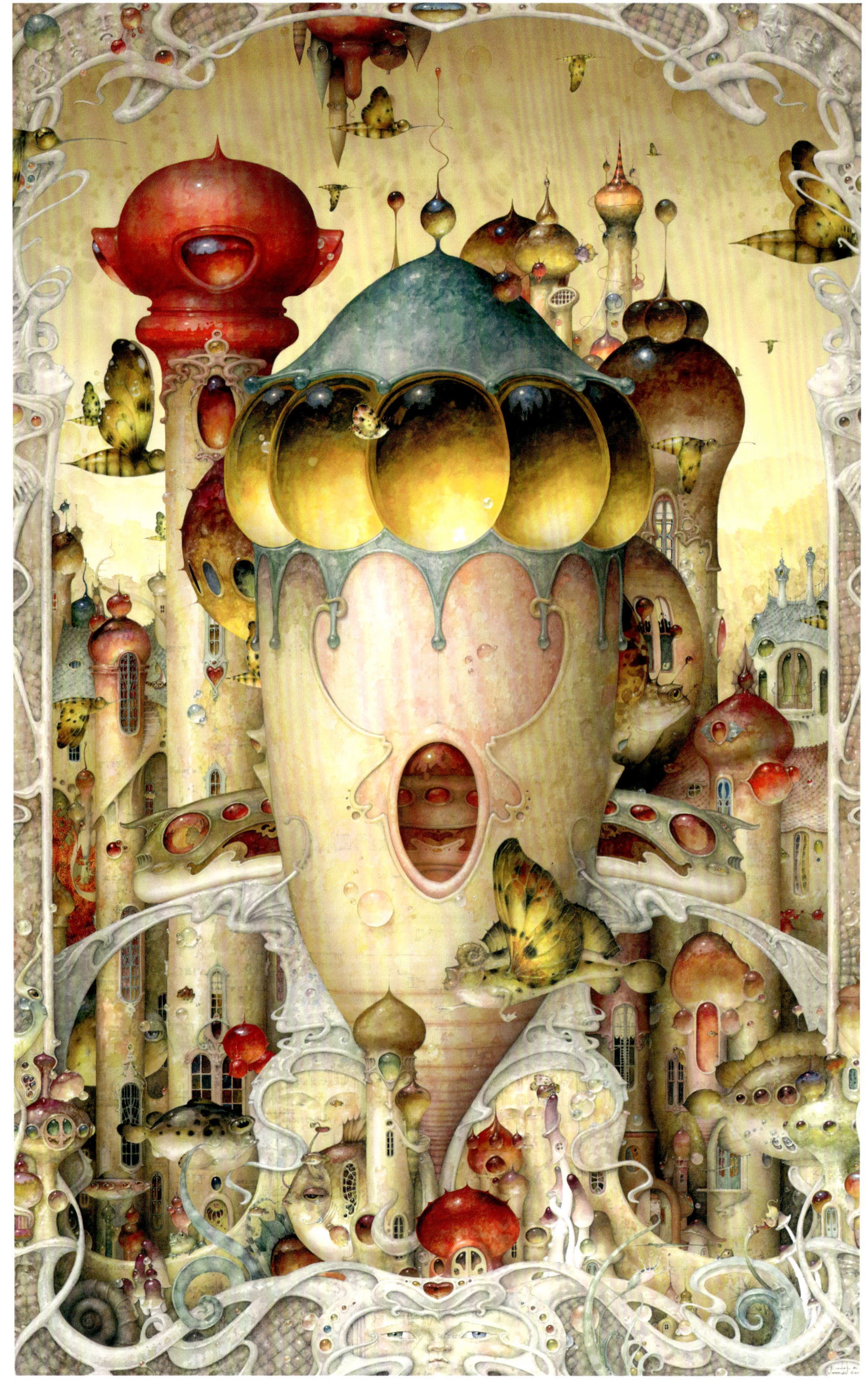

Metropolis
1997, watercolor on paper
56.5" x 36.75"

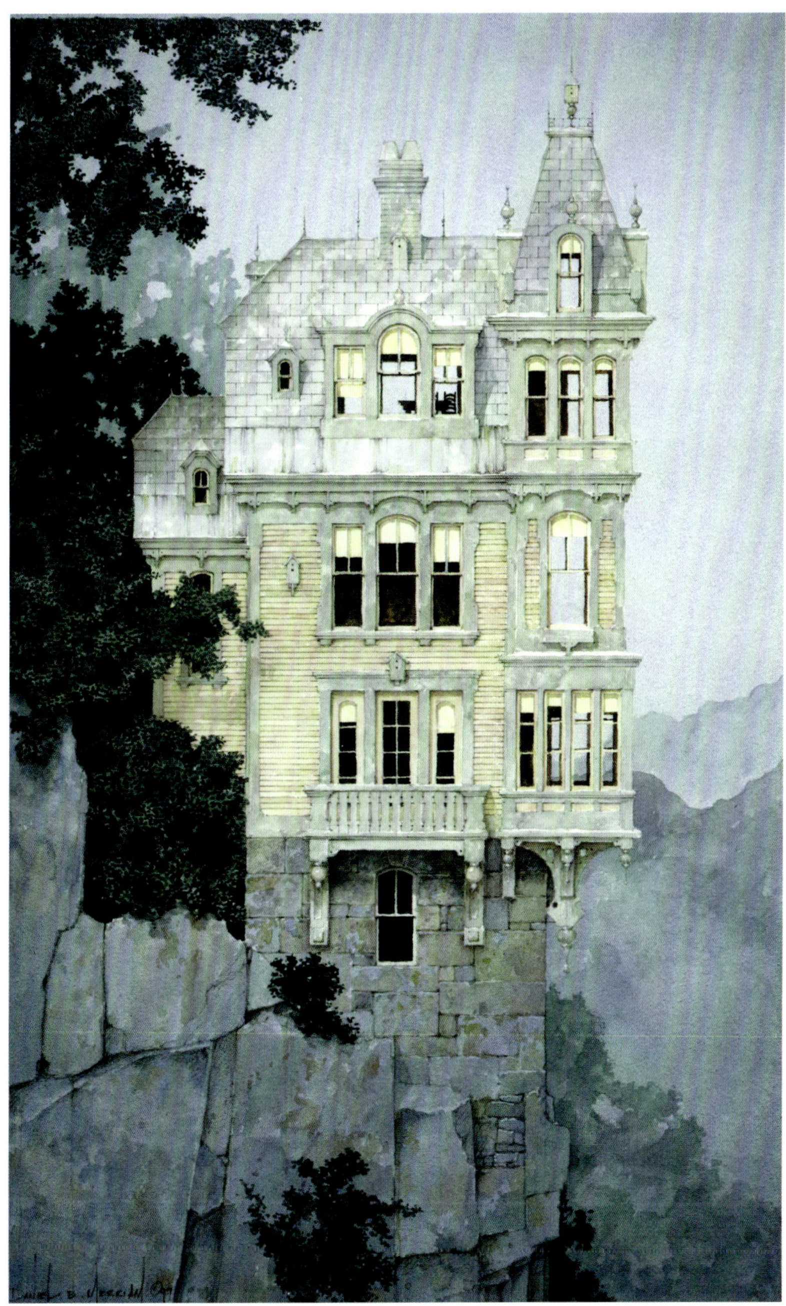

THE EMERALD EDGE
1997, WATERCOLOR ON PAPER
14" x 9"

DIVERSITY

Perhaps the future could take on a flavor different from that typically pictured in movies and comic books. I can imagine alternative orders to design that have within them all the diversity of our world today. After seeing what our society has built in the last fifty years -- the straight rows of identical houses, the grid work of modern farming -- I am compelled to once again curve and twist the lines to a more organic motif. The architectural designs of Antoni Gaudi suggest that I am not the first to imply this seeming impracticality. Within the confines of order, a periodic break or distraction seems to give the order more meaning.

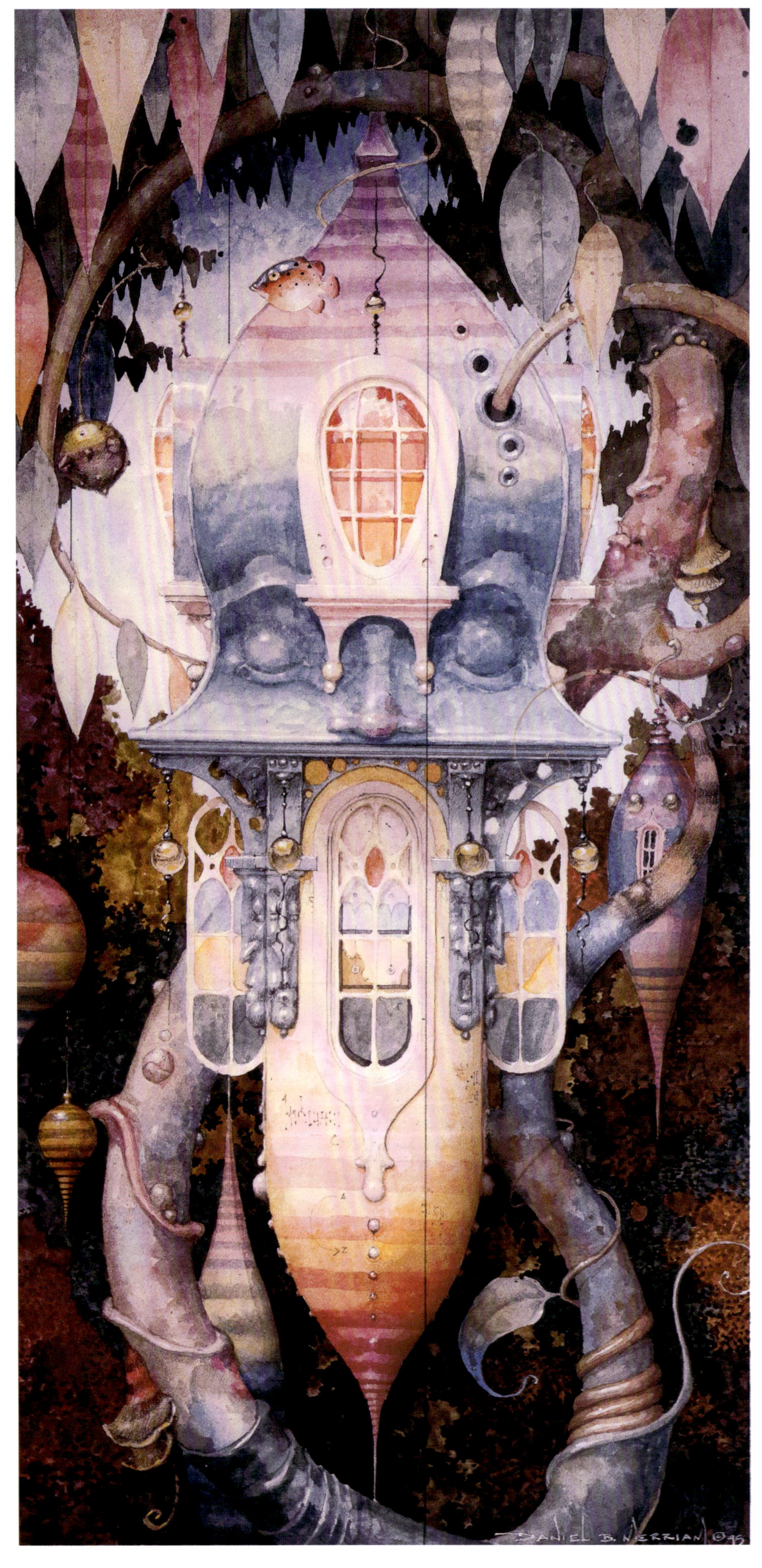

Treetops
1995, watercolor on paper
A. 16" x 8"

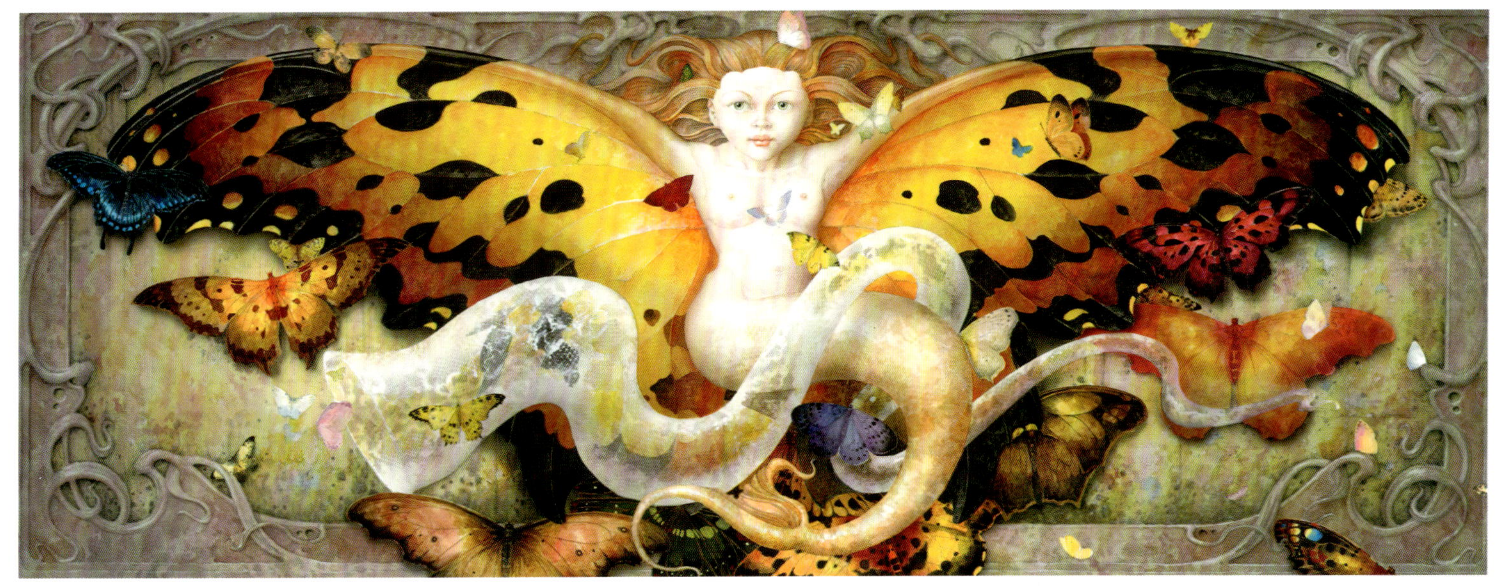

MYLITTA
1996, WATERCOLOR ON PAPER
22" X 52"

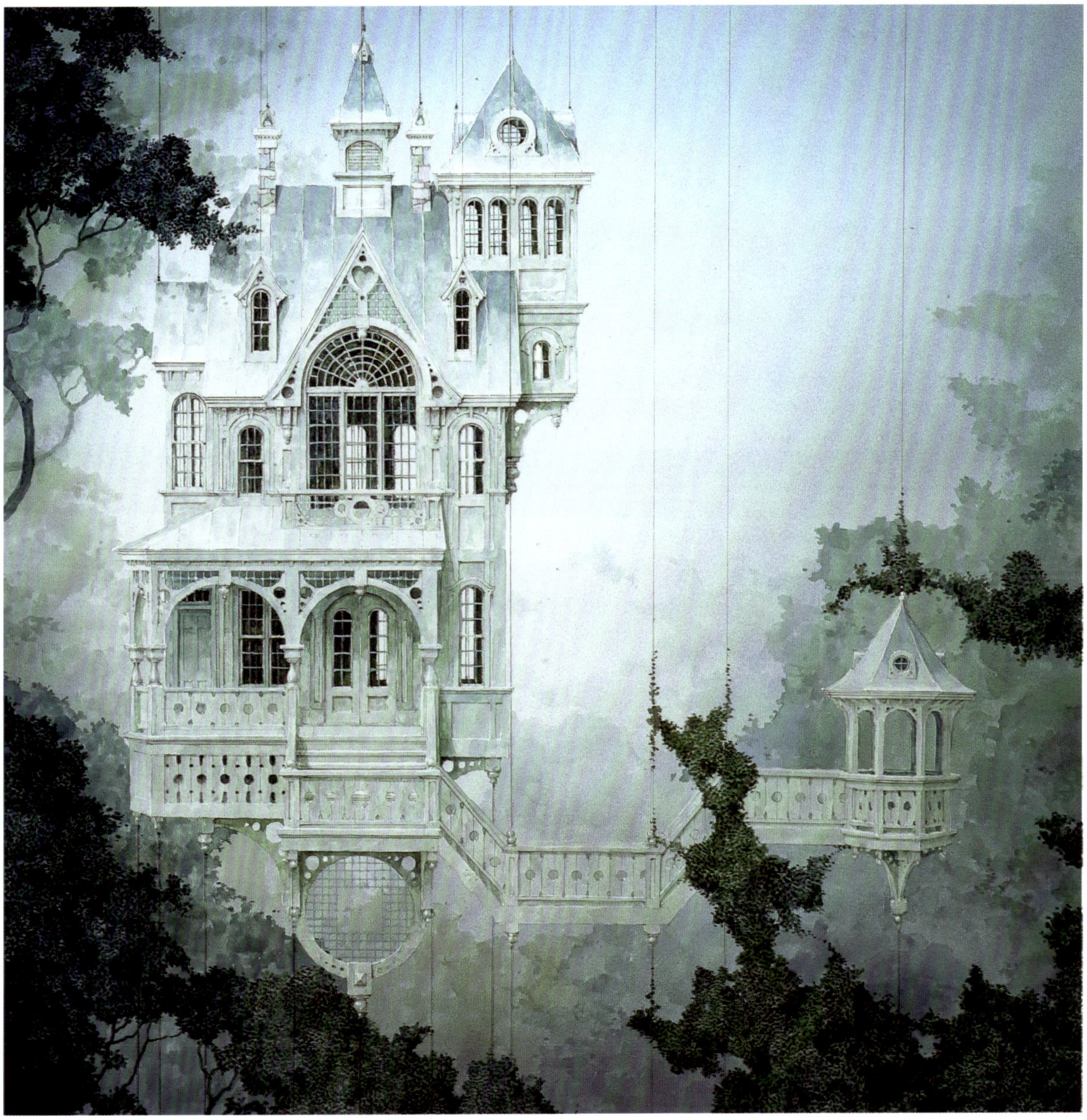

MY BACK YARD
1994, WATERCOLOR ON PAPER
A. 16" X 16"

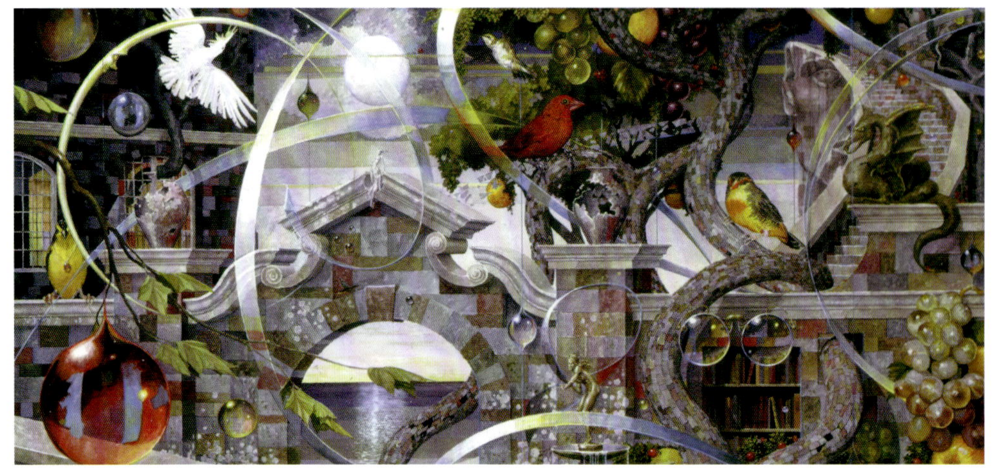

PATHWAYS
1988, WATERCOLOR ON PAPER
A. 16" X 31"

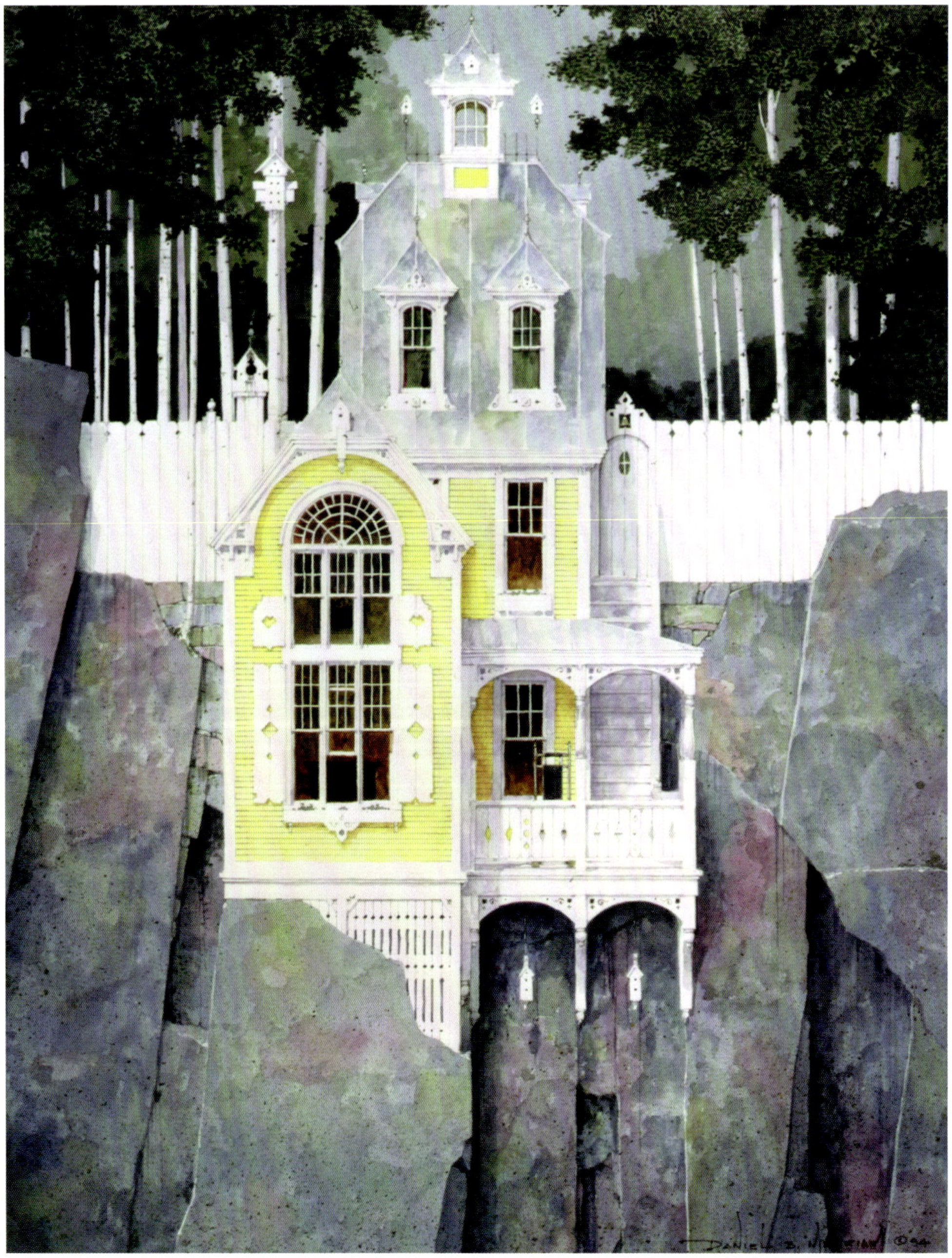

THE OTHER SIDE OF THE FENCE
1994, WATERCOLOR ON PAPER
A. 16" X 12"

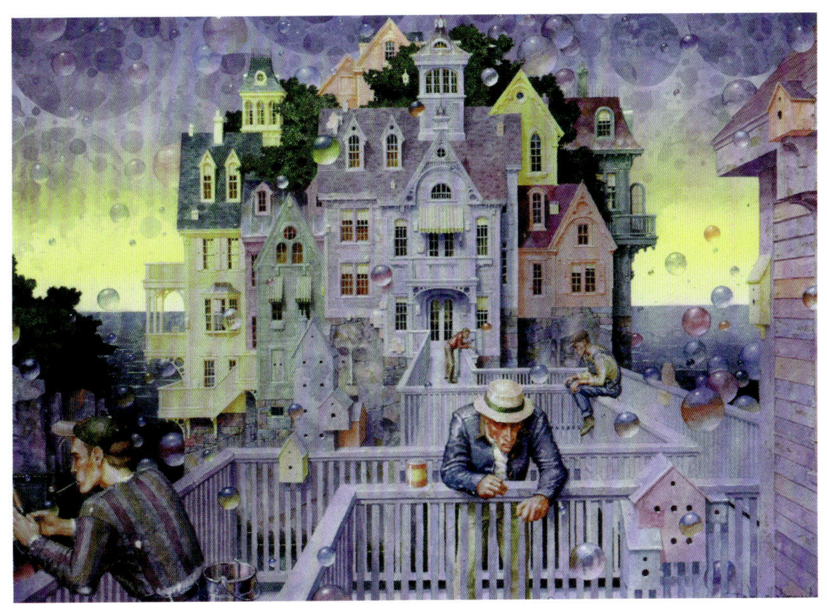

ISLAND
1993, WATERCOLOR ON PAPER
A. 20" X 30"

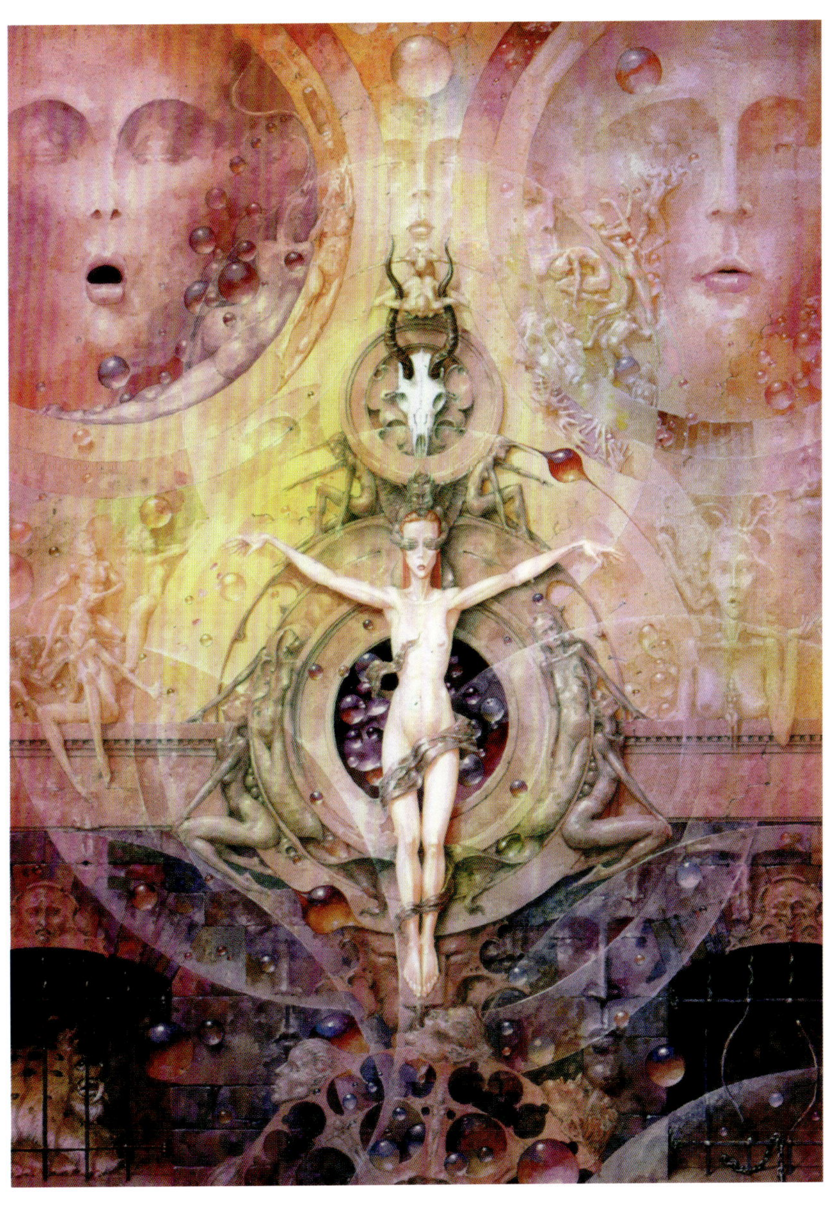

EUPHORIA
1993, WATERCOLOR ON PAPER
28" X 20.1"

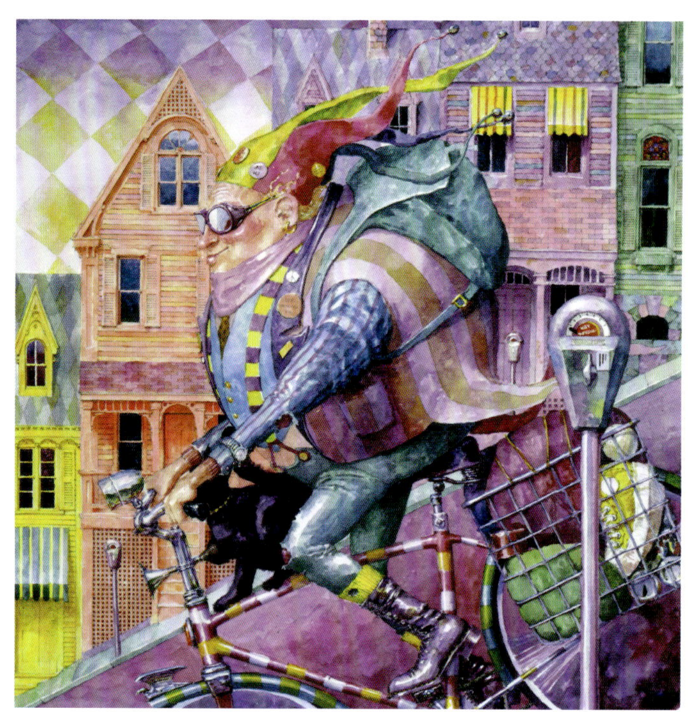

The Random Variable
1992, watercolor on paper
a. 16" x 16"

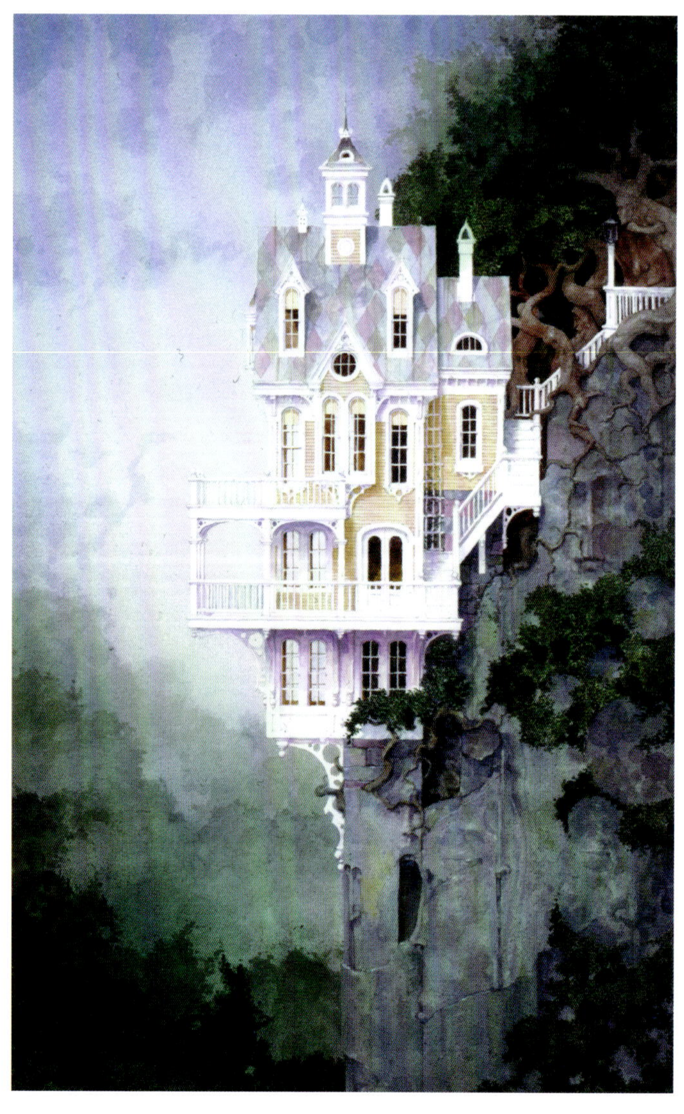

Facing The World
1993, watercolor on paper
a. 22" x 14"

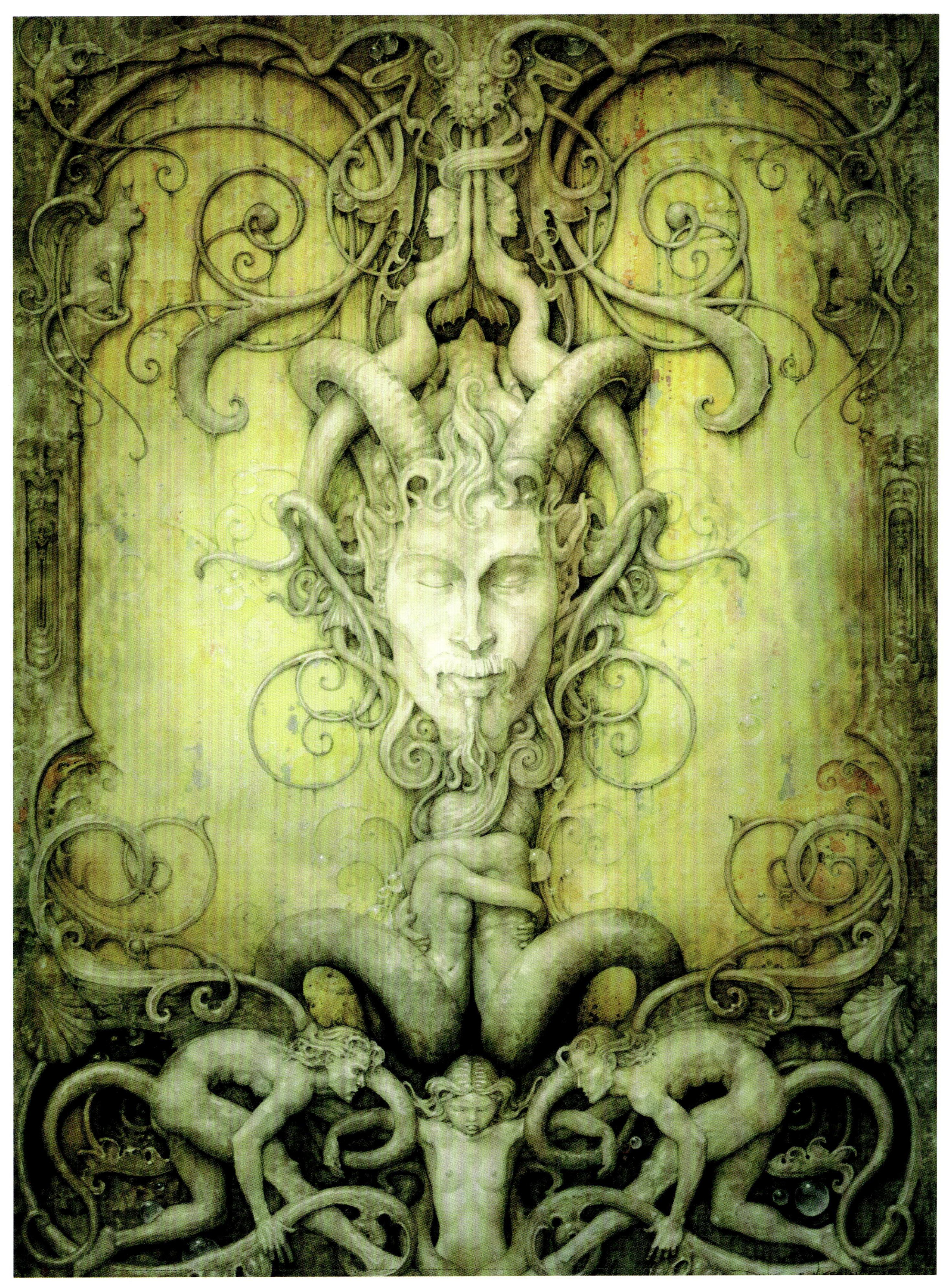

Entranced
1996, watercolor on paper
28.1" x 21.1"

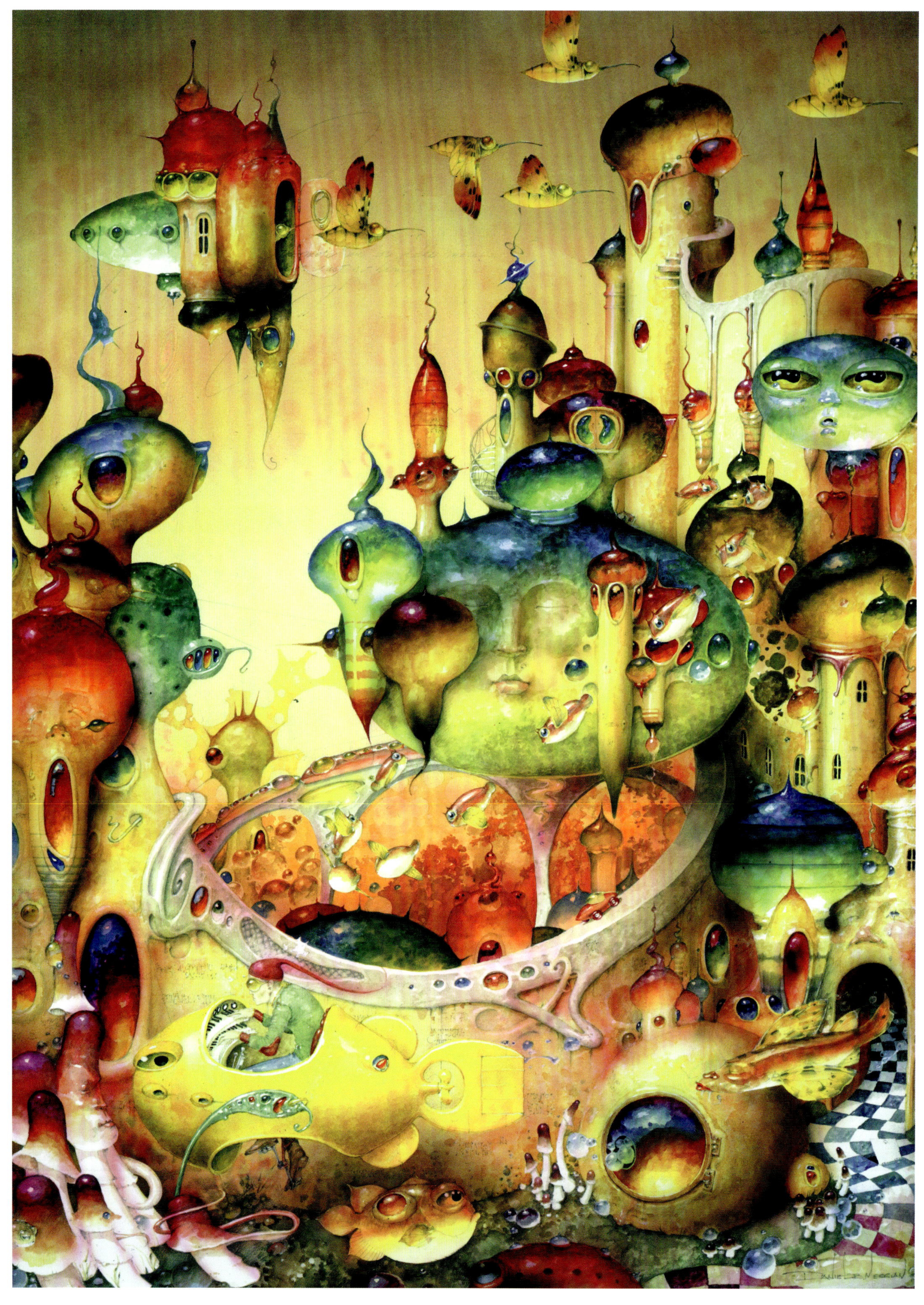

Fly Away
1996, watercolor on paper
28.1"x 21.1"

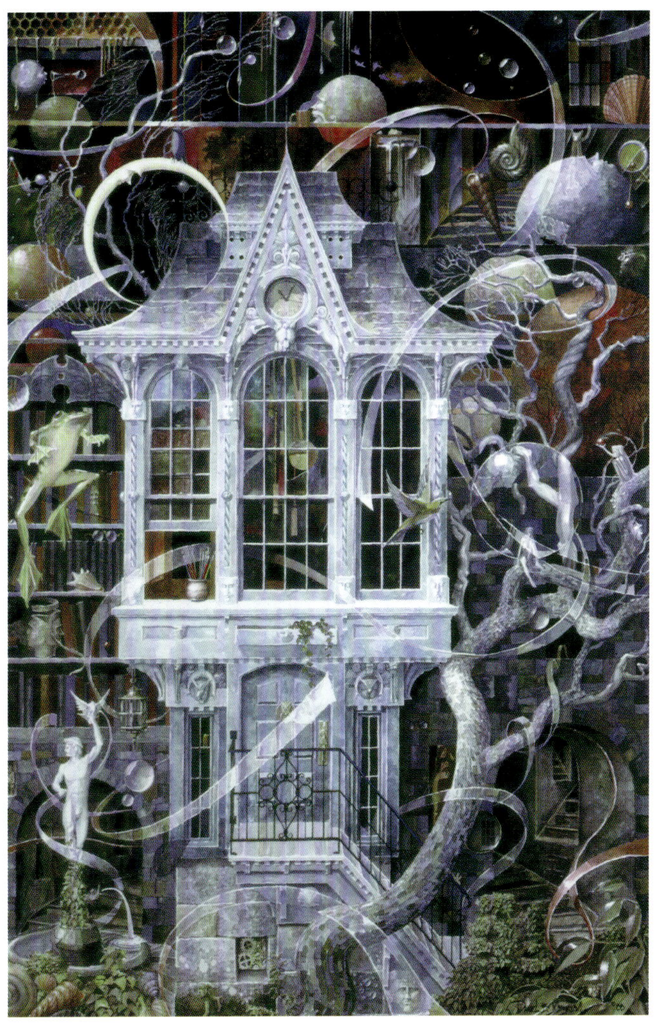

House of Knowledge
1988, watercolor on paper
a. 22" x 14"

Space

I find tranquility in depicting spaces where things are magical, and where softness breeds forgiveness of myself as well as others. I always have, and always will, wander out into the distant mind where the sky is filled with orbs, within each of which a nucleus of emotion converges into a universe of spiraling space. Throughout this enchanted world, gravity-defying thoughts move about freely, and spirits soar.

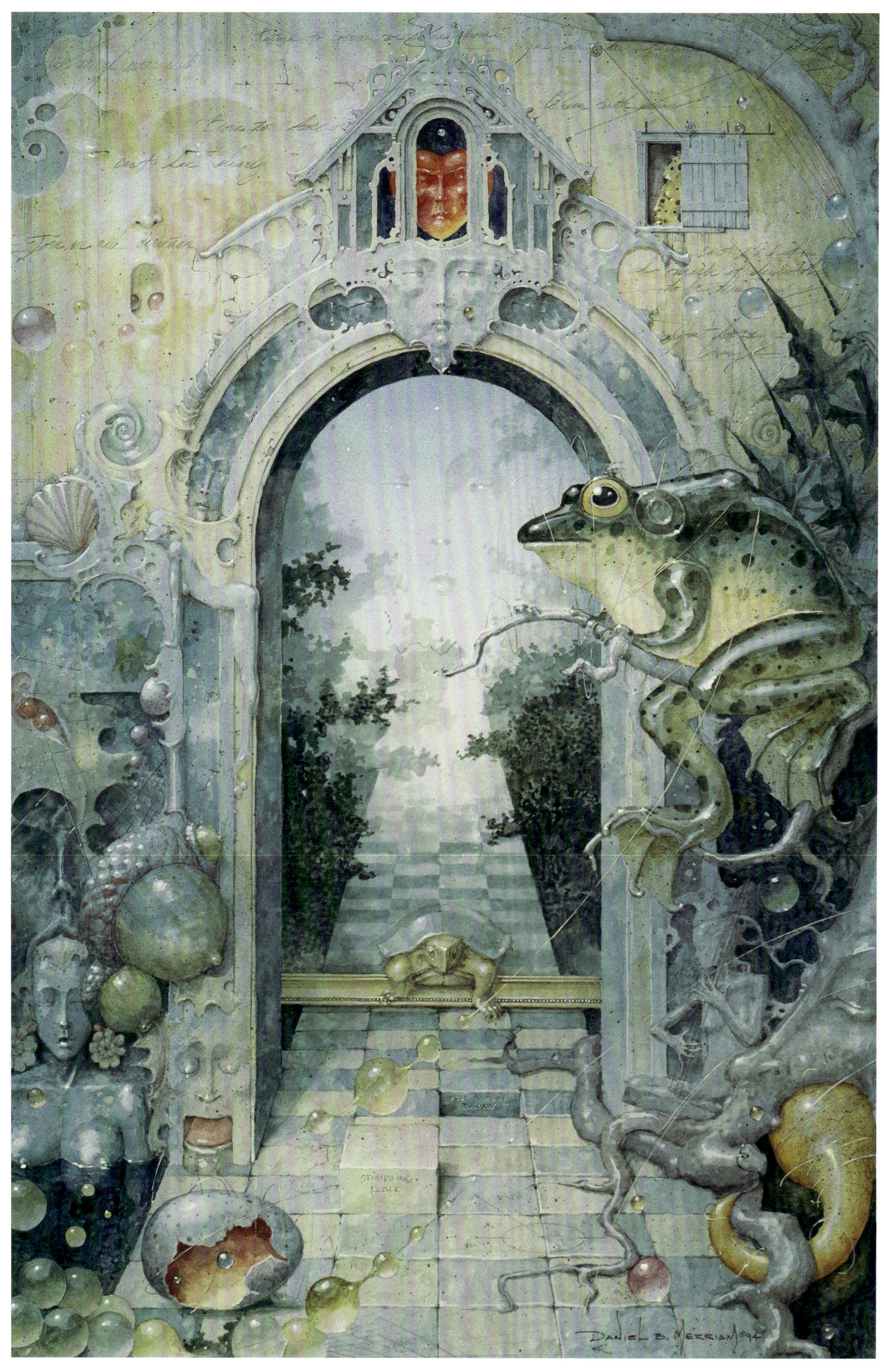

Whole in The Theory
1994, watercolor on paper
a. 18" x 12"

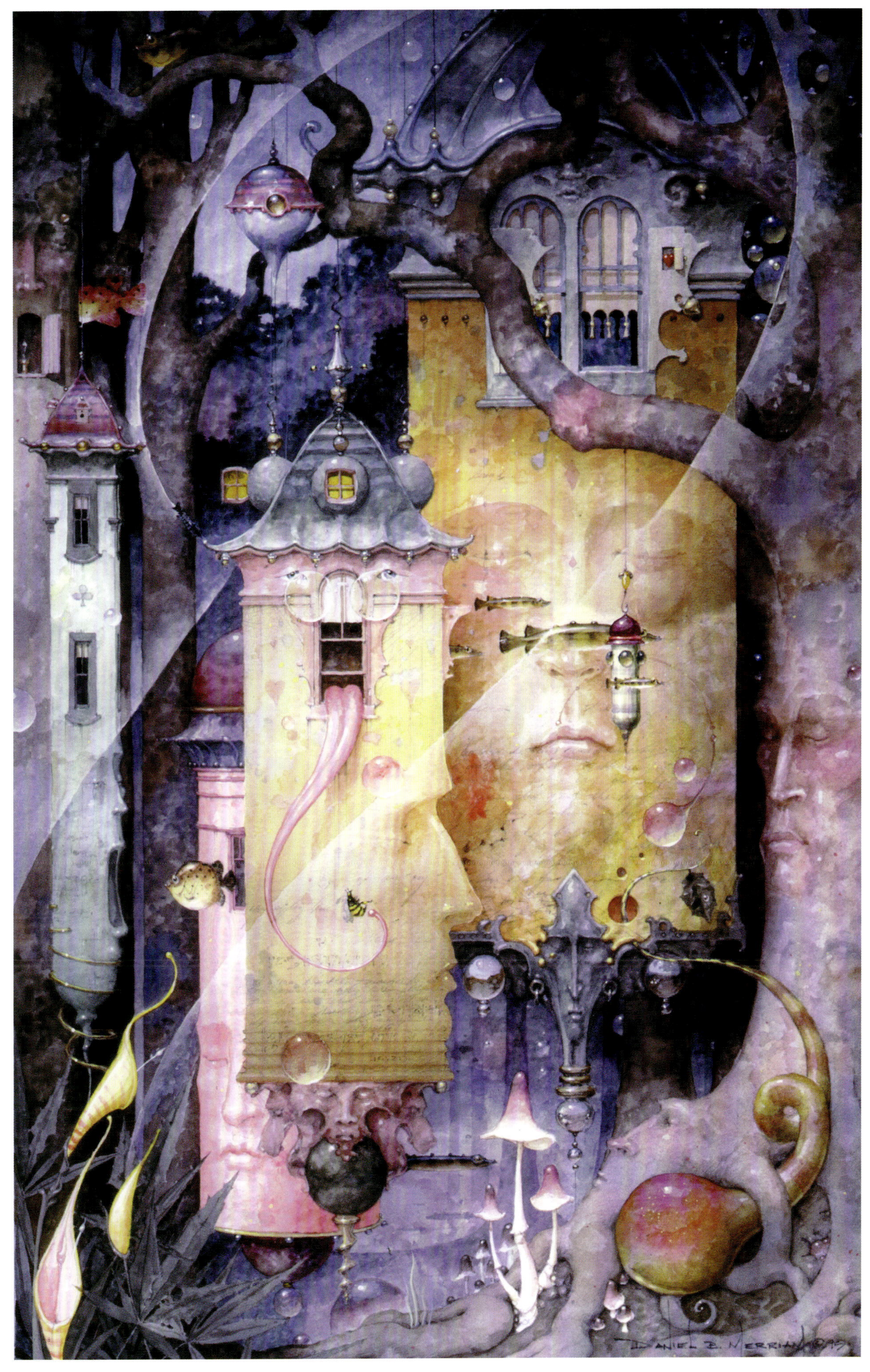

SLIP OF THE TONGUE
1995, WATERCOLOR ON PAPER
20" X 12.8"

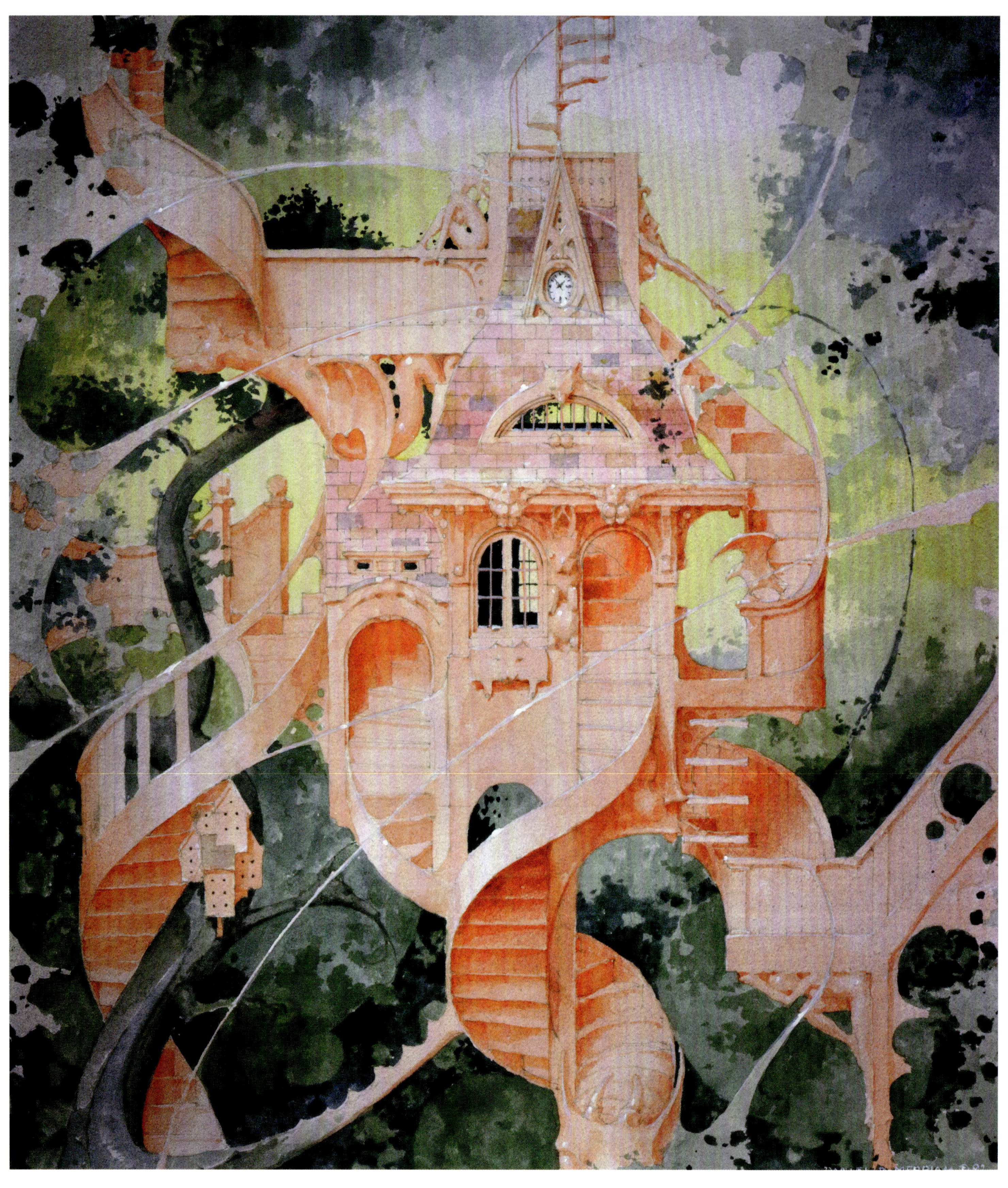

HYSTERIA
1991, WATERCOLOR ON PAPER
10.5" X 9.25"

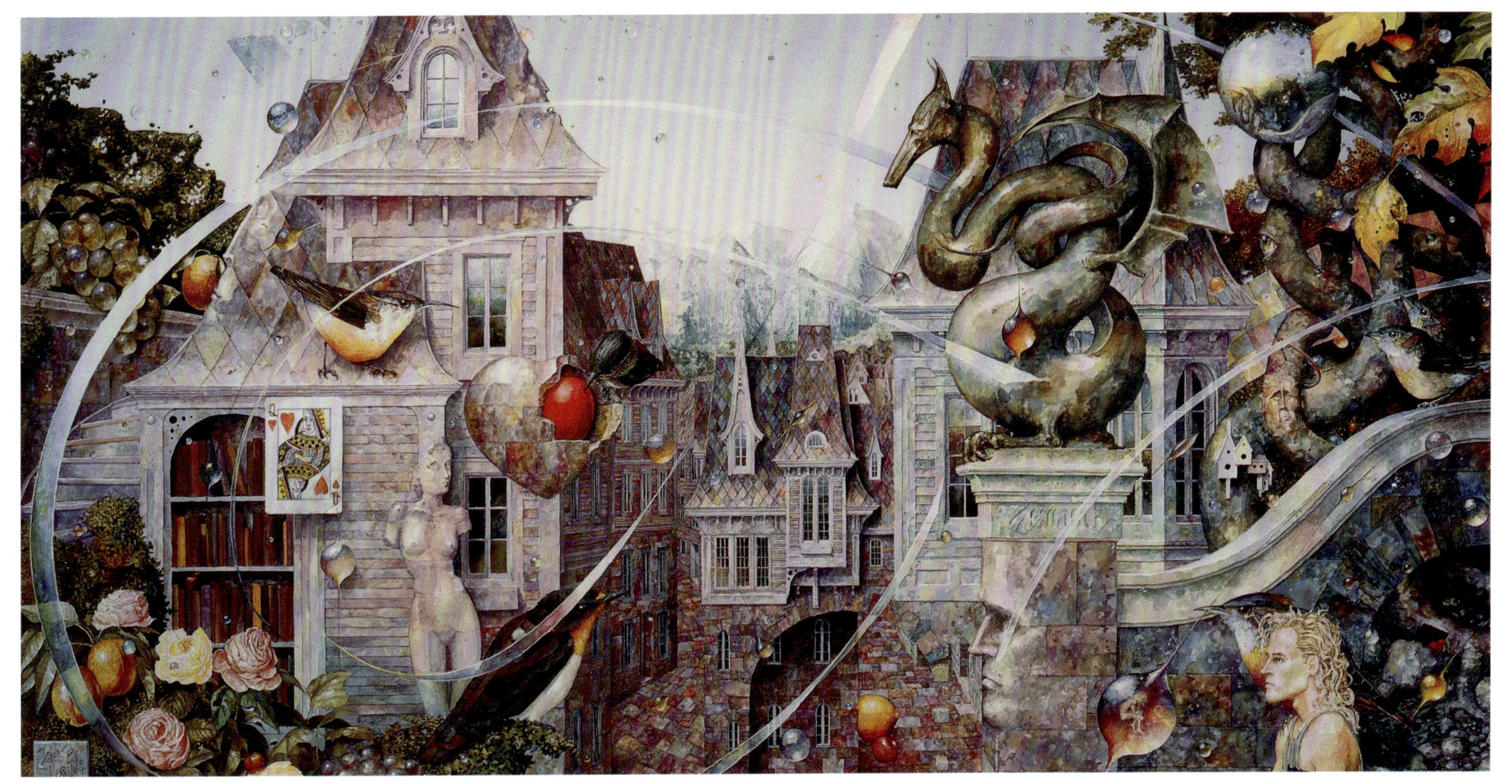

When Birds Cry
1992, watercolor on paper
a. 18" x 40"

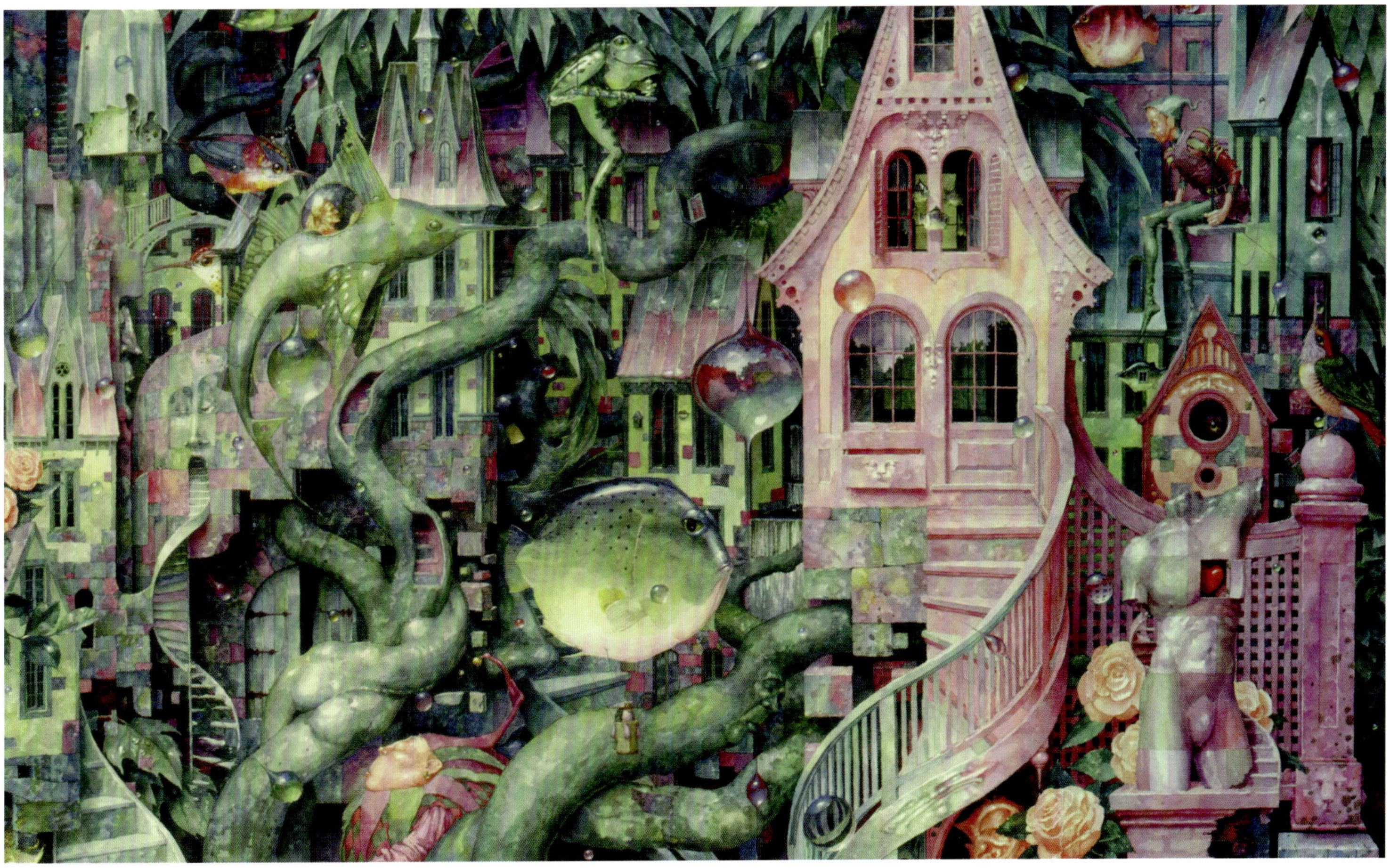

Atlantis
1992, watercolor on paper
a. 24" x 40"

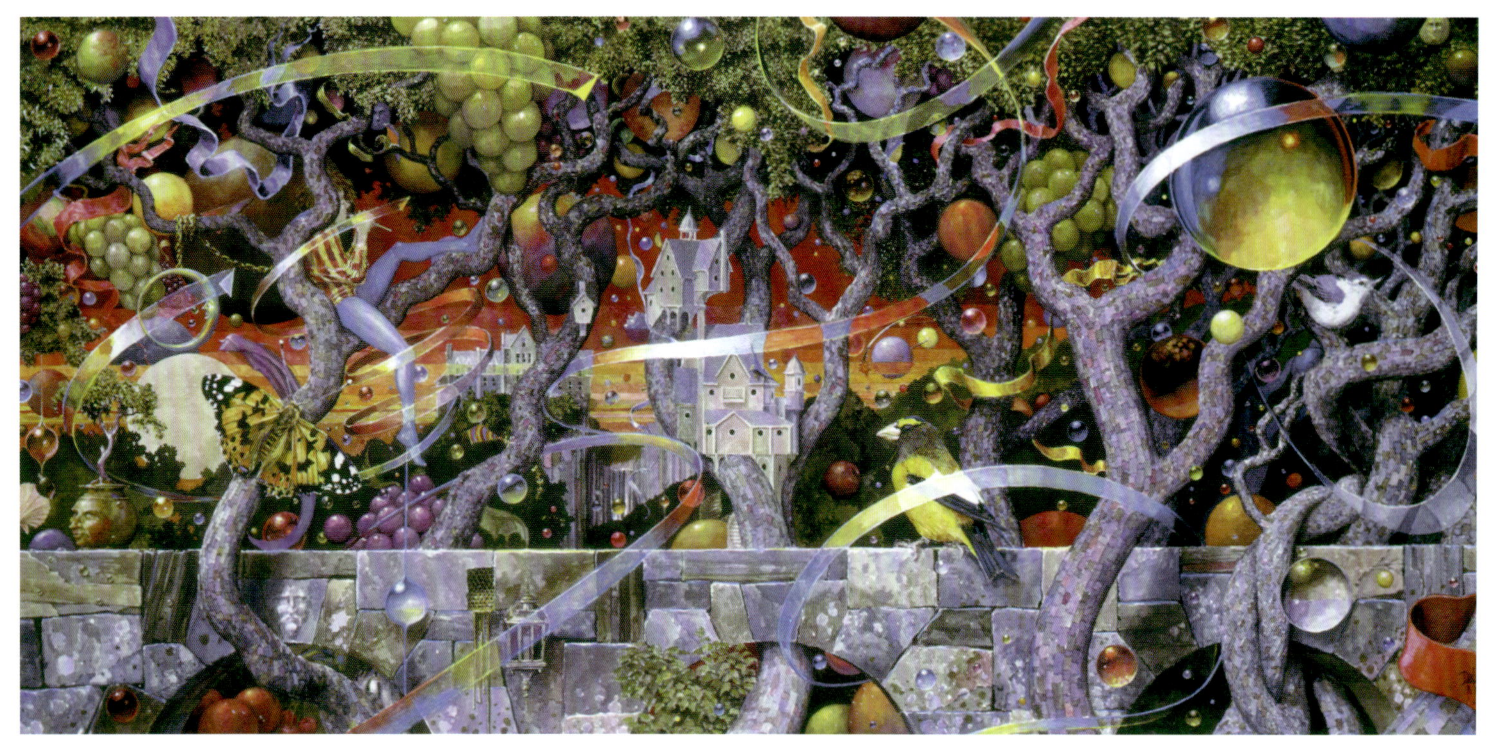

Danny's Song
1988, watercolor on paper
a. 12" x 30"

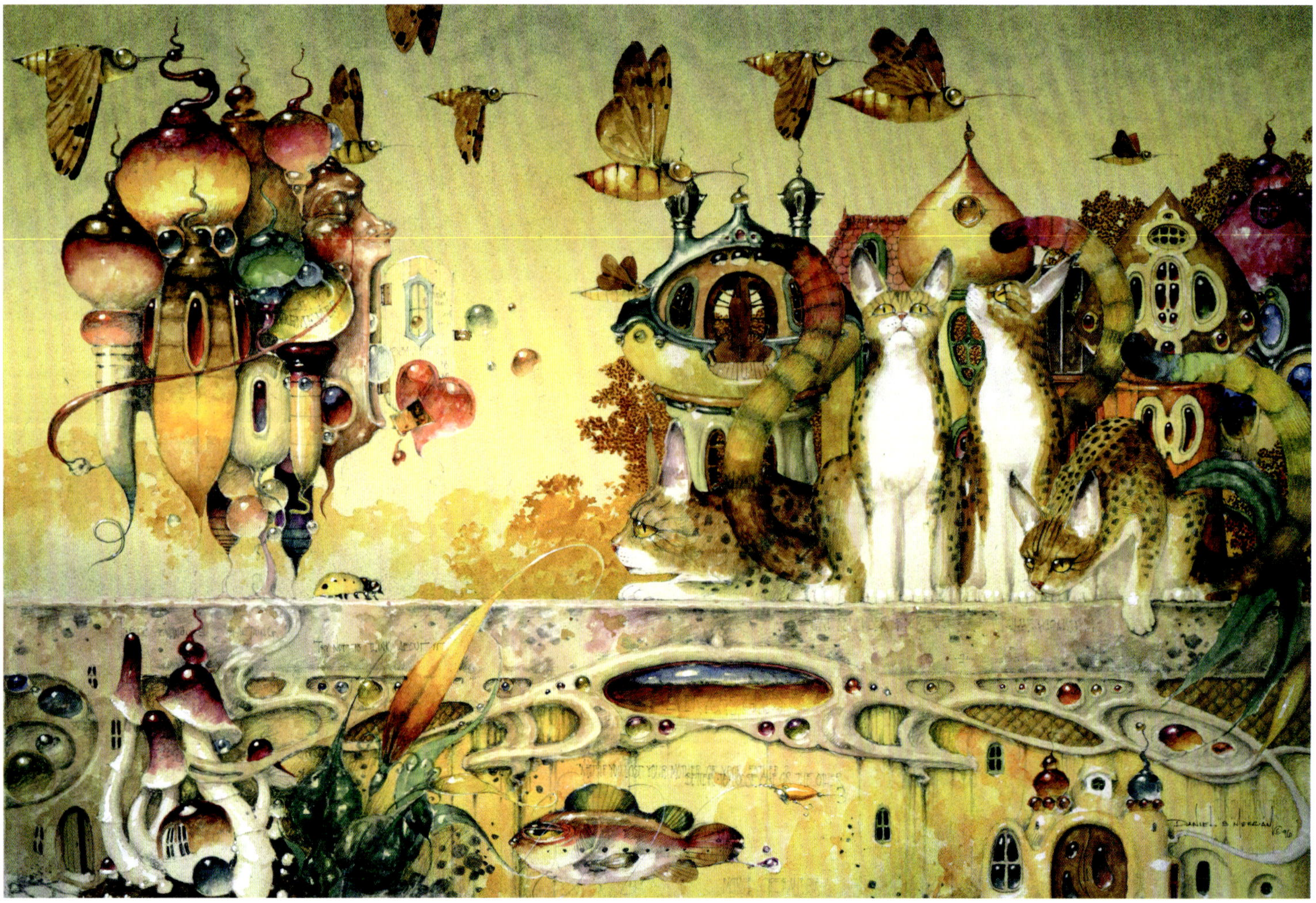

Busquito Row
1996, watercolor on paper
a. 11" x 17"

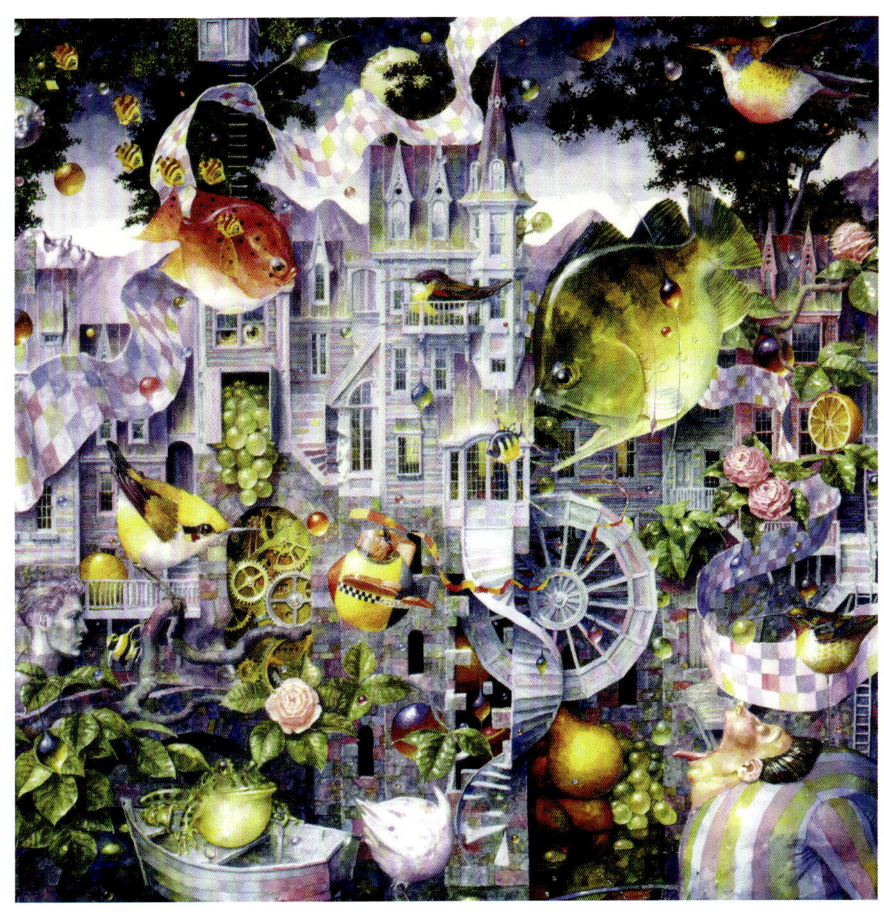

FULL CIRCLE
1991, WATERCOLOR ON PAPER
A. 20" X 20"

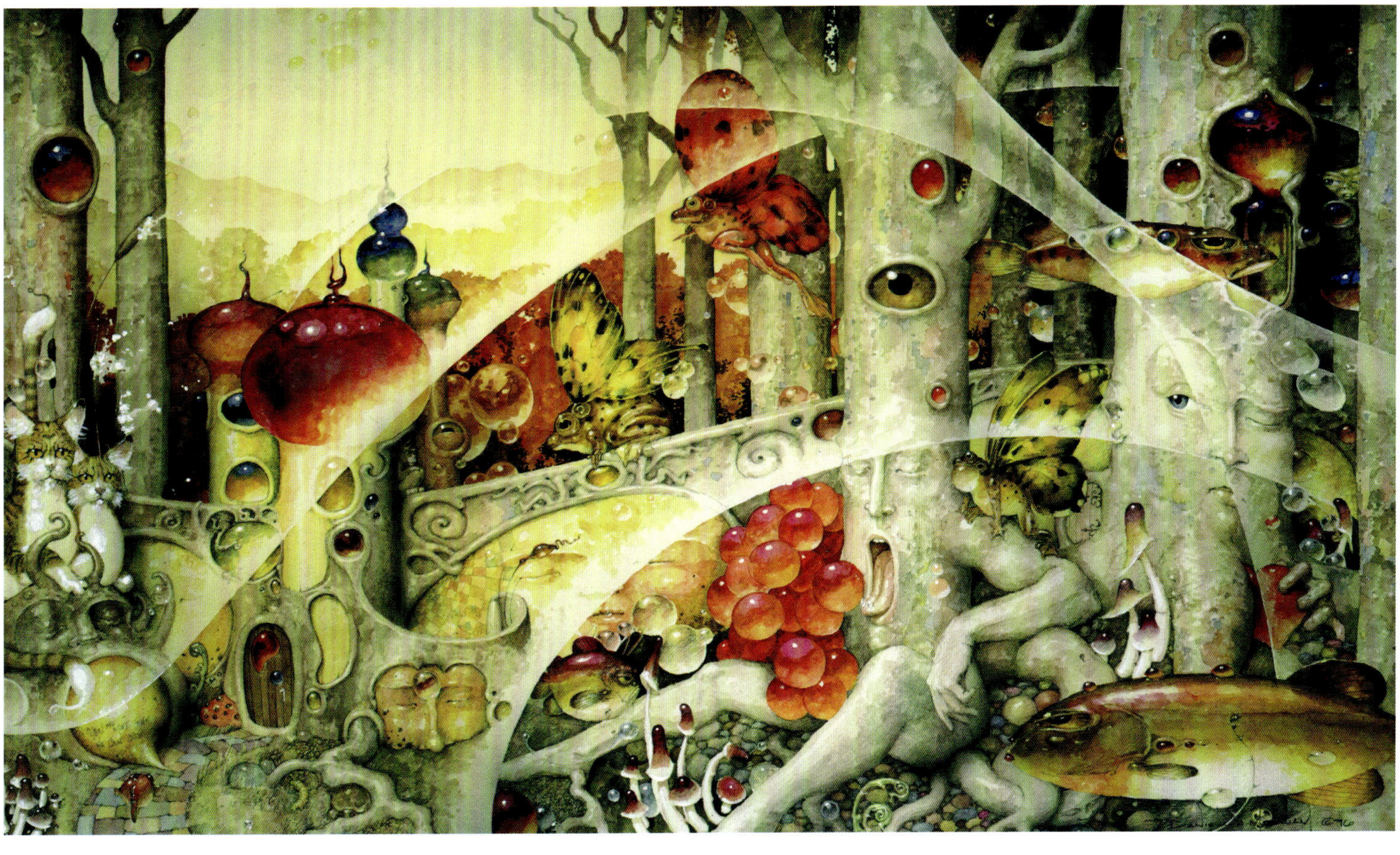

LEAP FROG
1996, WATERCOLOR ON PAPER
14" X 24"

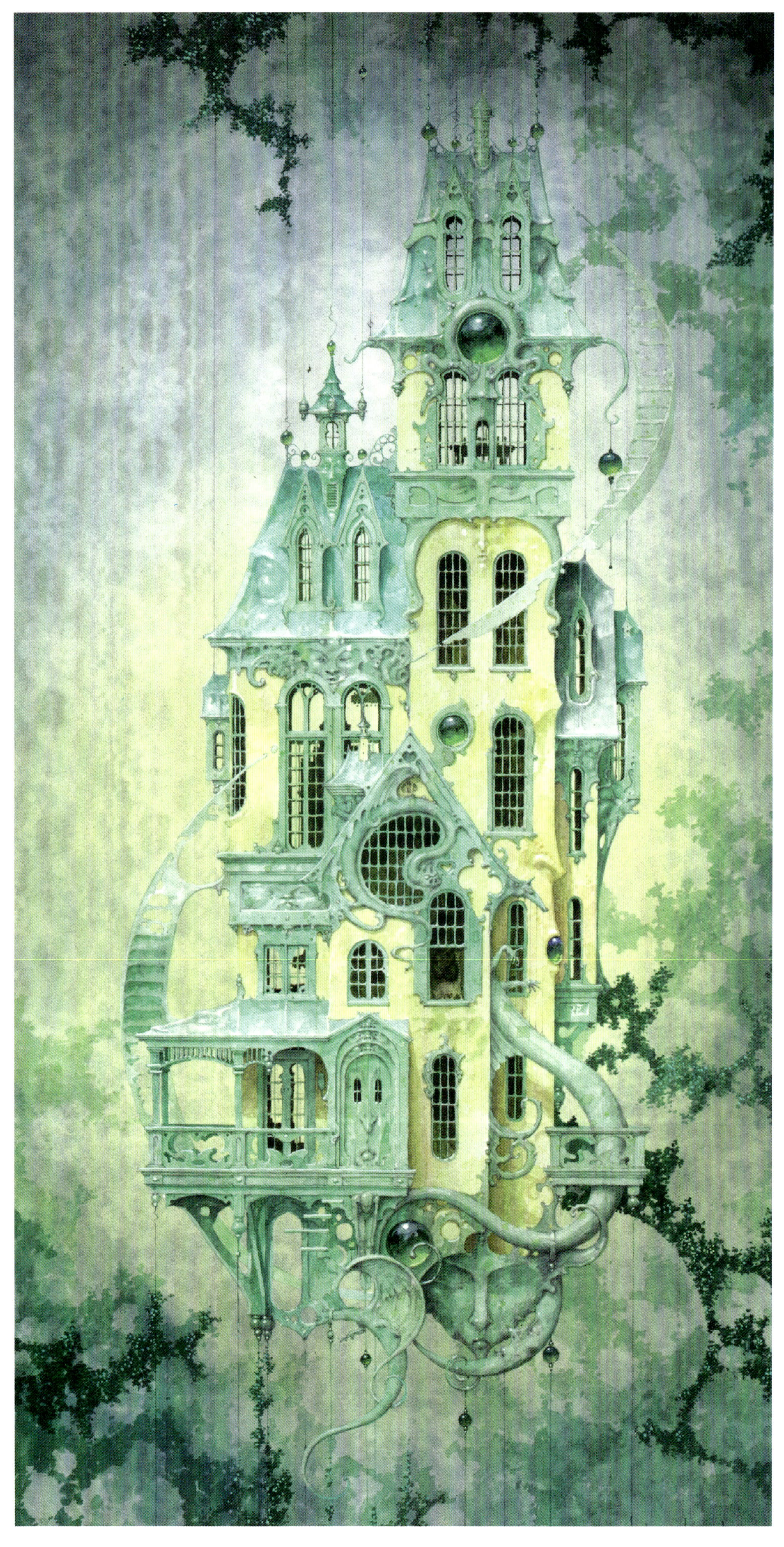

Laurel's Lair
1995, watercolor on paper
24" x 15"

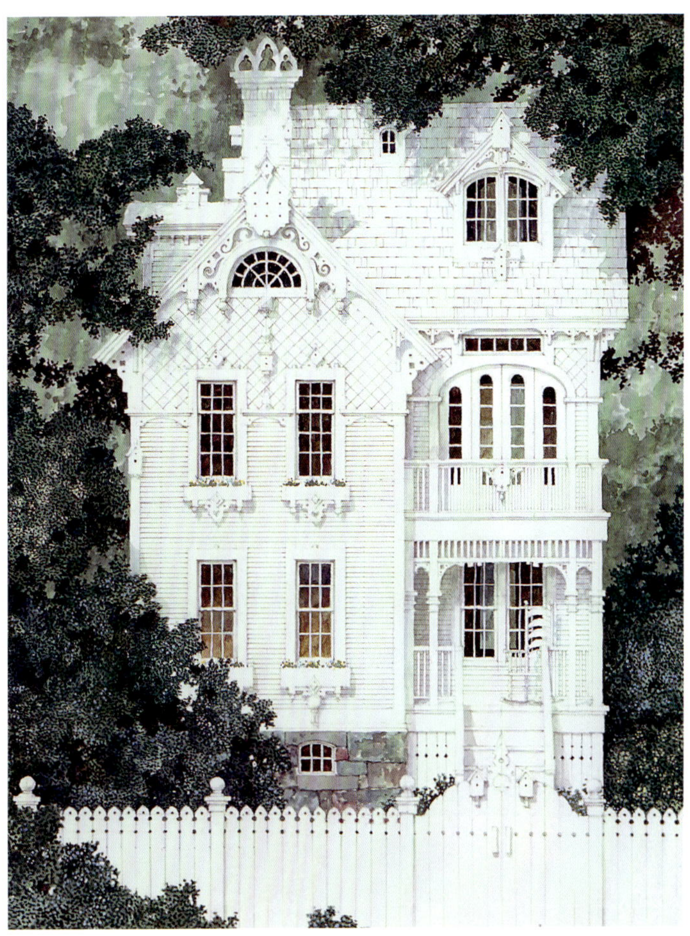

THE WHITE HOUSE
1996, WATERCOLOR ON PAPER
12" X 9"

STRUCTURE

Within the facades of architectural ornamentation are the scriptings of human ideals, marked of the time from which they came. These are our motifs in their grandest form, and they engulf our lives not only in body but also in spirit. We began in caves and painted on the walls, and we may soon live in spaceships of the oddest designs. My architectural subjects are dwellings that display the importance of home and the use of its space. They are not structures of status; they are, instead, the monuments to family that shelter us from harm and keep us warm.

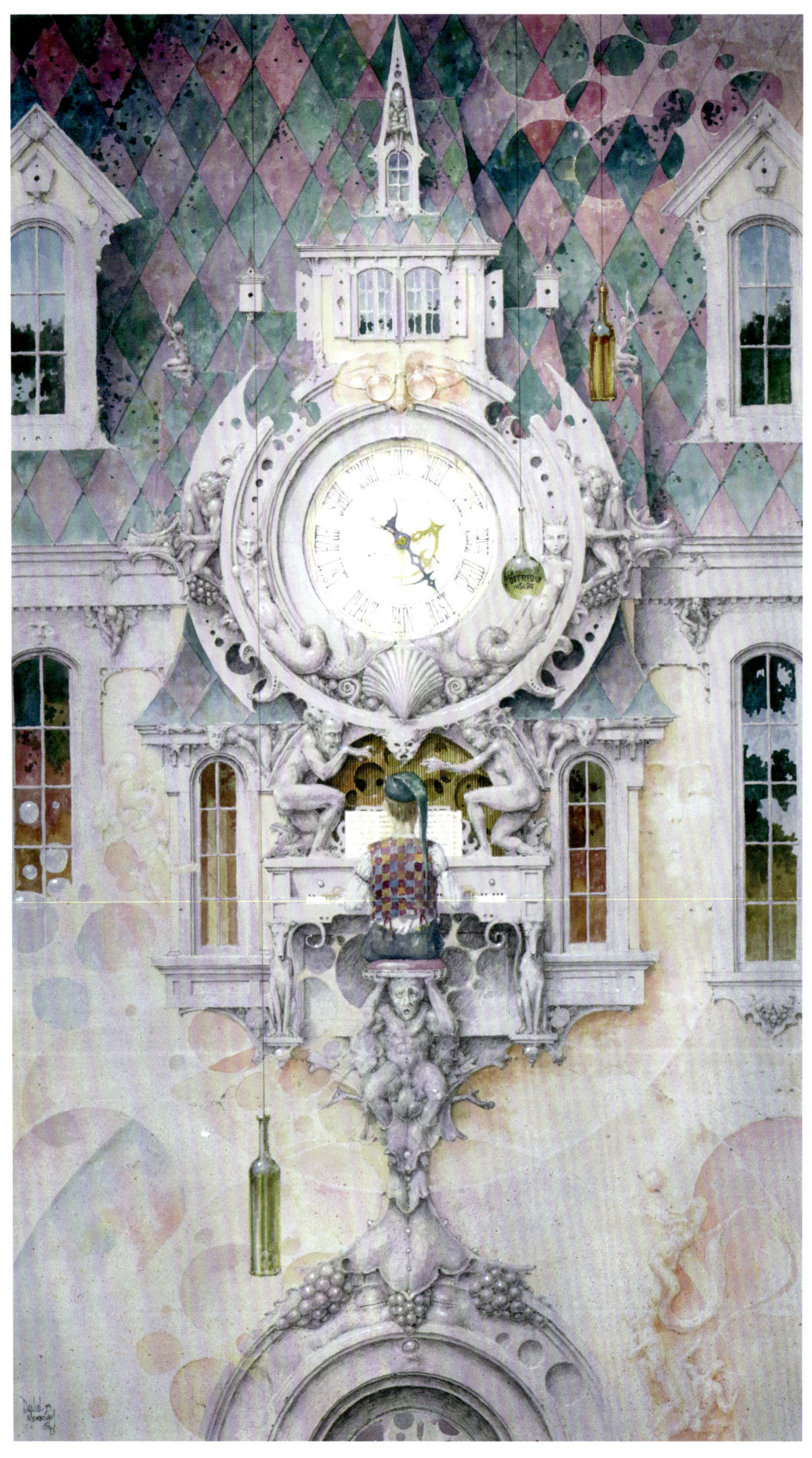

EMOTIONAL CLOCK
1993, WATERCOLOR ON PAPER
A. 26" X 15"

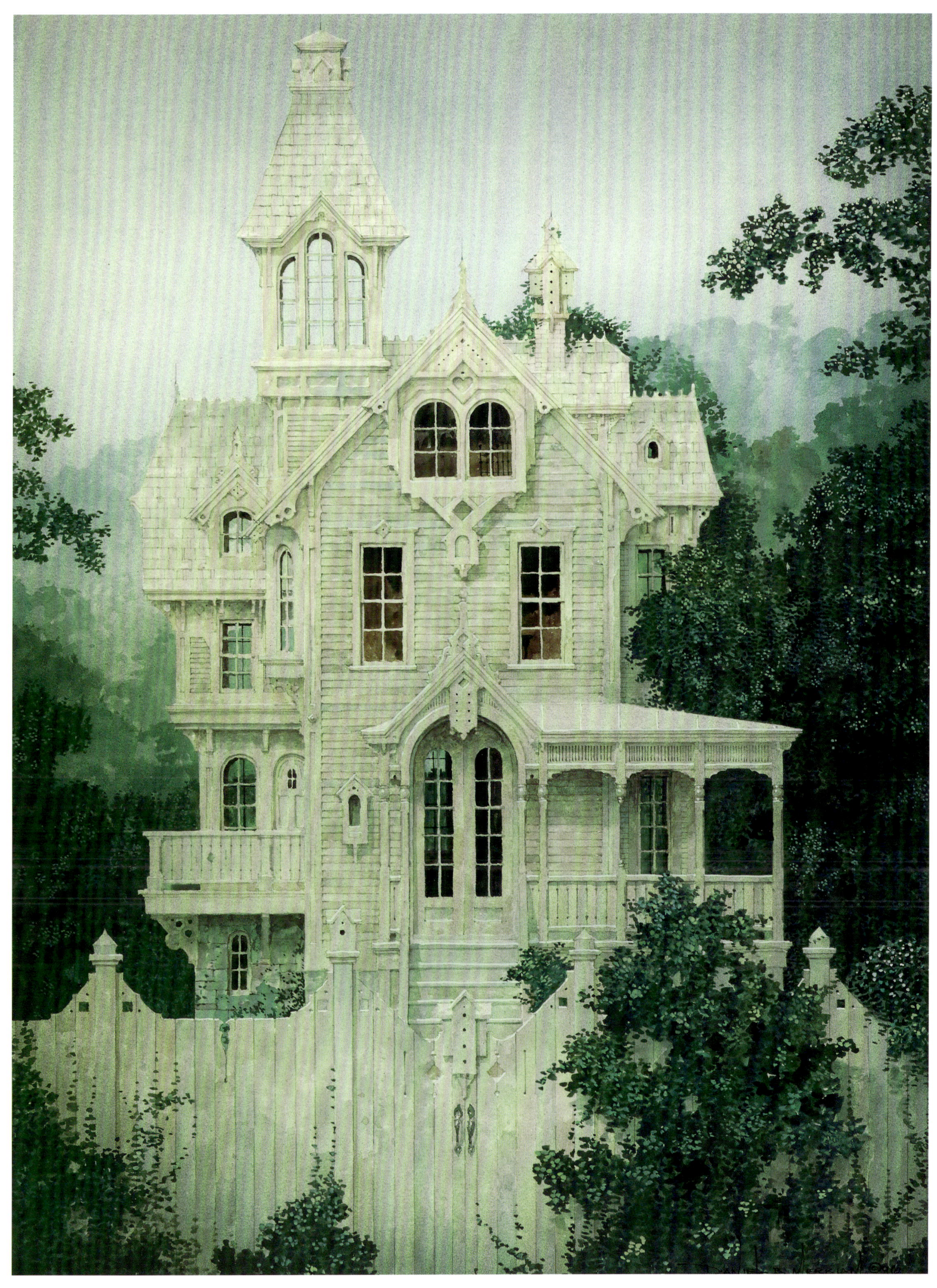

Right At Home
1996, watercolor on paper
15.5" x 11.5"

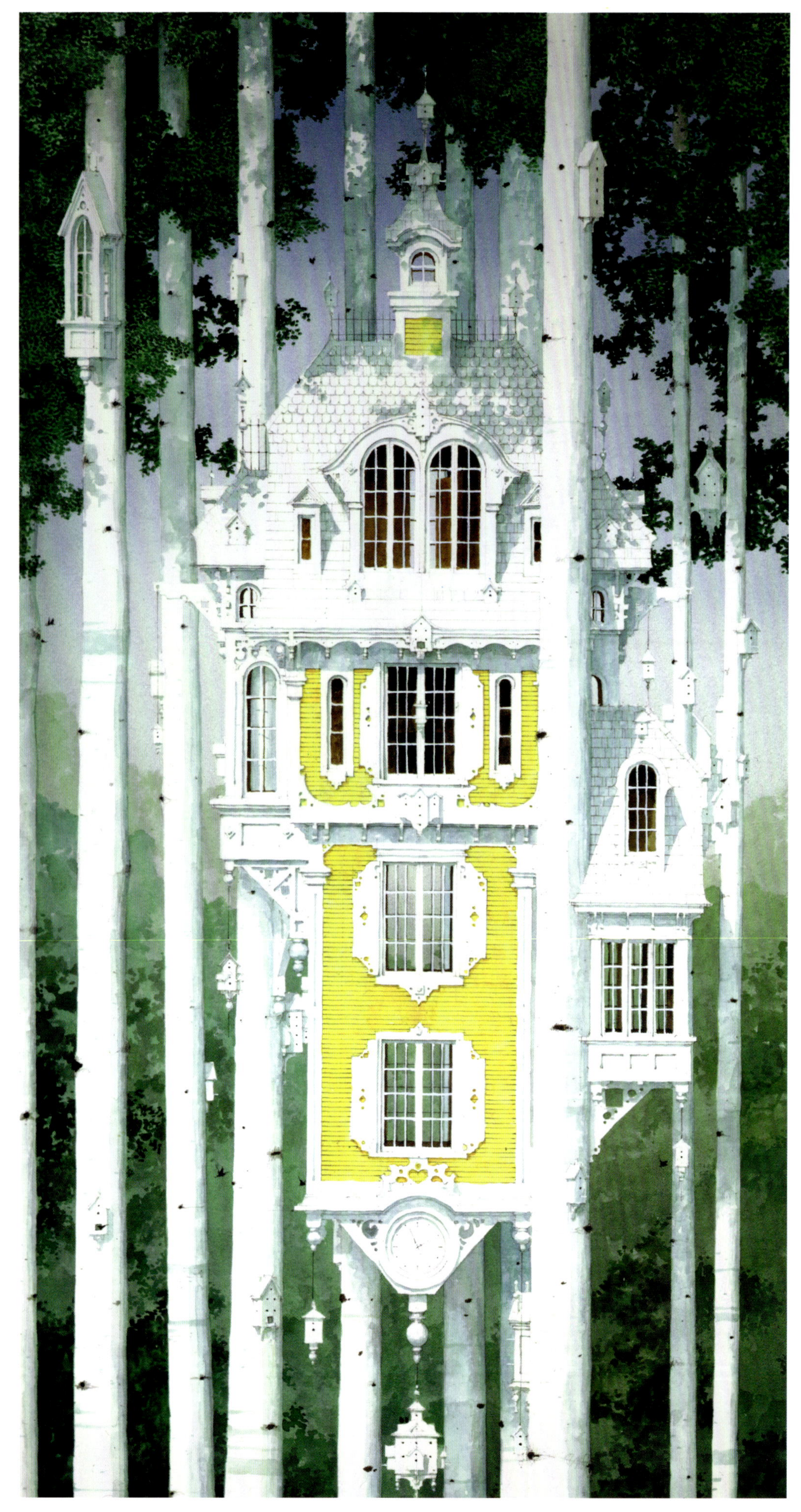

Lost in the Trees
1995, watercolor on paper
20.5" x 11.1"

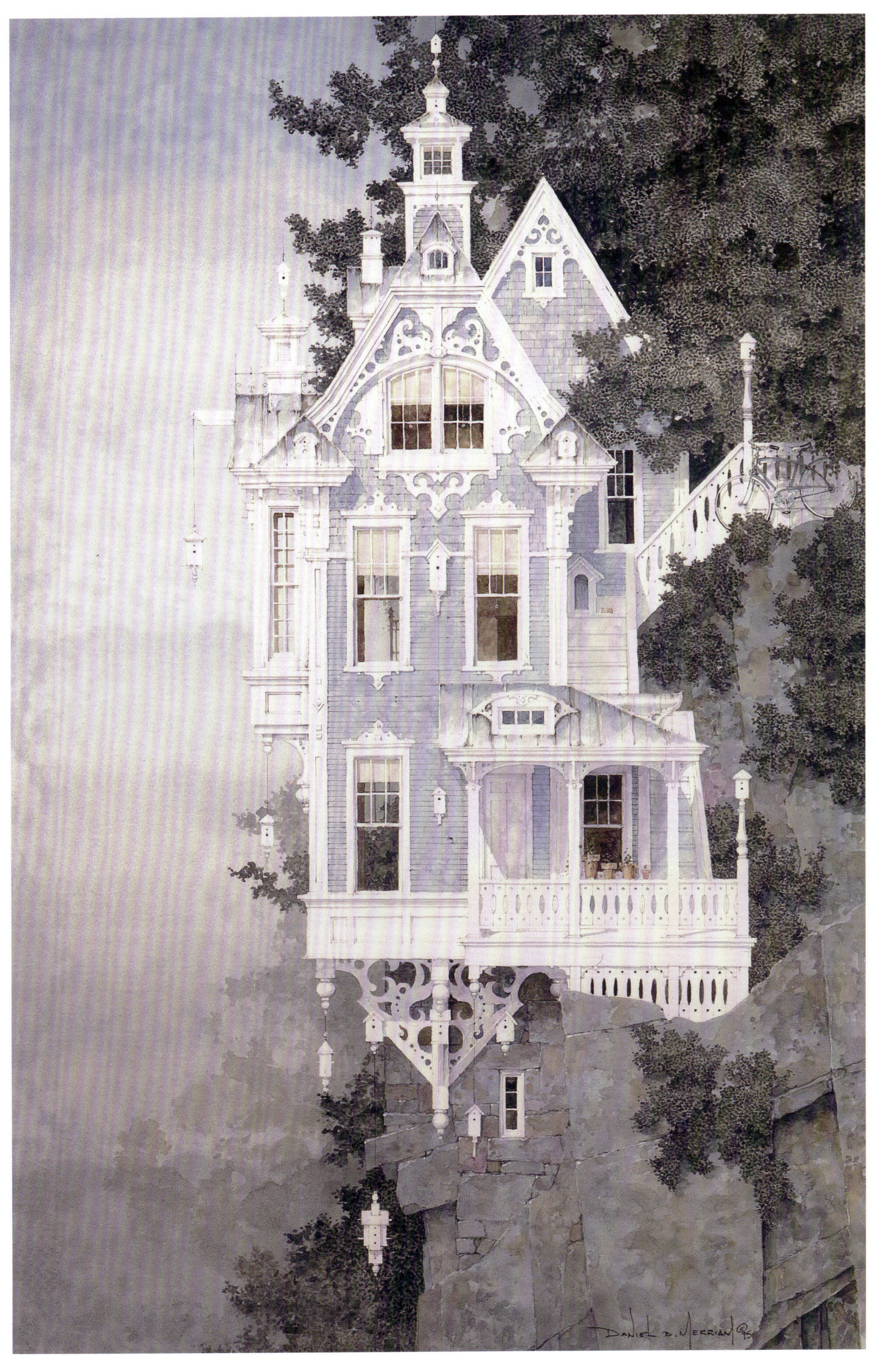

LOOKING OUT FROM MYSELF
1995, WATERCOLOR ON PAPER
A. 18" X 12"

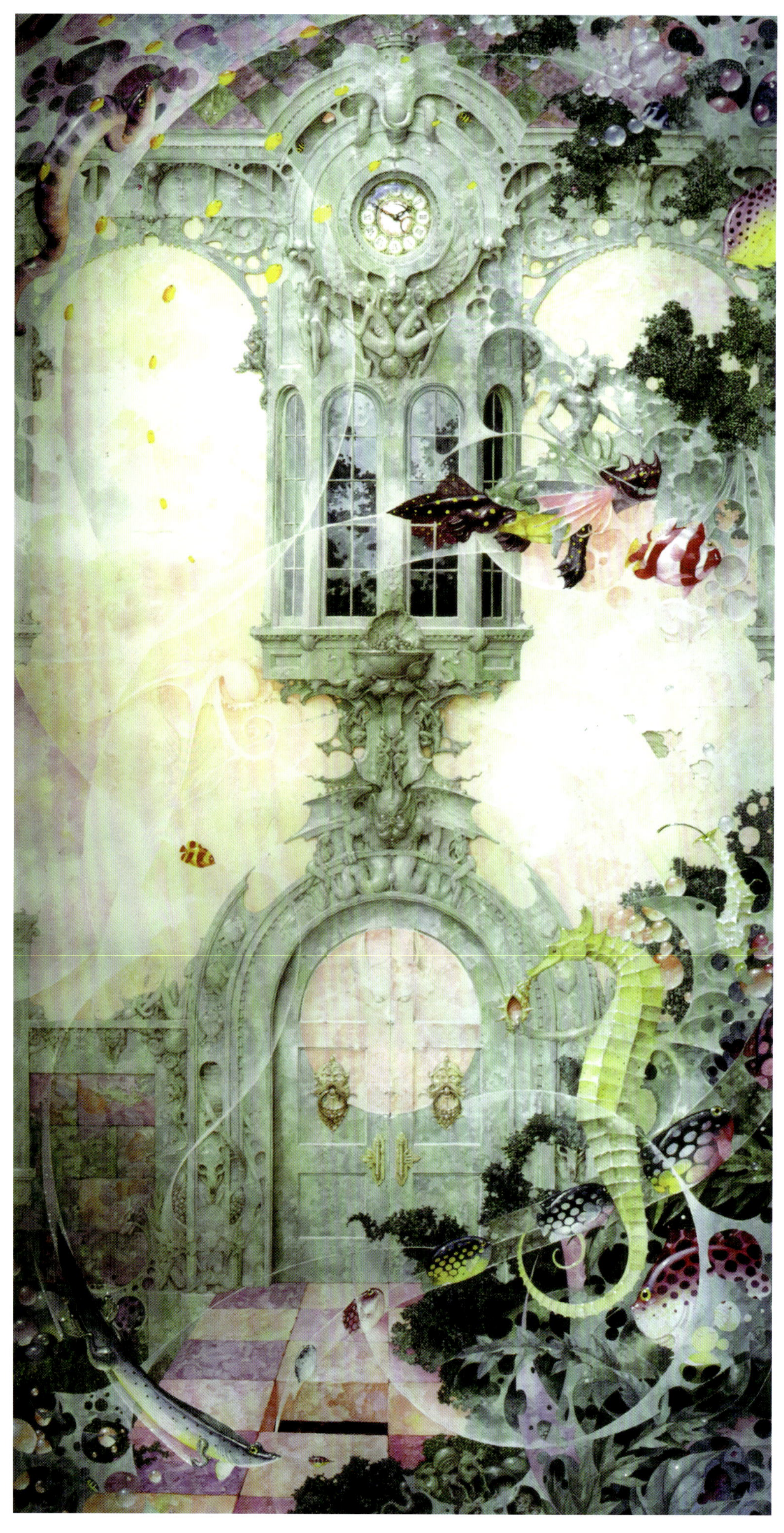

Infinite Possibilities
1993, watercolor on paper
a. 50" x 30"

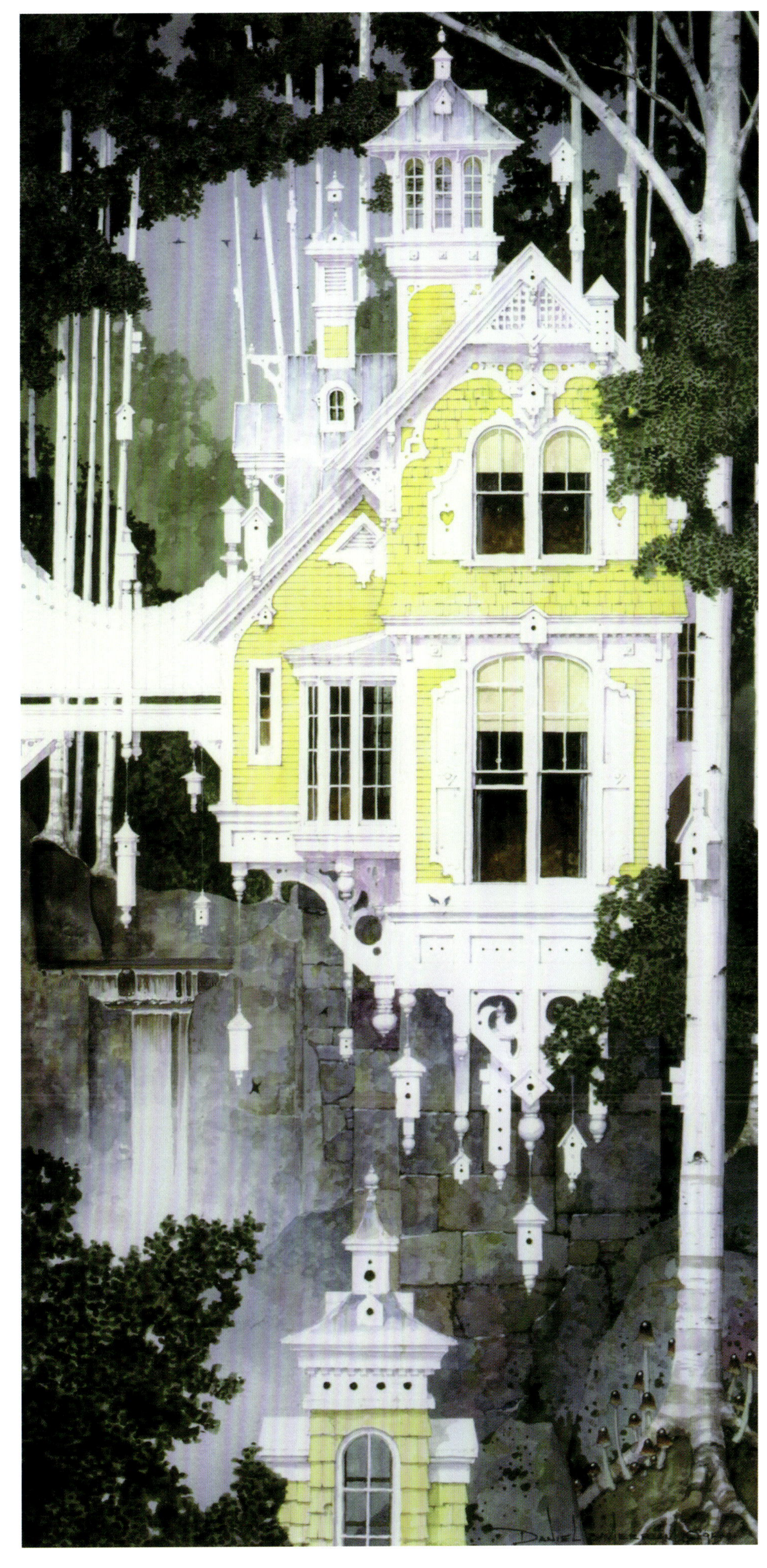

Over the Falls
1995, watercolor on paper
A. 22" x 11"

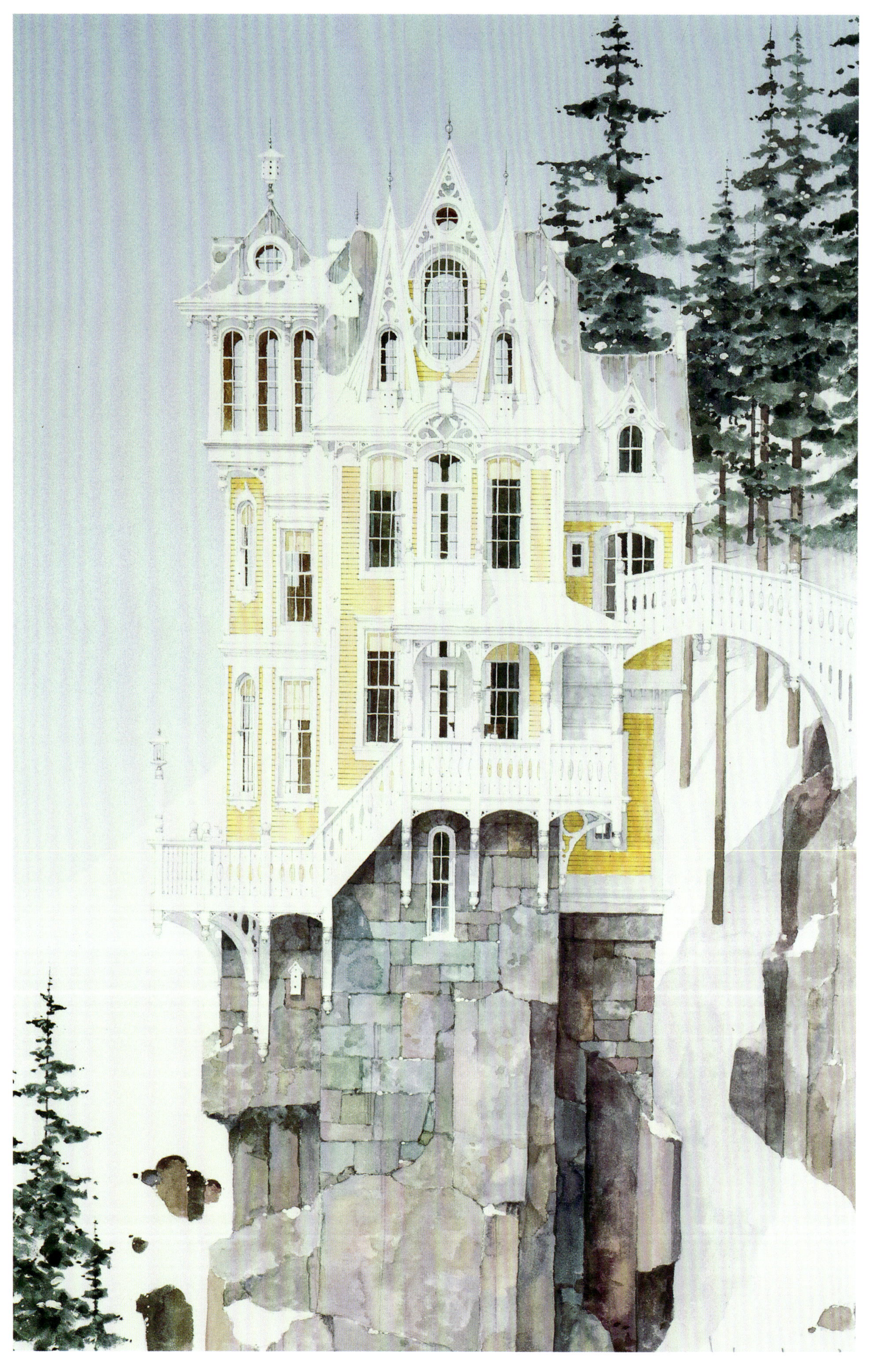

Half Way Up
1994, watercolor on paper
a. 18" x 12"

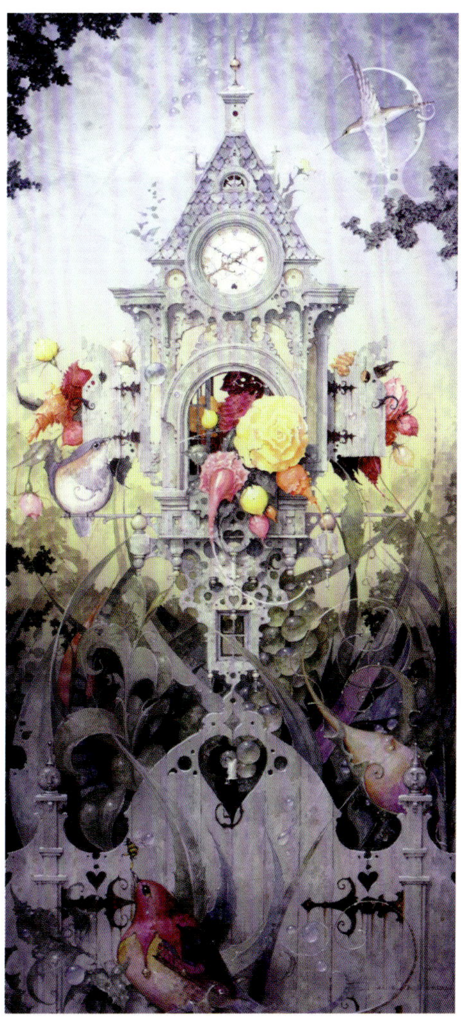

Overgrown
1995, watercolor on paper
a. 28" x 14"

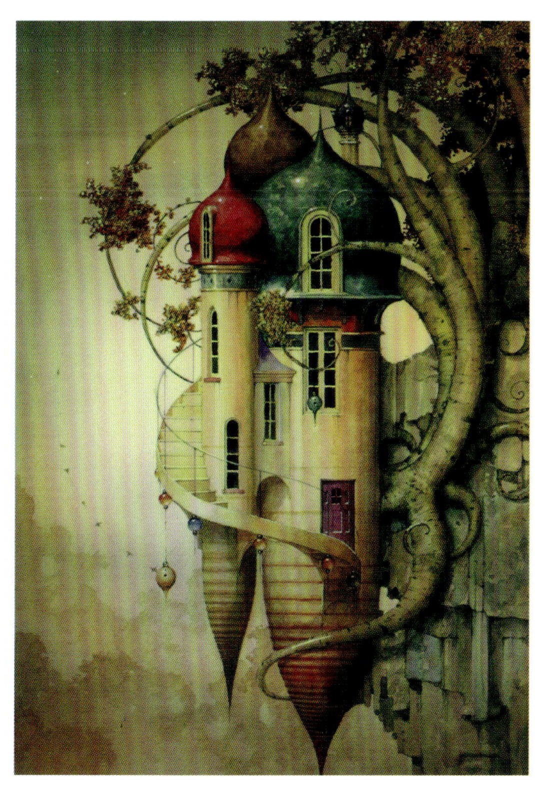

Over the Edge
1996, watercolor on paper
a. 15" x 10"

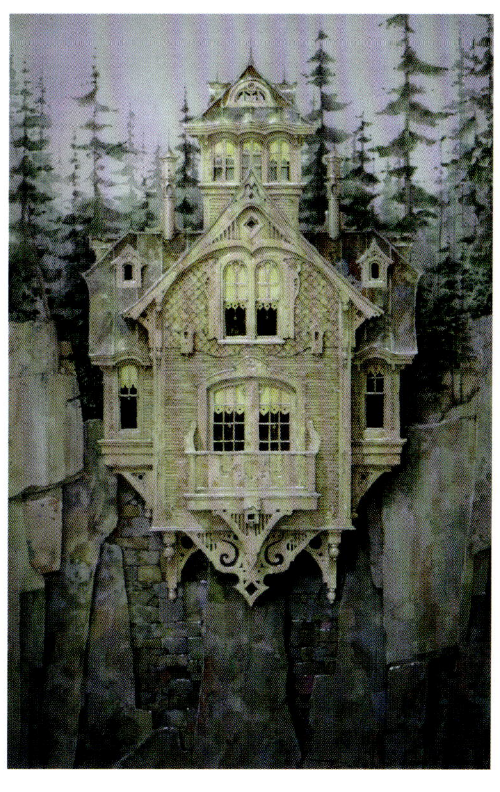

Aloft
1996, watercolor on paper
15" x 10"

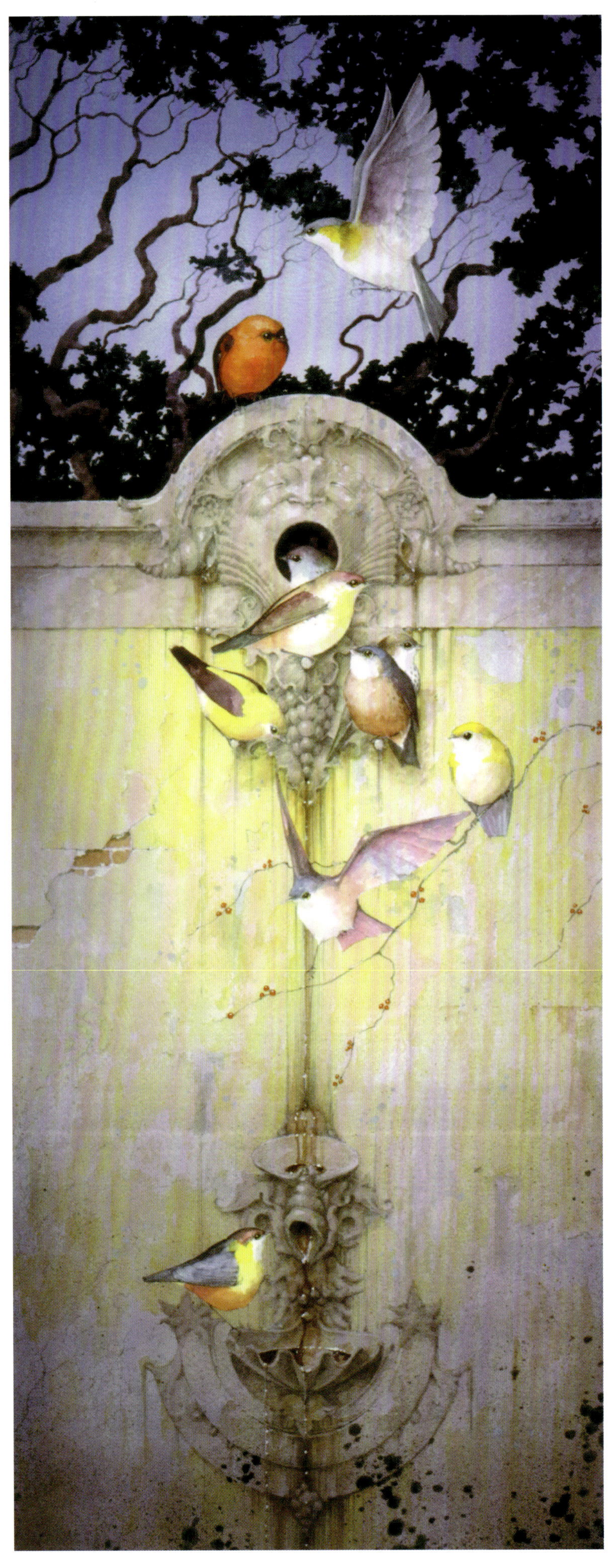

Aviary
1995, watercolor on paper
a. 30" x 12"

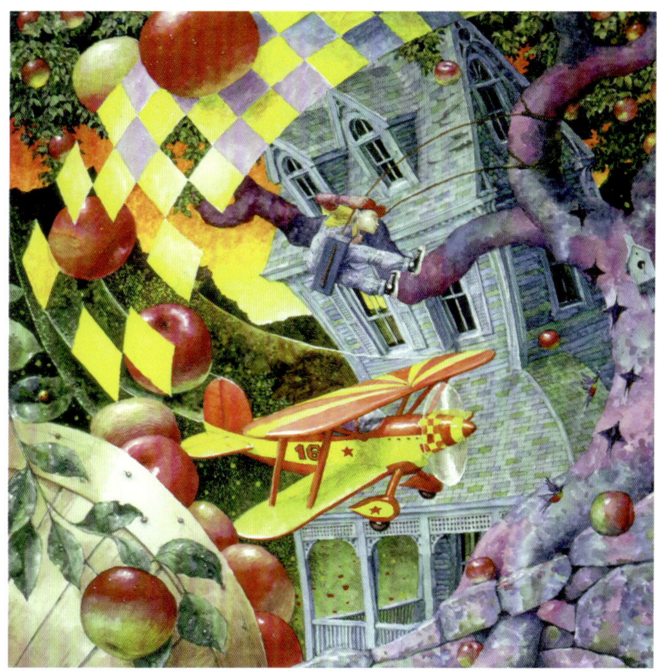

Apple Toss
1992, watercolor on paper
a. 14" x 14"

Flight

In my dream, I started with a gentle descent from the railing of a third-story balcony. By flapping my arms I was able to delay my falling. After encountering a number of dream sequences where I had taken to flight, I found myself flying increasingly higher. It seemed the more confident I was, the higher I could fly. Eventually I realized that I could stay aloft without moving my arms. As long as I didn't think about falling, I would float above the clouds for hours.

Today, I can at will close my eyes and soar from where I sit -- just traveling about at any speed, anywhere, performing elaborate swoops and ascending turns. Over the rooftops I fly, cresting hills and gliding off the edges of canyons.

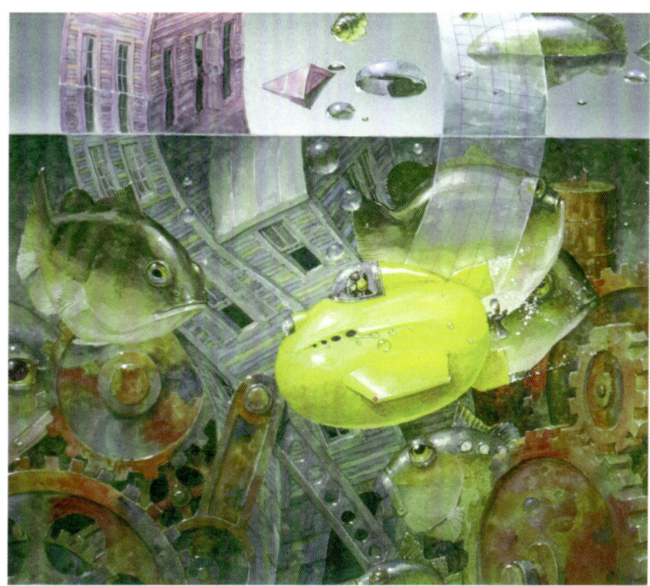

The World Below Us
1992, watercolor on paper
a. 16" x 16"

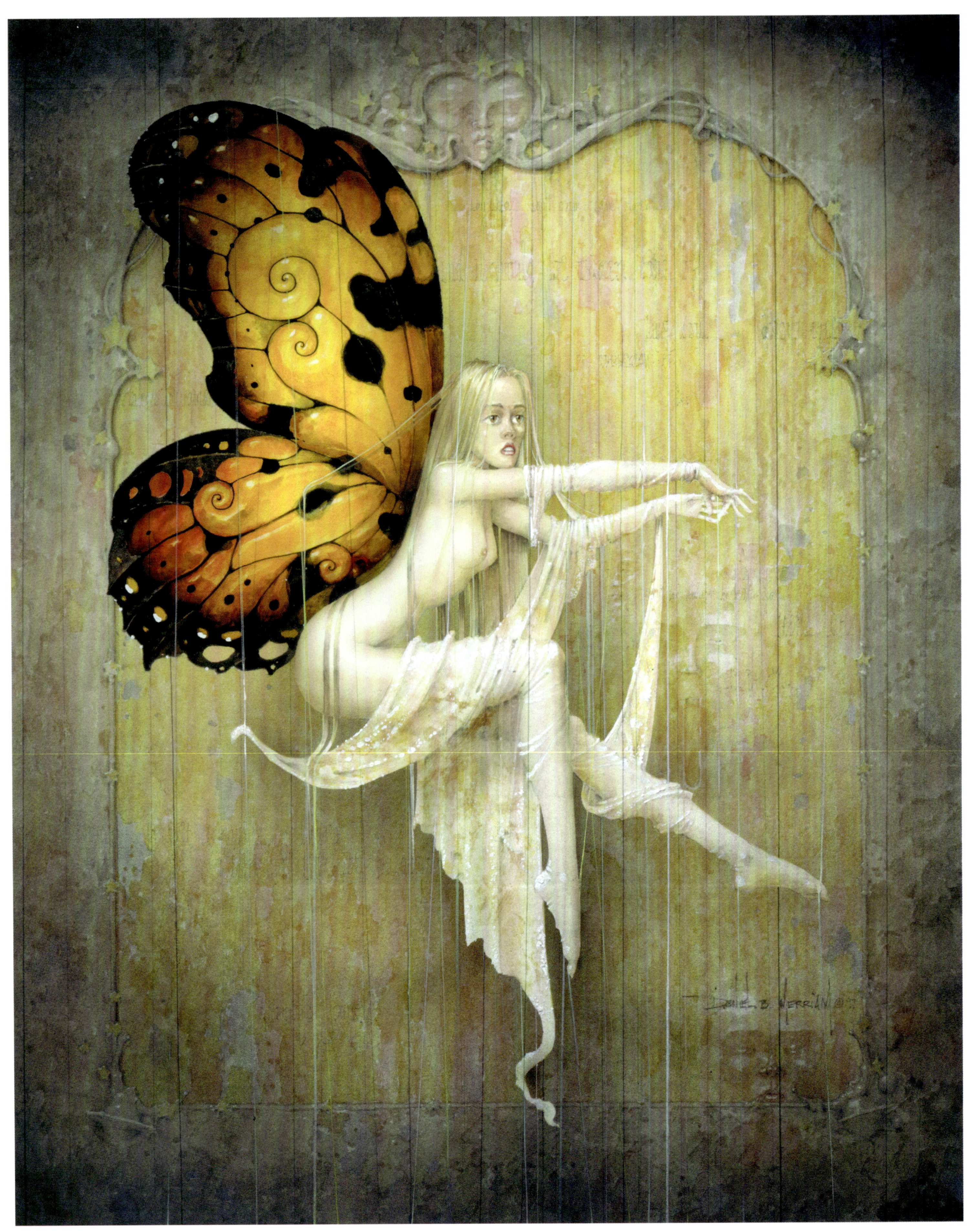

METAMORPHOSIS
1997, WATERCOLOR ON PAPER
22" X 18"

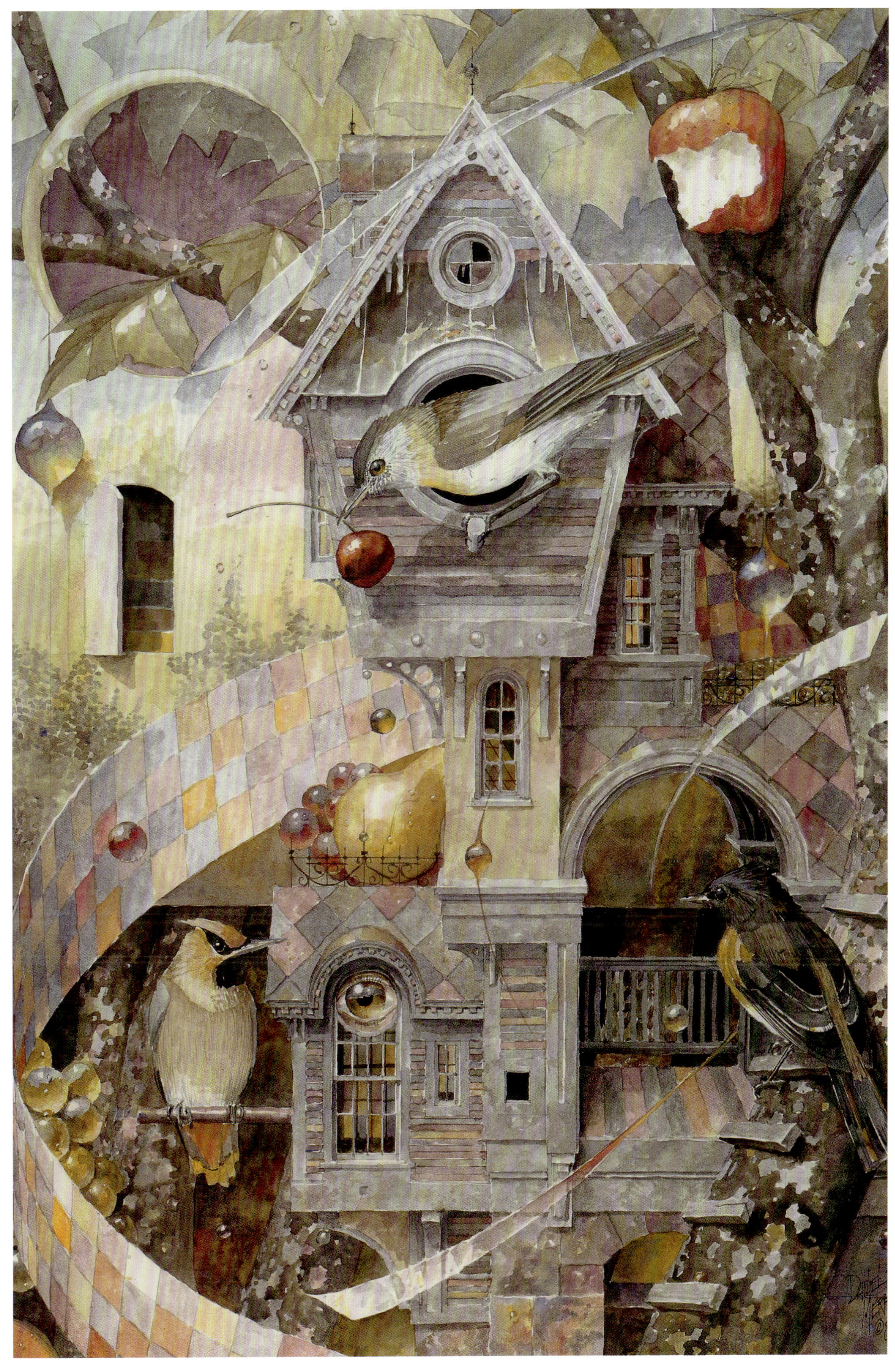

Birdhouse
1992, watercolor on paper
a. 20" x 14"

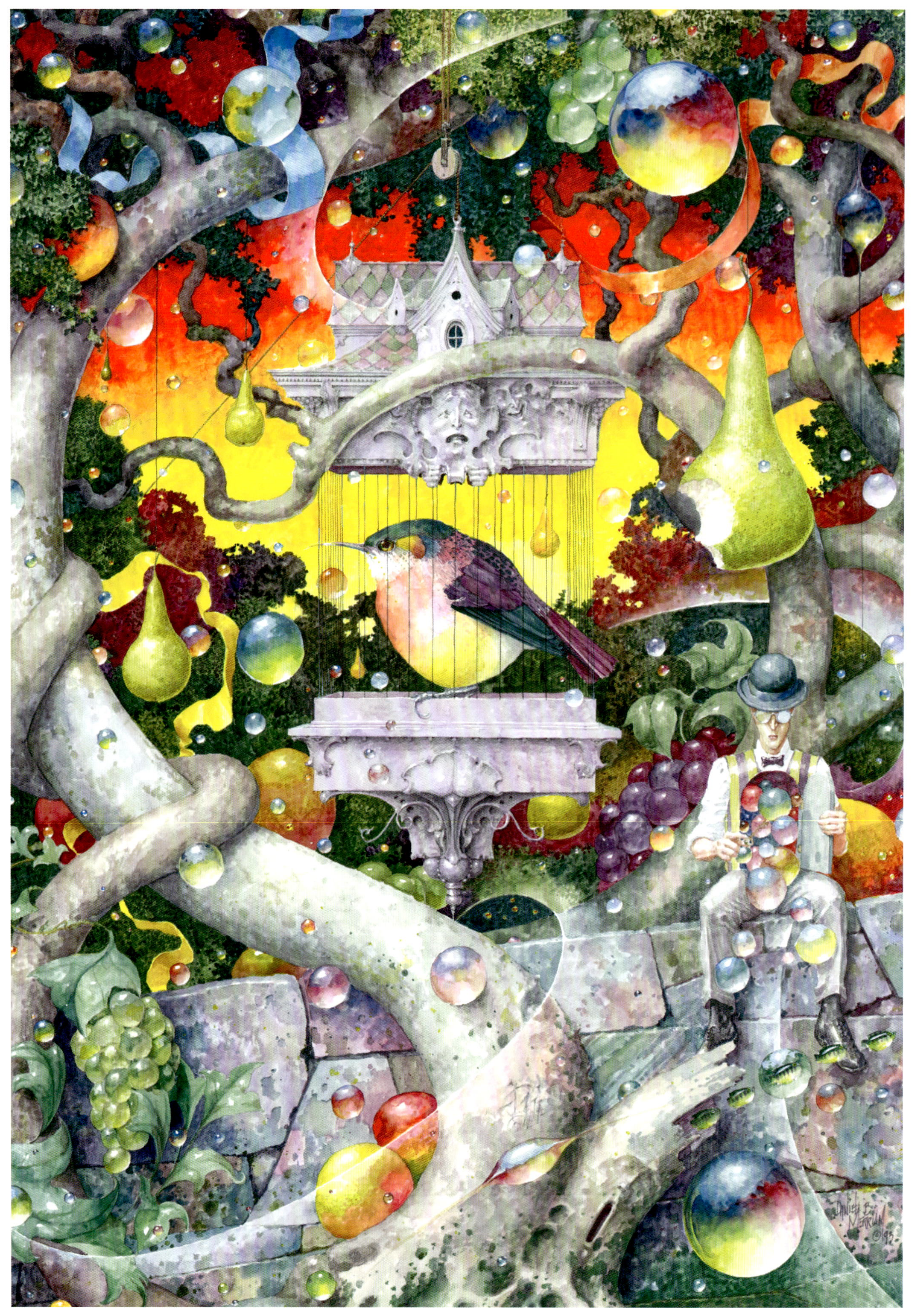

Thoughts Considered
1993, watercolor on paper
27.5" x 16.5"

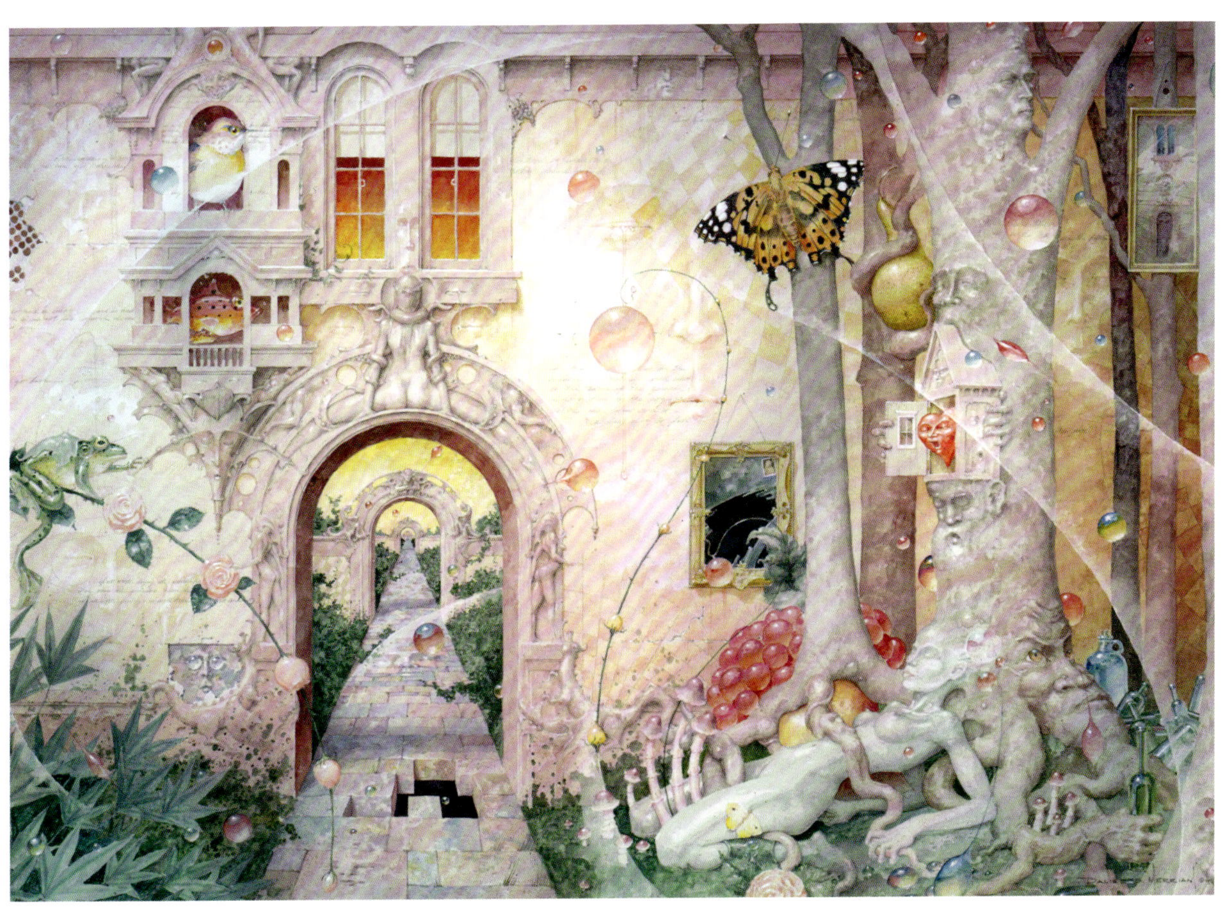

INSIDE OUT
1995, WATERCOLOR ON PAPER
22" X 30"

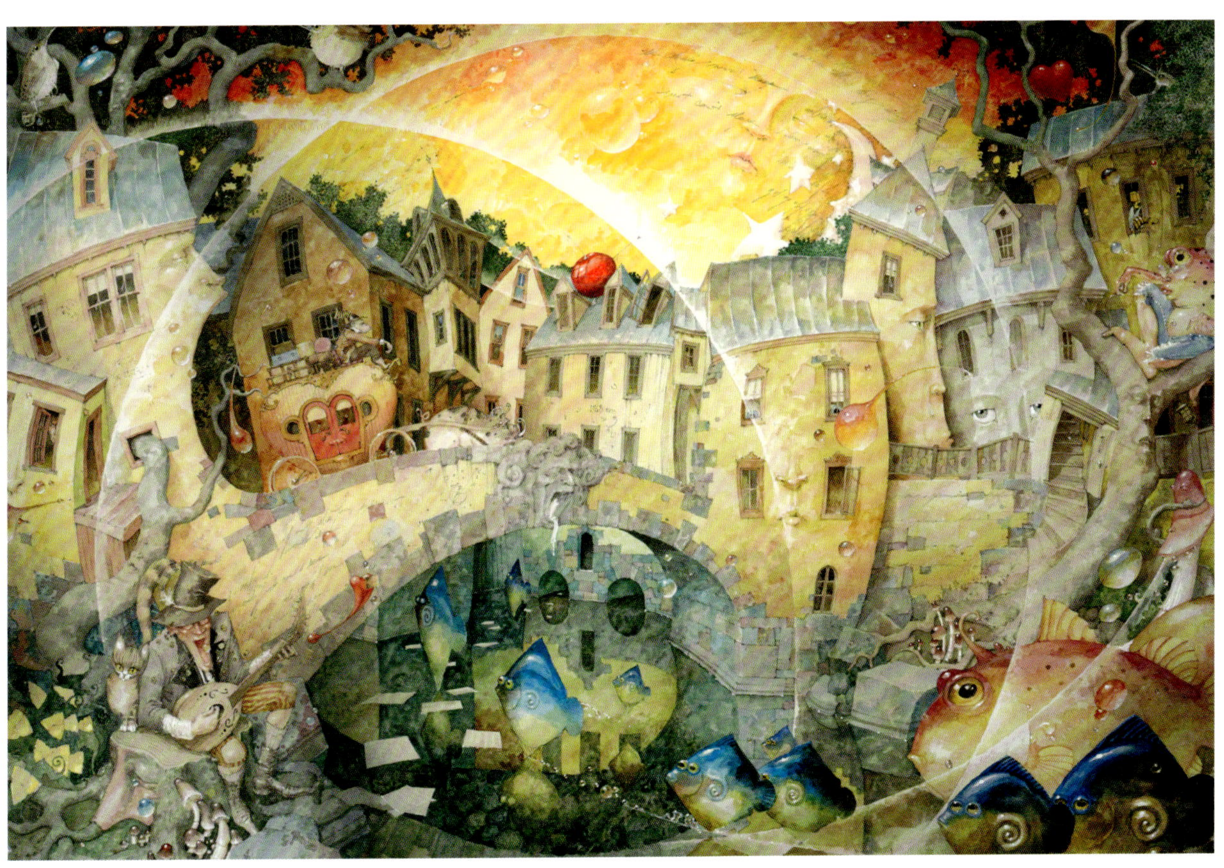

MANDOLIN
1995, WATERCOLOR ON PAPER
22" X 30"

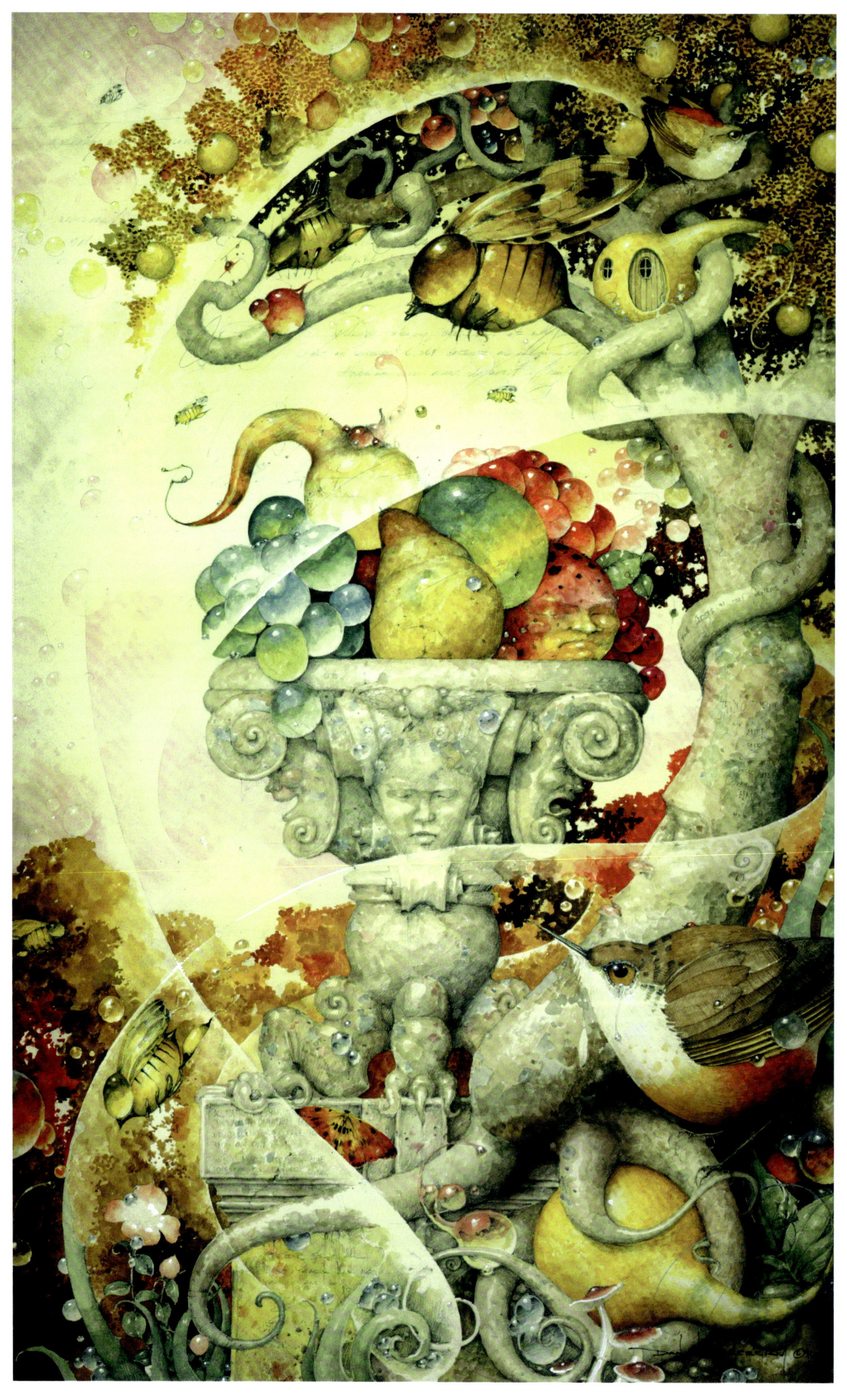

Summer Daze
1996, watercolor on paper
23.75" x 14"

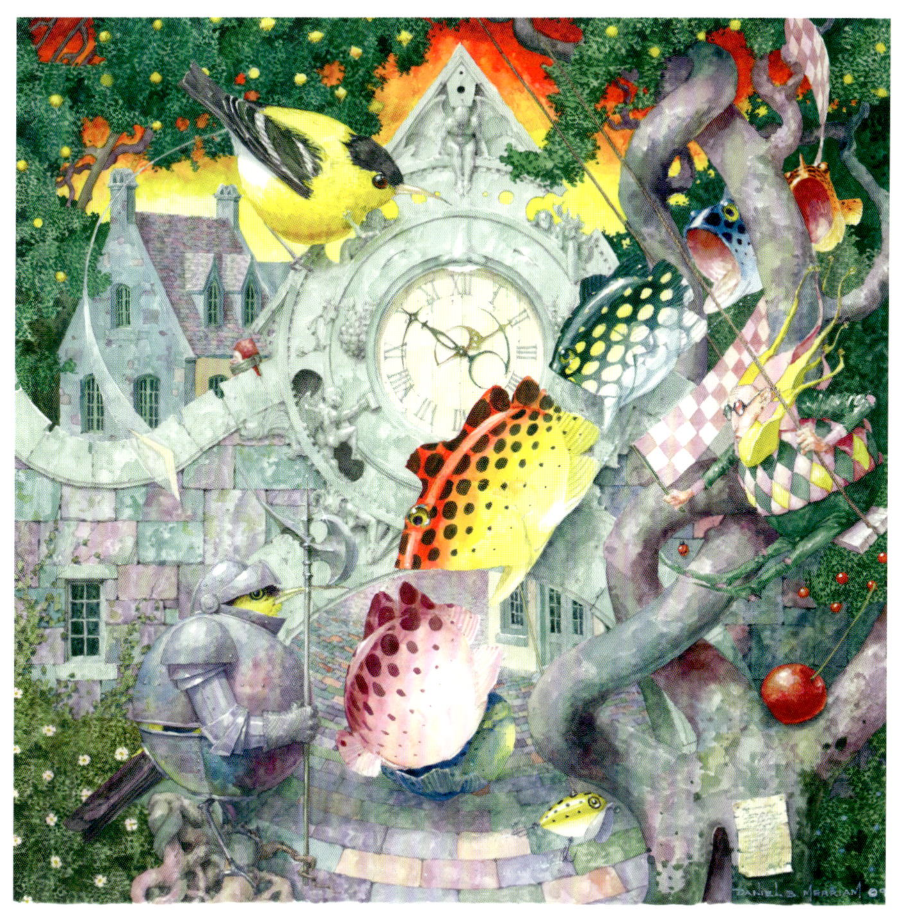

CROSSING UNDER
1993, WATERCOLOR ON PAPER
14.75" X 14.75"

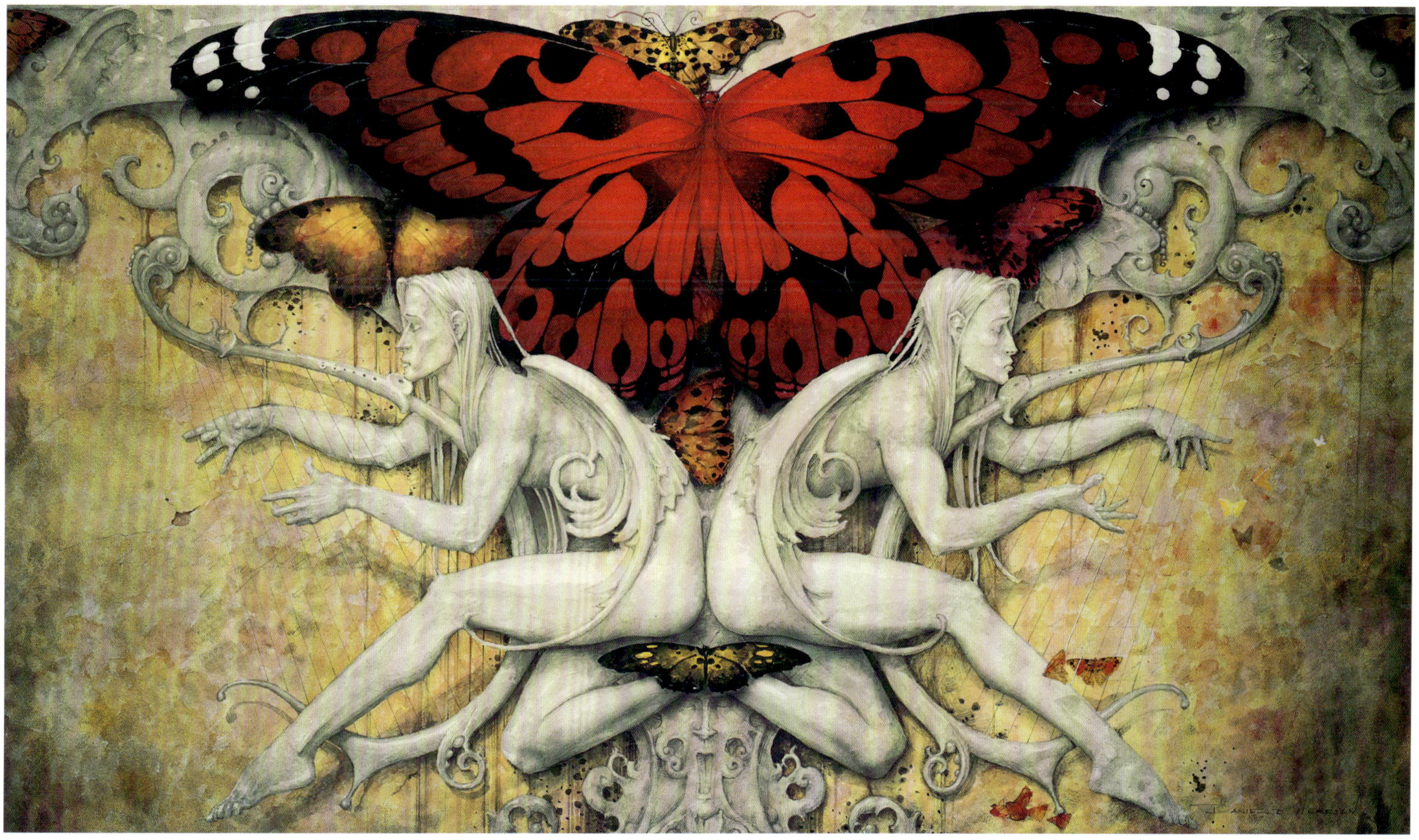

DUET
1995, WATERCOLOR ON PAPER
A. 14" X 22"

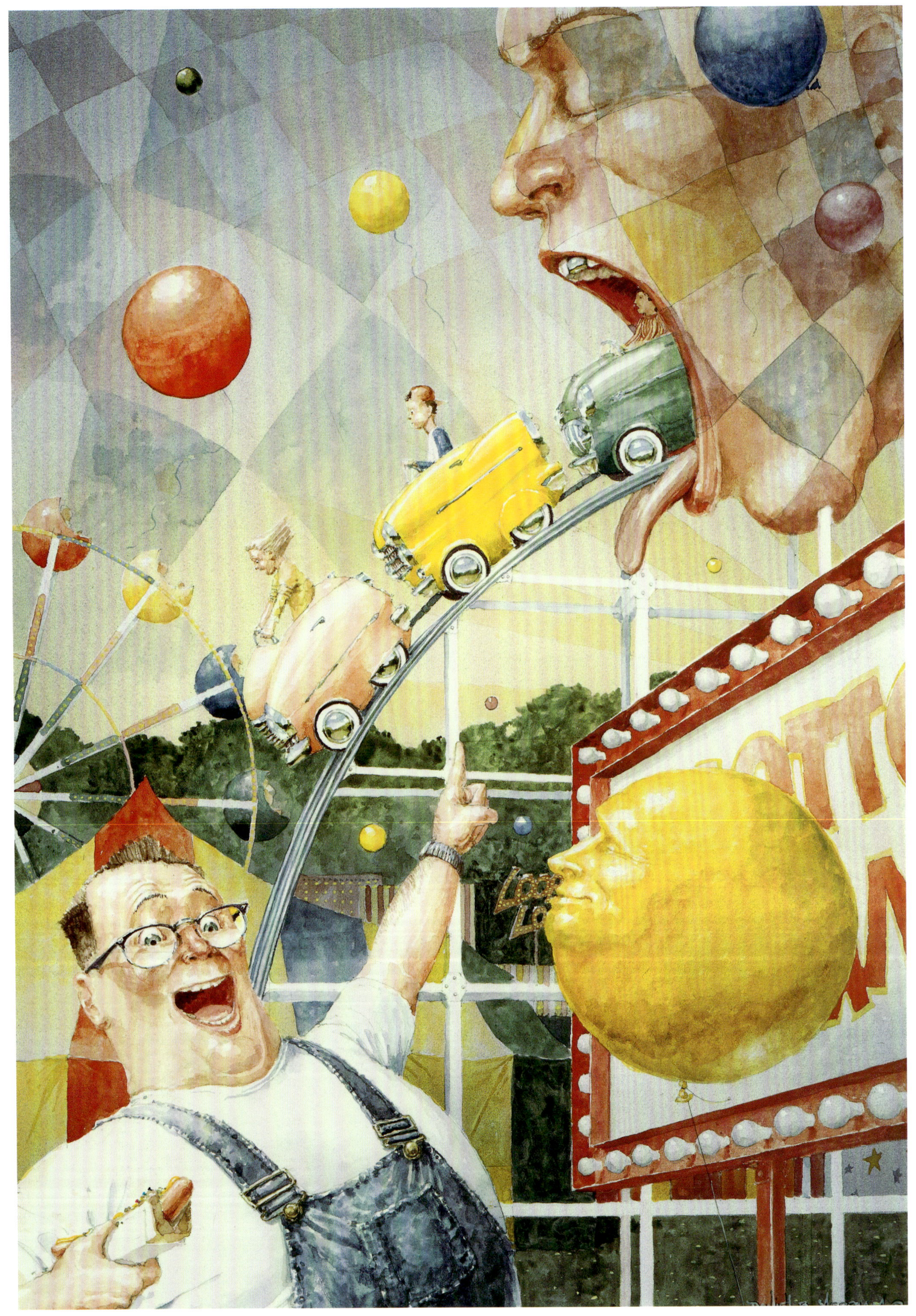

THE RIDE

1993, WATERCOLOR ON PAPER

13.5" X 9.5"

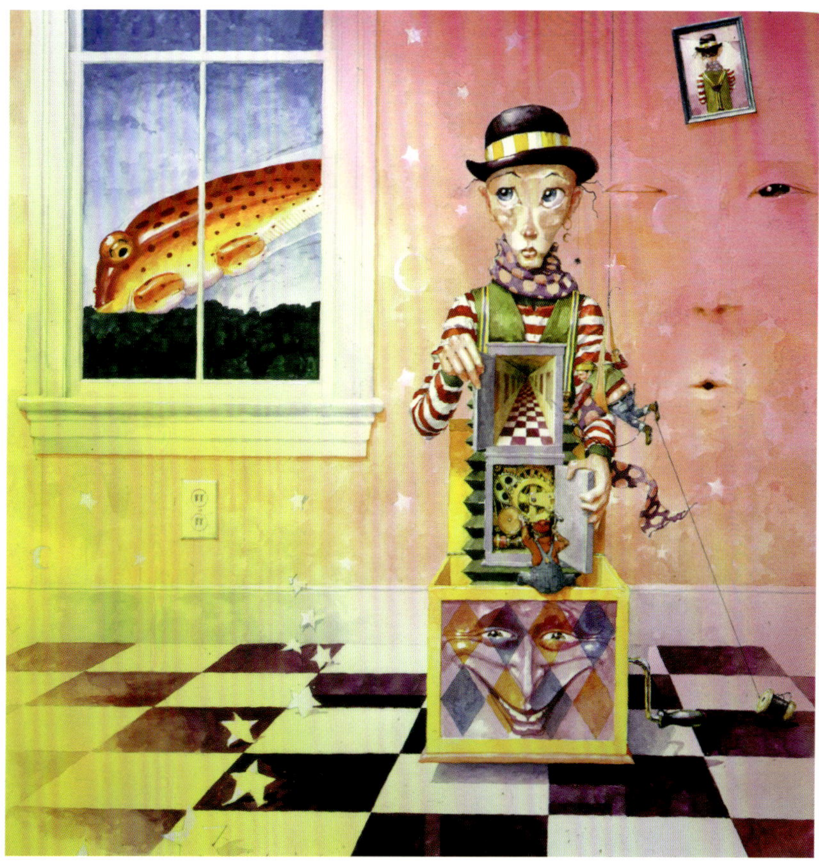

Fly By My Window
1993, watercolor on paper
a. 14" x 14"

Humor

Since I was a child, I could not resist picturing the most awkward scenarios at the most inappropriate times. In fact, I could not resist the fantasy, as it would force its irony into my mind. In some way, I am compelled to express a bit of humor as a regular part of my day. I find it does the body and soul a lot of good.

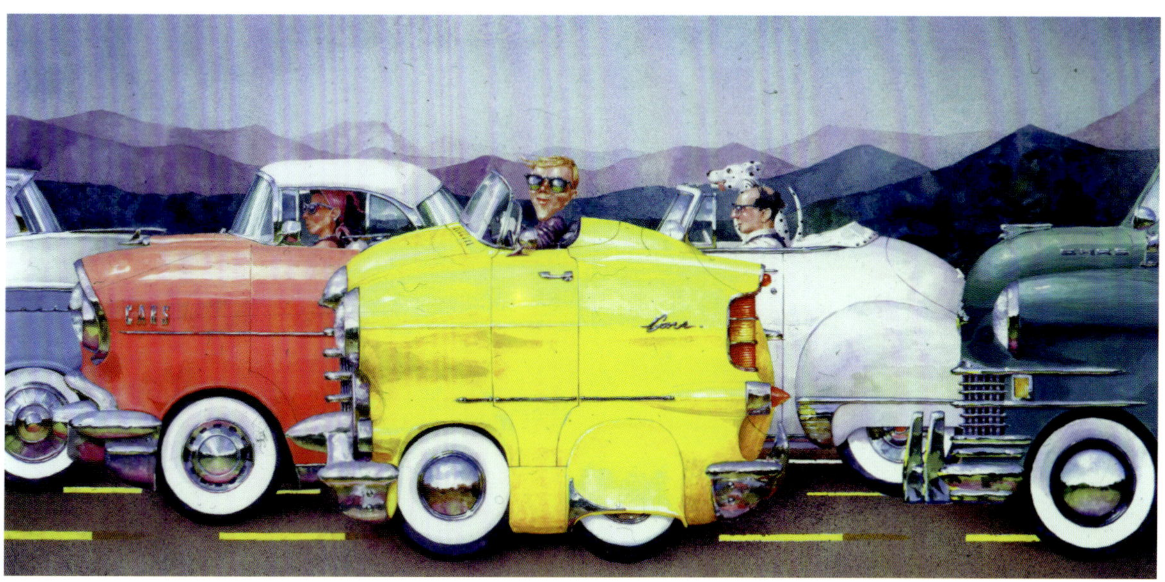

Sunday Drive By
1993, watercolor on paper
a. 15" x 30"

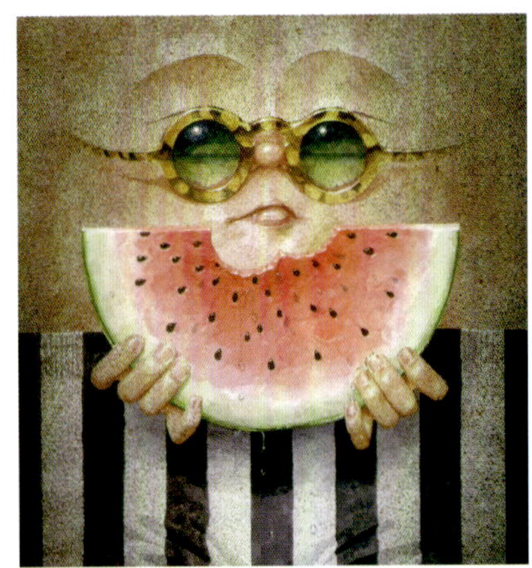

Spitting Image
1992, watercolor on paper
a. 16" x 16"

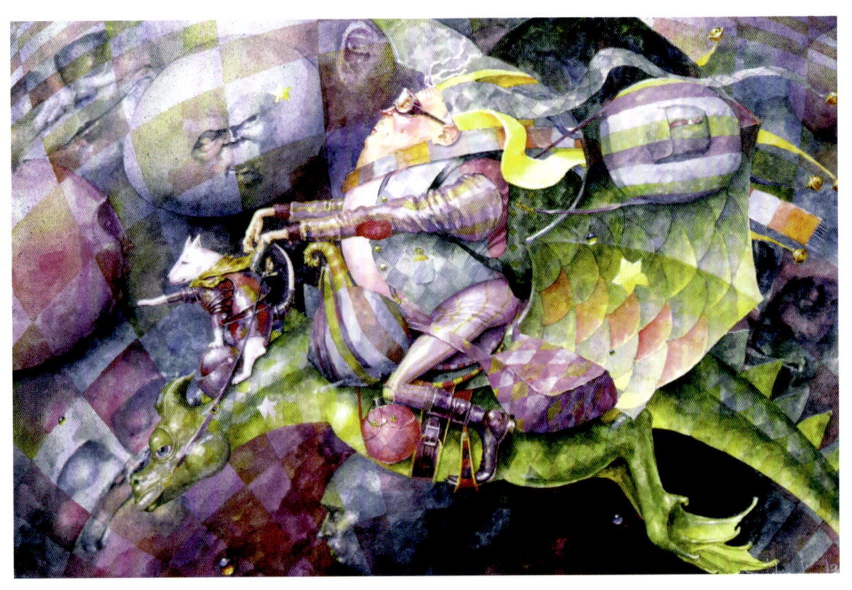

Heart of a Full Moon
1991, watercolor on paper
a. 16" x 22"

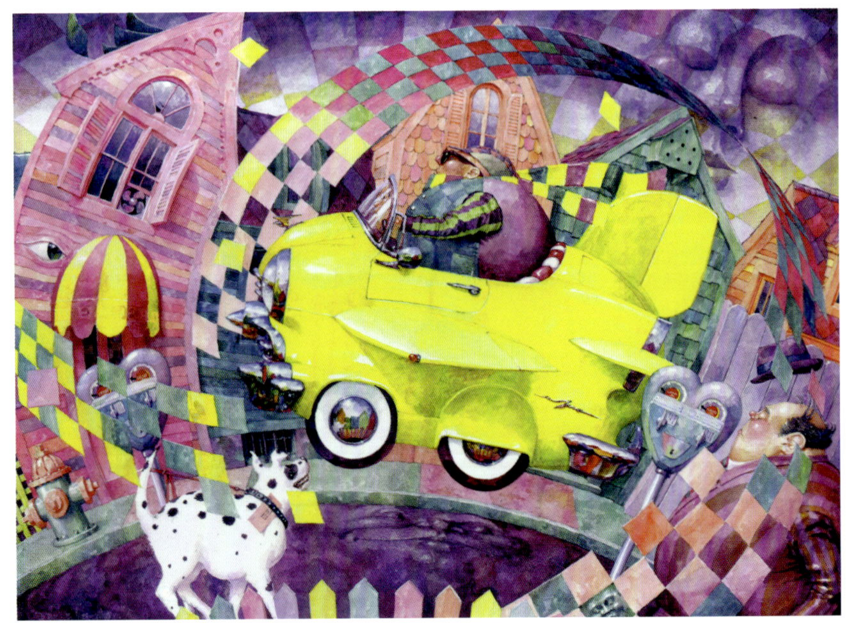

No Parking
1992, watercolor on paper
20" x 28"

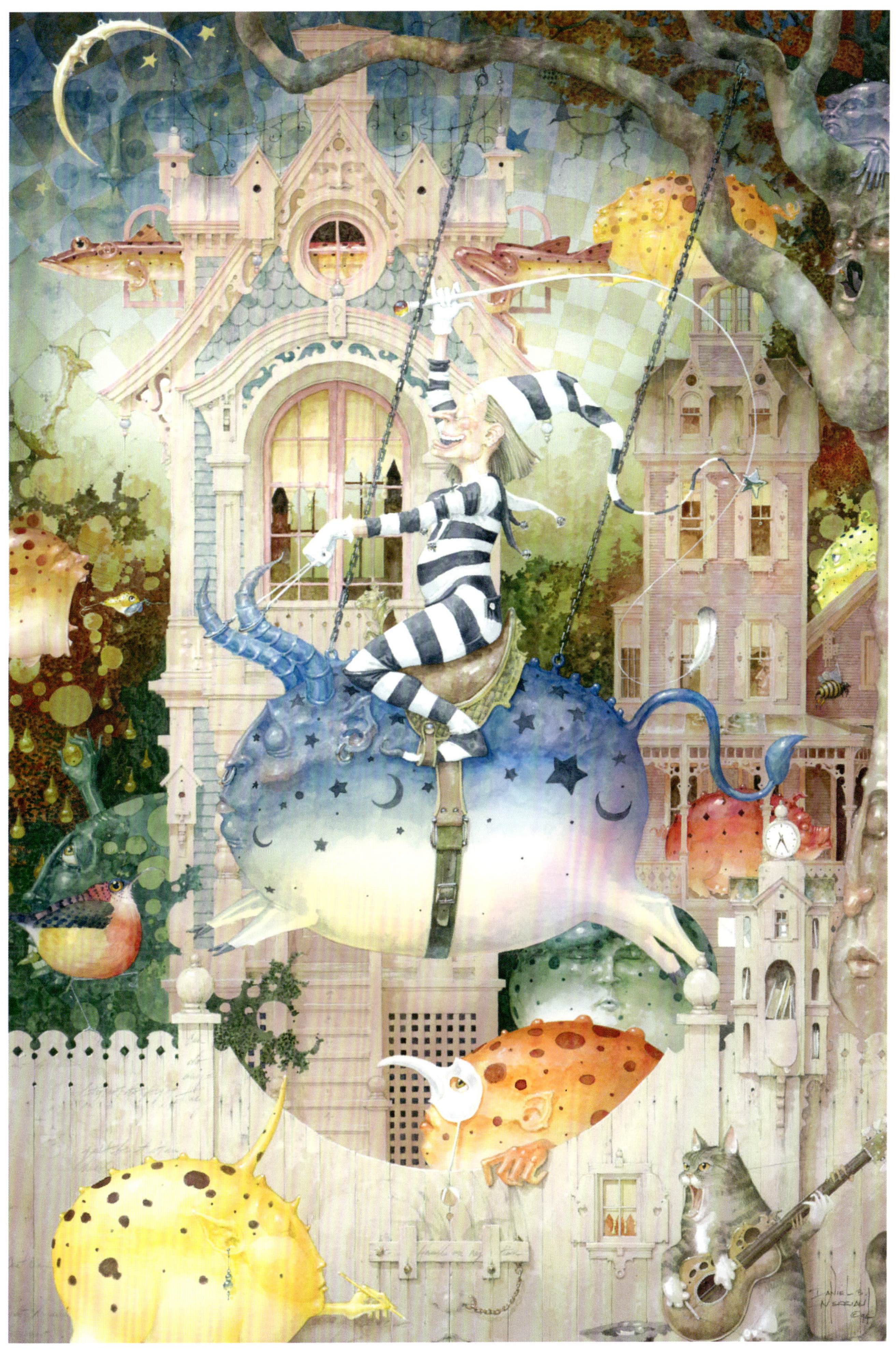

Handle On Rejection
1994, watercolor on paper
28" x 19"

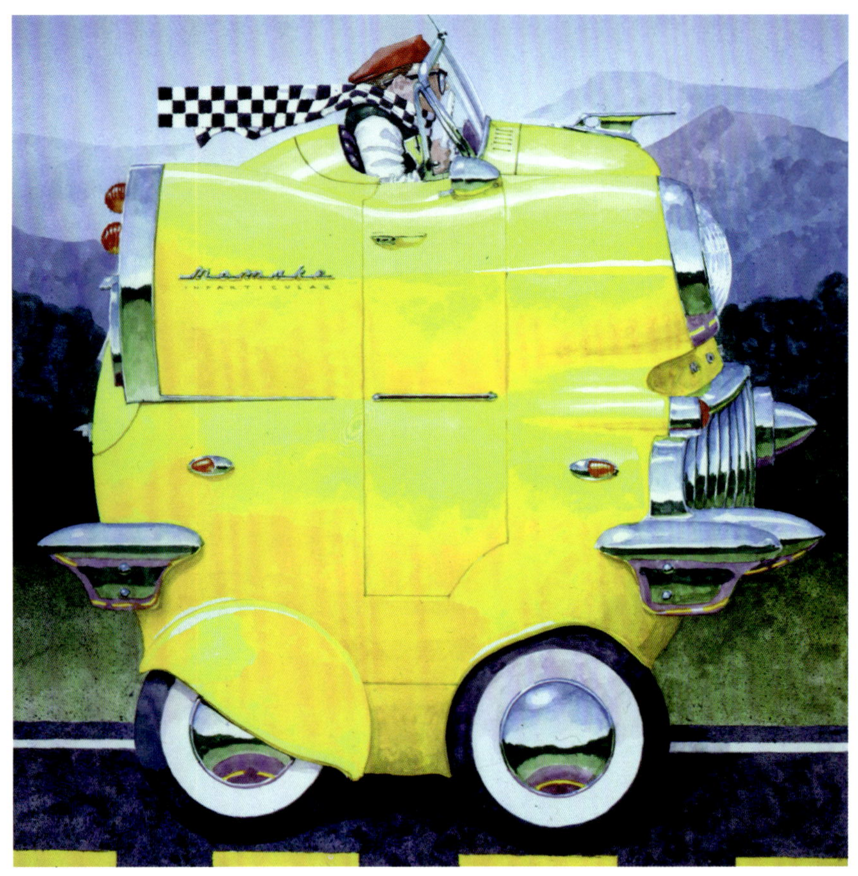

No Make Inparticular
1993, watercolor on paper
12" x 12"

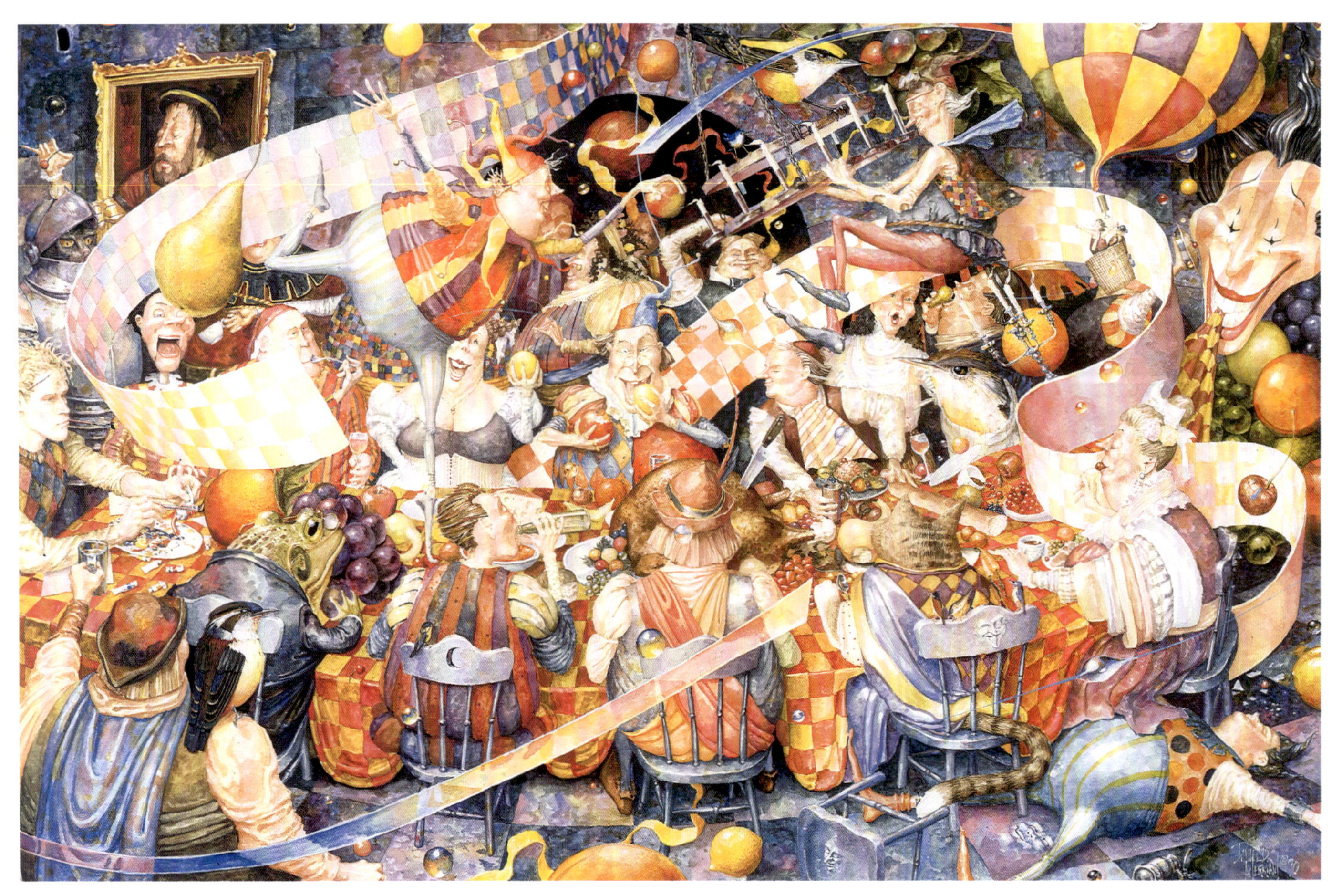

Feast of Frenzy
1990, watercolor on paper
20" x 28"

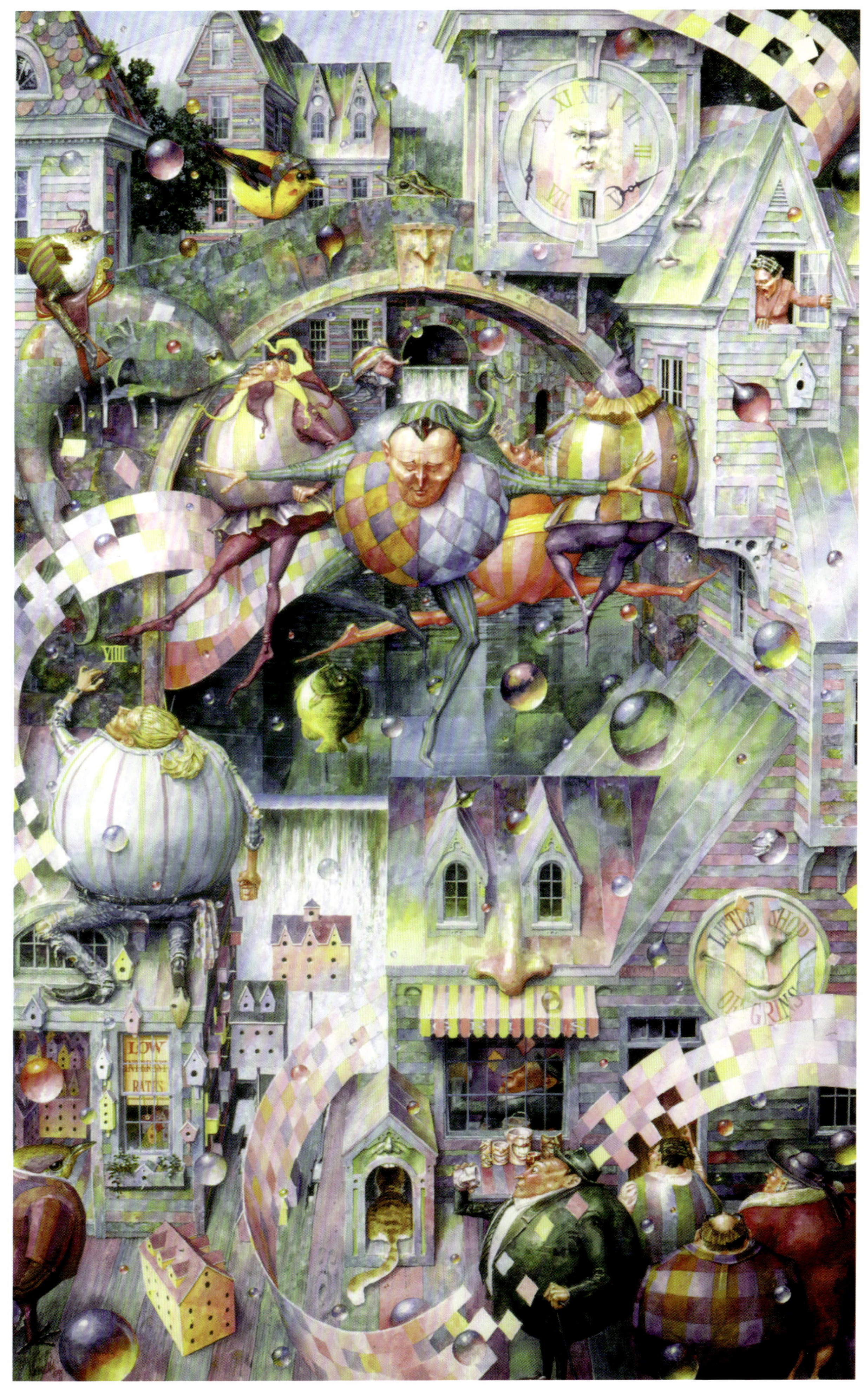

Little Shop of Grins
1991, watercolor on paper
a. 40" x 24"

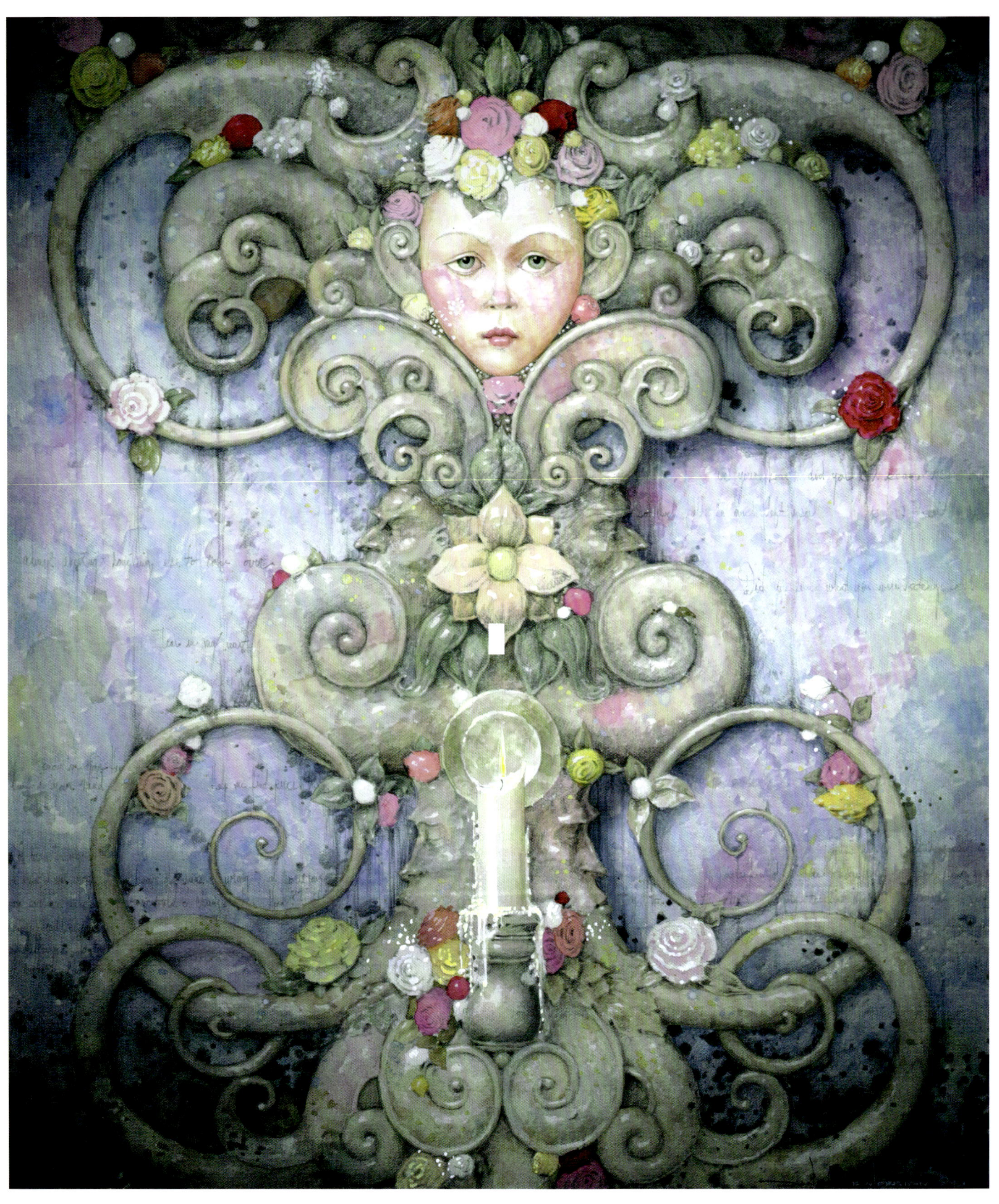

FARAWAY EYES
1995, WATERCOLOR ON PAPER
20" X 17.5"

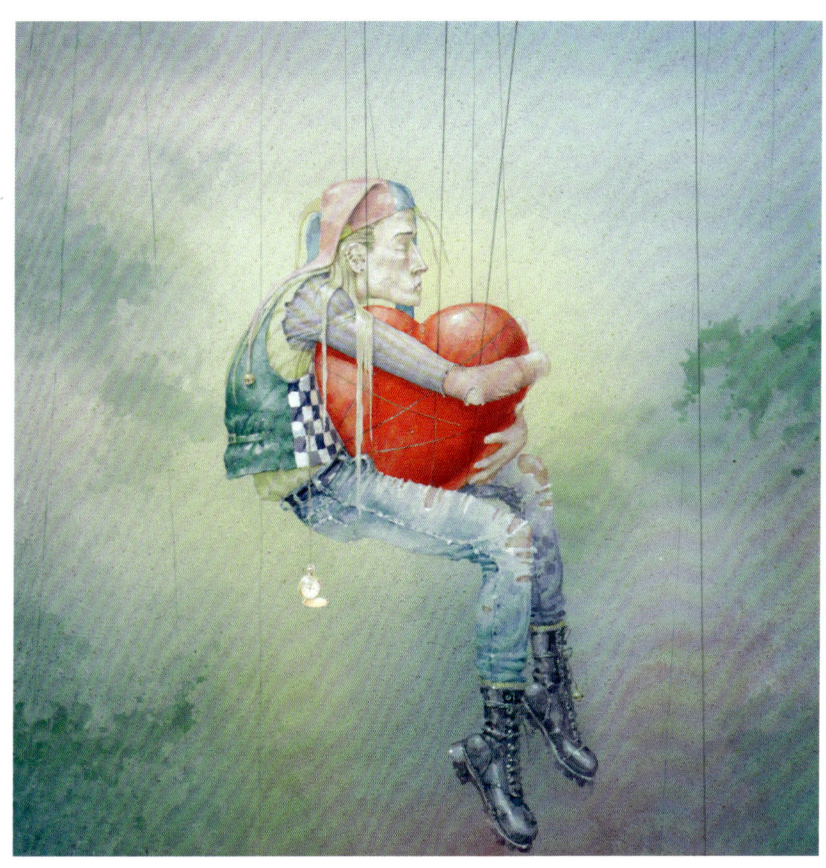

HEARTSTRINGS
1993, WATERCOLOR ON PAPER
A. 12" X 12"

LOVE

Love is a difficult thing to define, but I know it is there. Running through my life's work is a common thread of motivation. Before embarking on the journey of each painting, I carefully survey my repertoire of feelings and emotions. Within those moments I find myself completely at the mercy of my sensations. To search for the optimum expression poses a problem that can only be overcome with love. To go forth with this one thing in mind is to be guided by a force that has its own way of taking care of itself. It does not need my direction. It only needs my support.

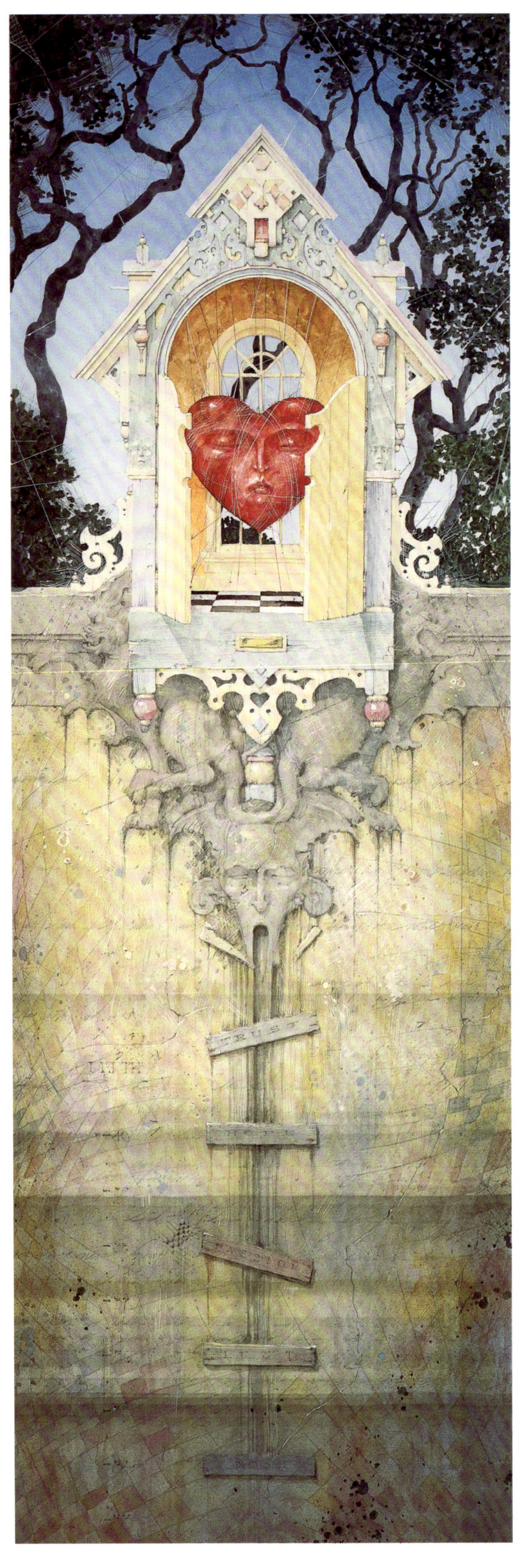

Caught Up in Myself
1995, watercolor on paper
a. 30" x 9"

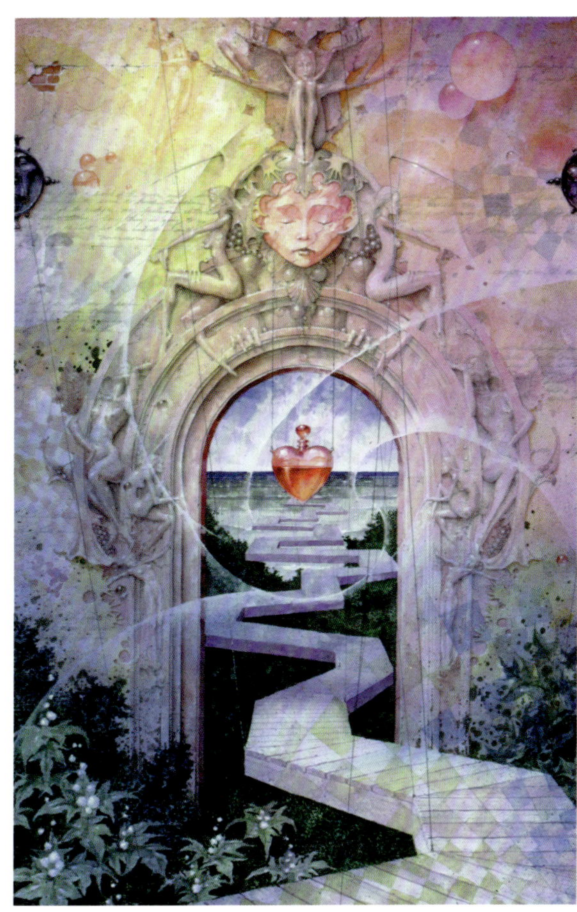

Glass Heart
1994, watercolor on paper
a. 20" x 12"

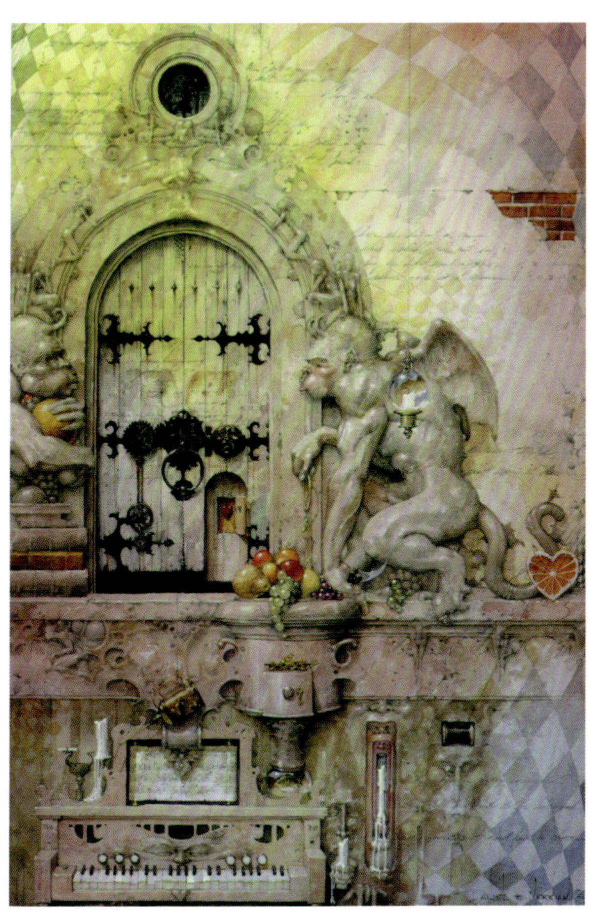

The Keeper
1995, watercolor on paper
18" x 16.5"

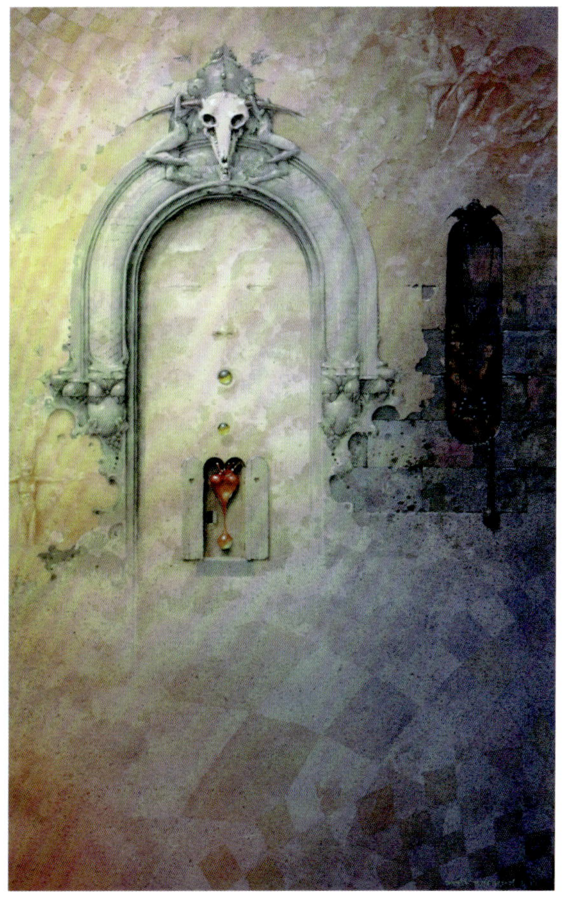

Rendered Soul
1993, watercolor on paper
19.5" x 13"

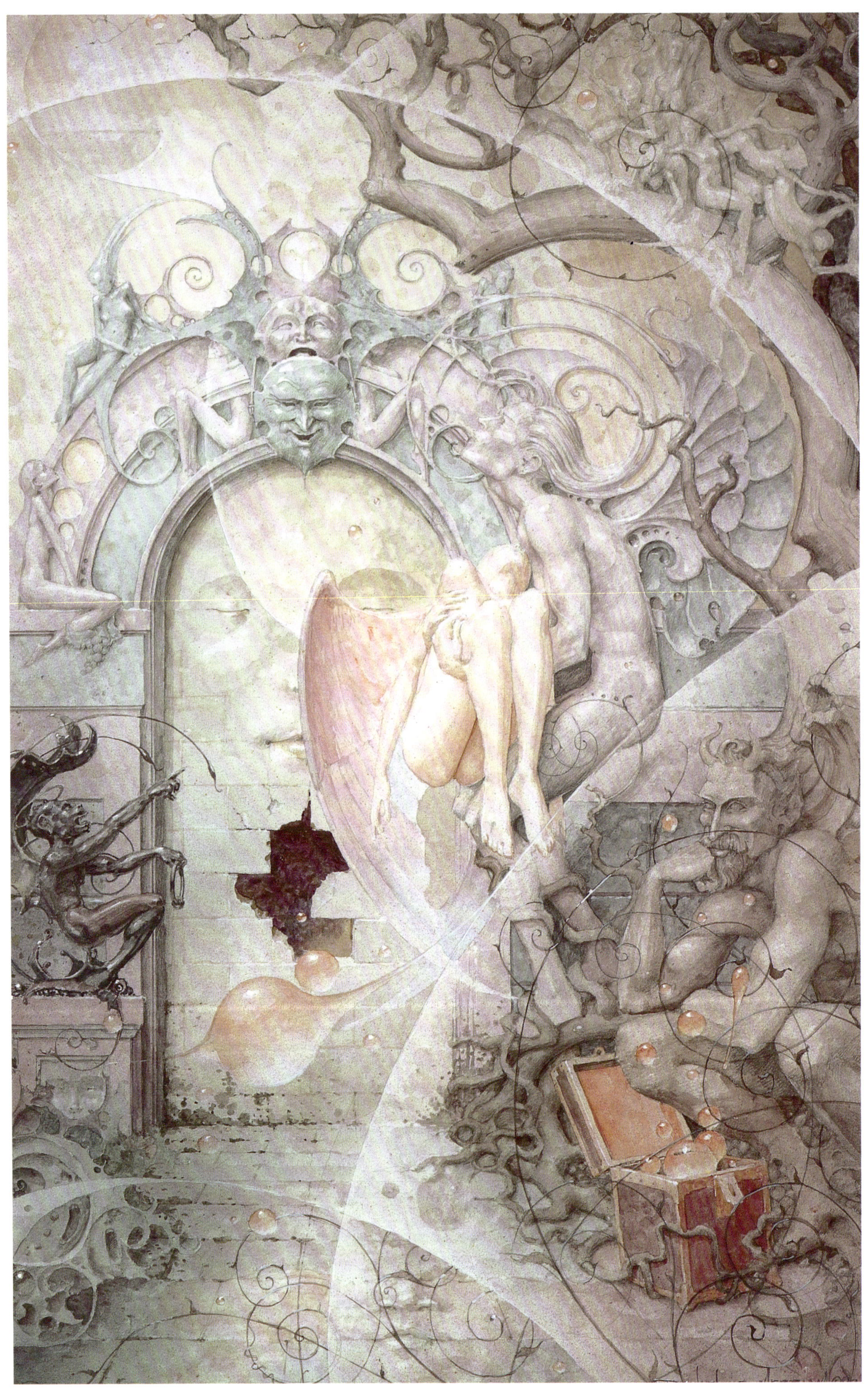

Fallen From Love
1993, watercolor on paper
a. 20" x 12"

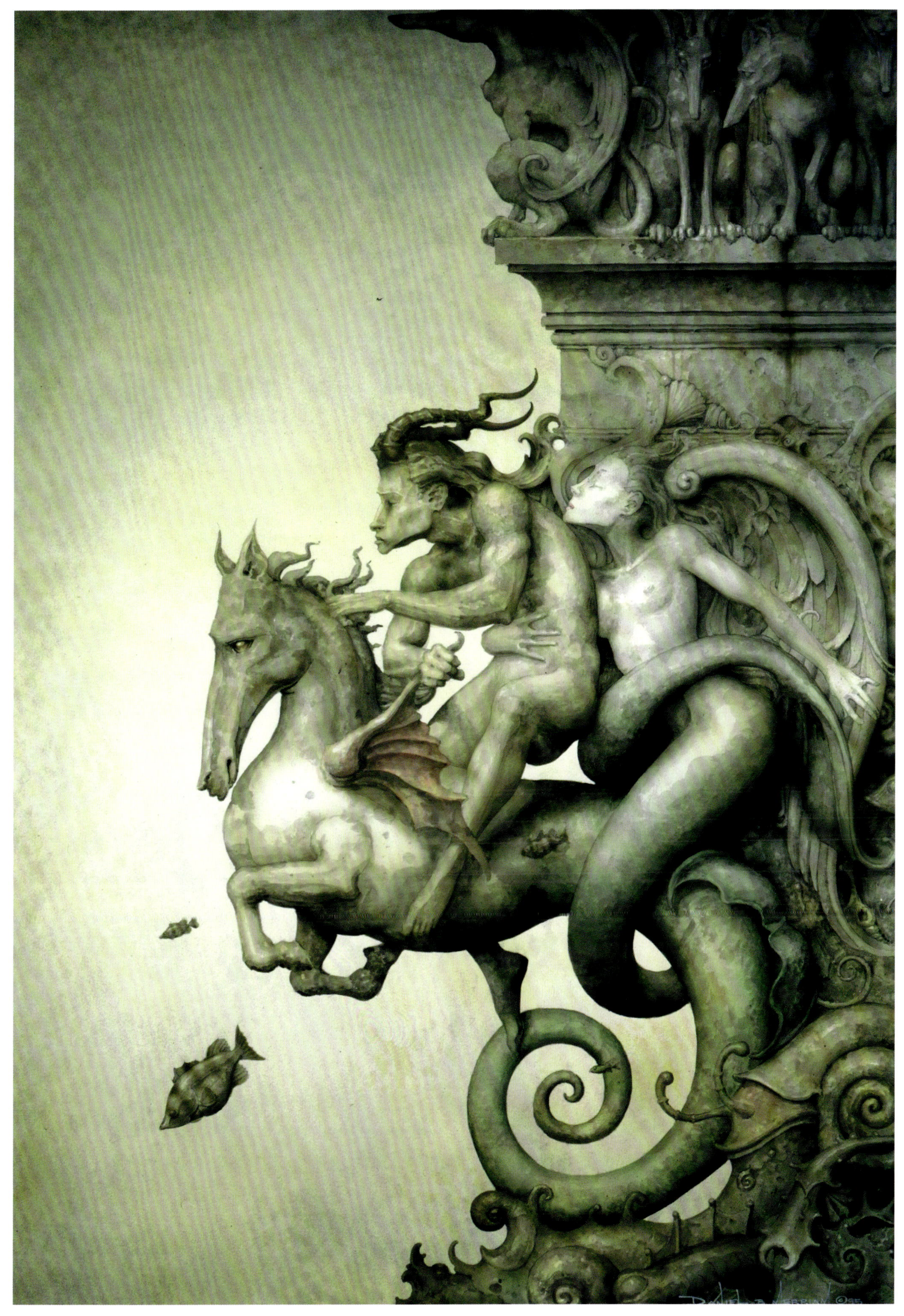

Ebb Tide
1995, watercolor on paper
A. 30" x 20"

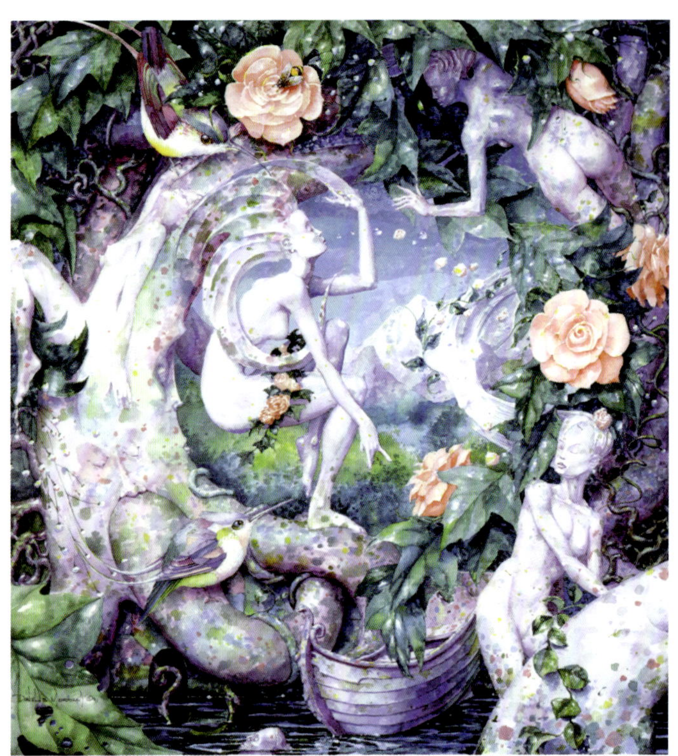

Pandora's Bath
1991, watercolor on paper
a. 22" x 20"

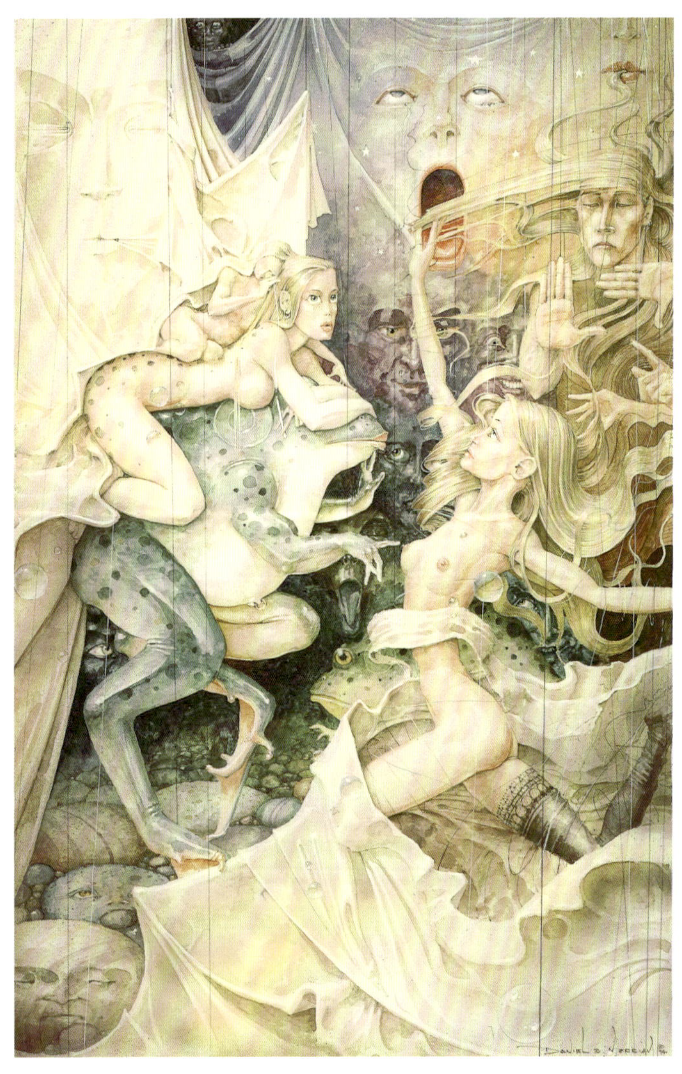

The Kiss
1994, watercolor on paper
a. 20" x 12"

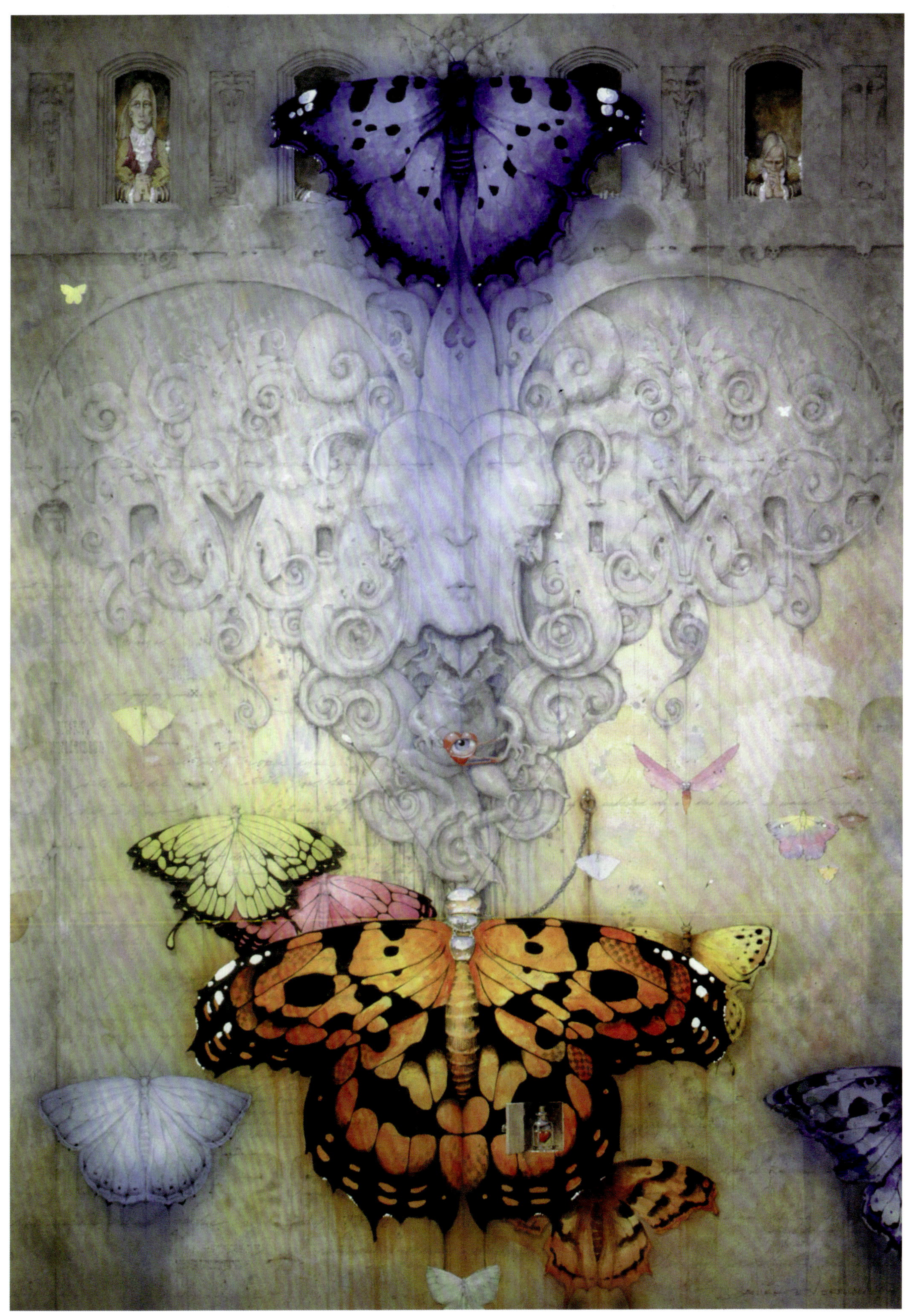

Beginning to End
1992, watercolor on paper
a. 36" x 22"

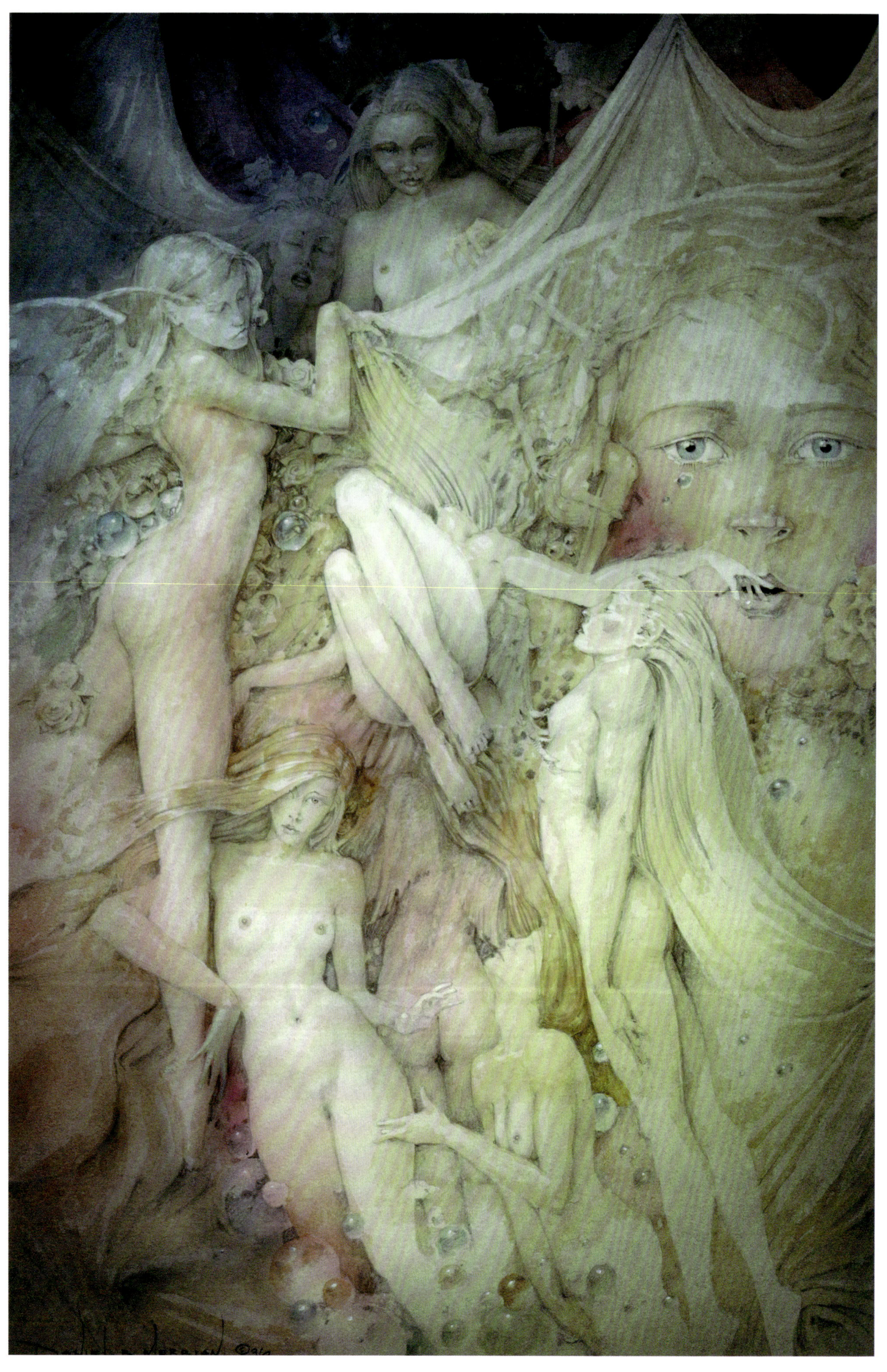

Forbidden Touch
1996, watercolor on paper
a. 17" x 10"

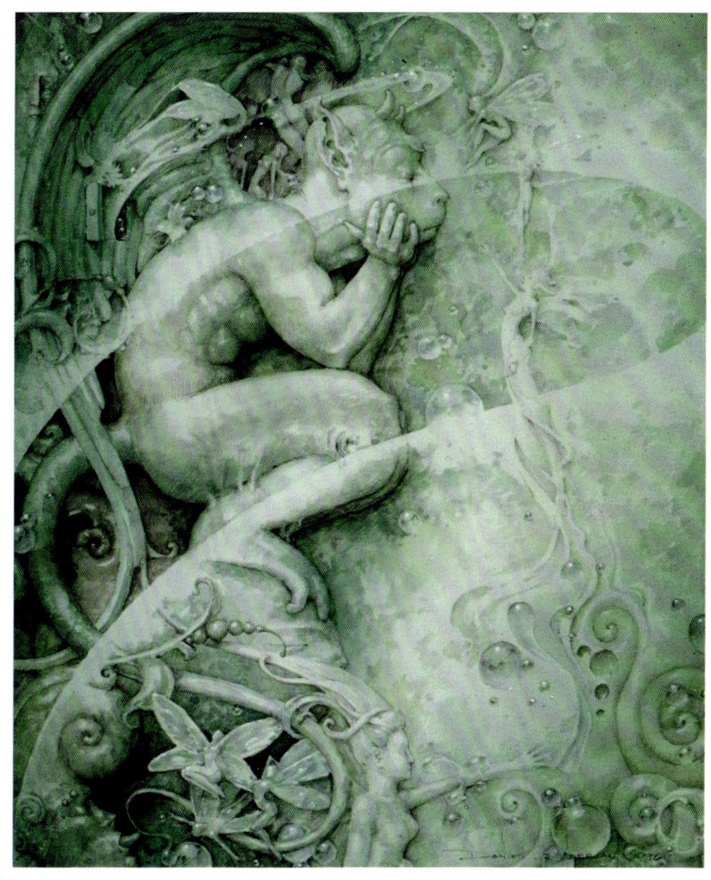

ENCHANTED
1996, WATERCOLOR ON PAPER
14" X 12"

SENSUALITY

Since I was a child, life's vibrancy has come to me in waves of emotion. My daydreams clung to my erotic nature, leaving me vulnerable, balanced between sensuality and shame. Some of my fondest memories were not of things I had done, but of fantasies. My urge to see and to touch embraced the sight and texture of everything that surrounded me. These feelings, in their innocence or their vanity, have become an integral part of who I am. Acceptance of that which comes naturally to me has allowed me to create my own euphoric Eden within an otherwise unsettled world.

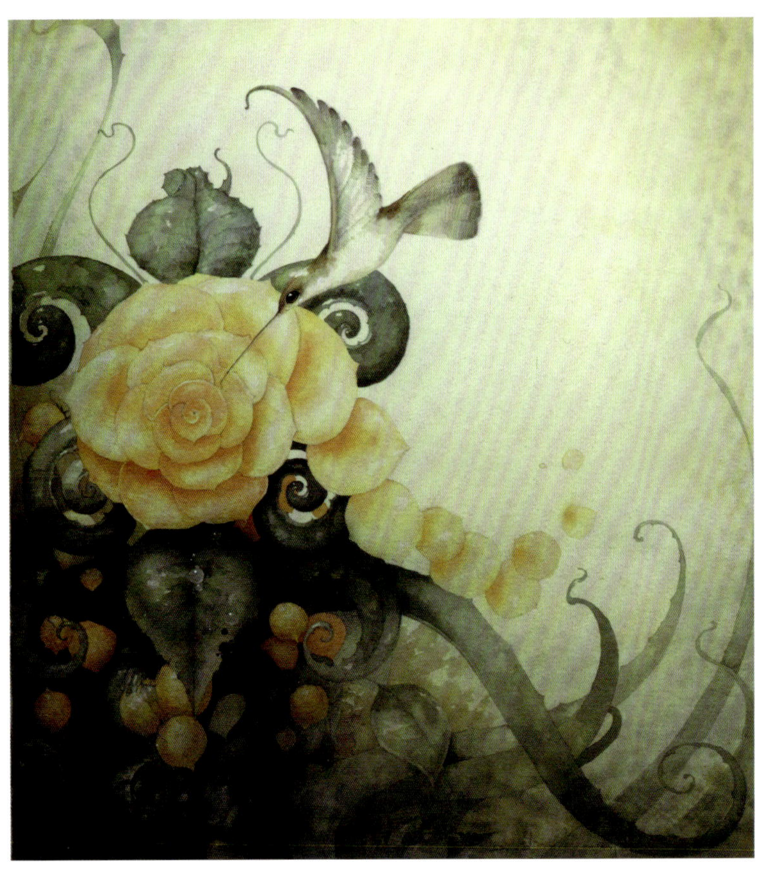

The Hummingbird
1997, watercolor on paper
15.4" x 13.4"

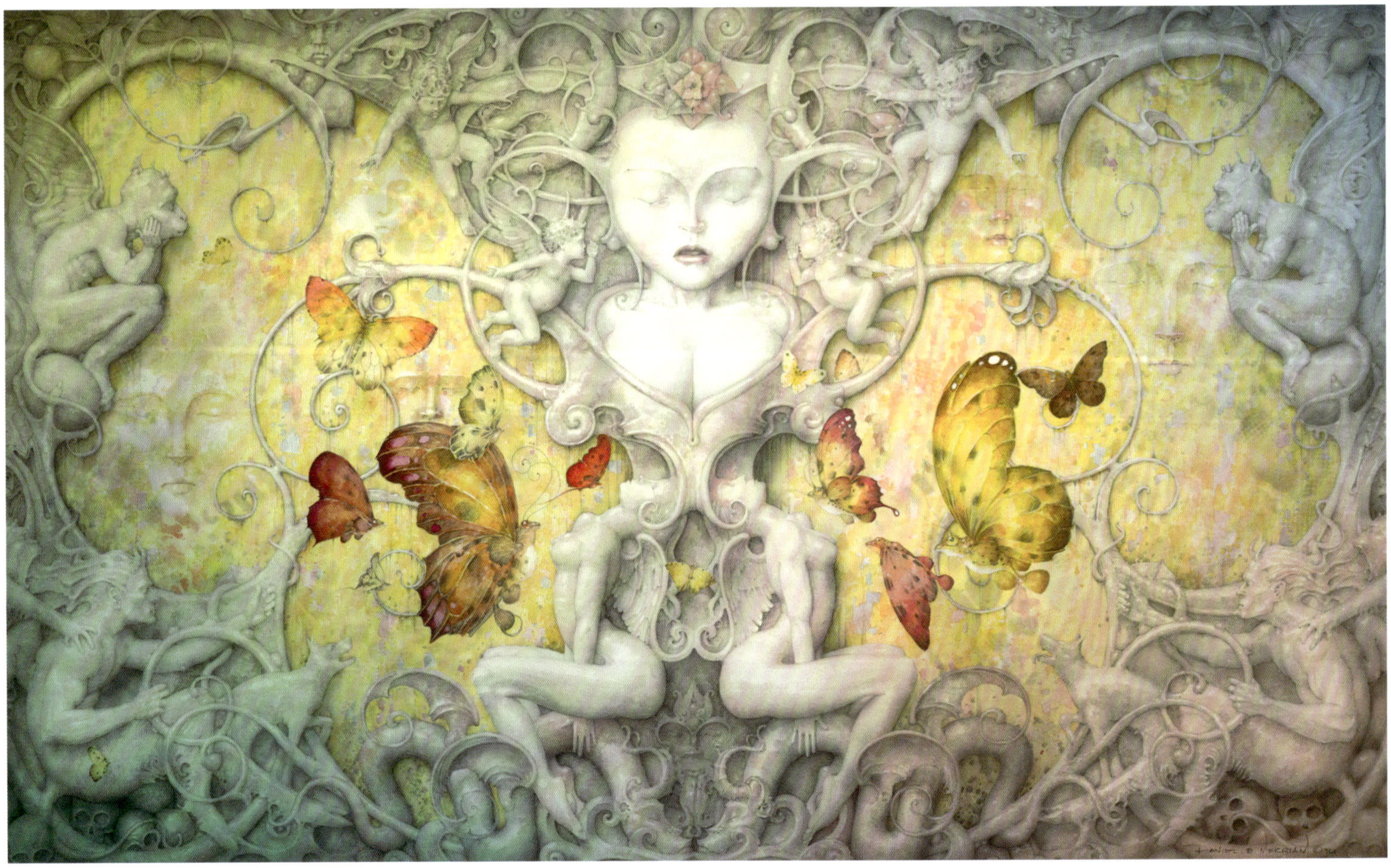

Seduction
1997, watercolor on paper
23" x 39"

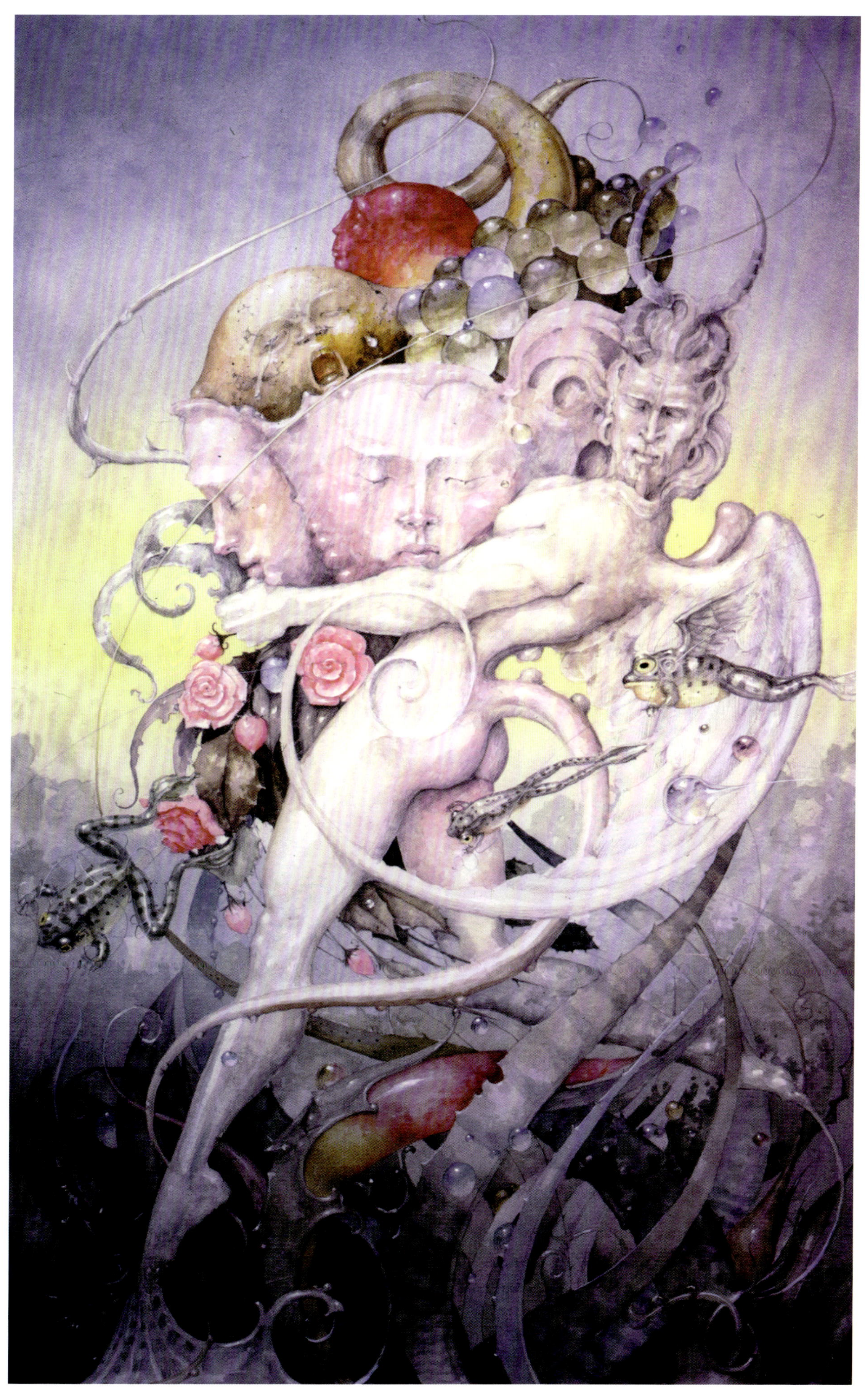

HARVEST
1995, WATERCOLOR ON PAPER
20" X 12.5"

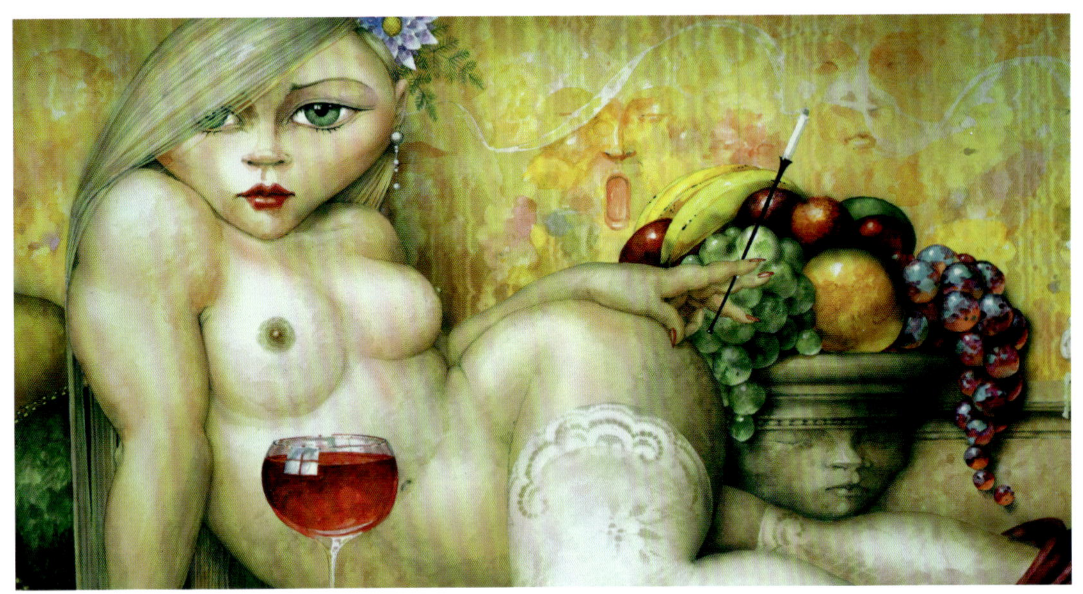

EVANGELINE
1995, WATERCOLOR ON PAPER
A. 12" X 24"

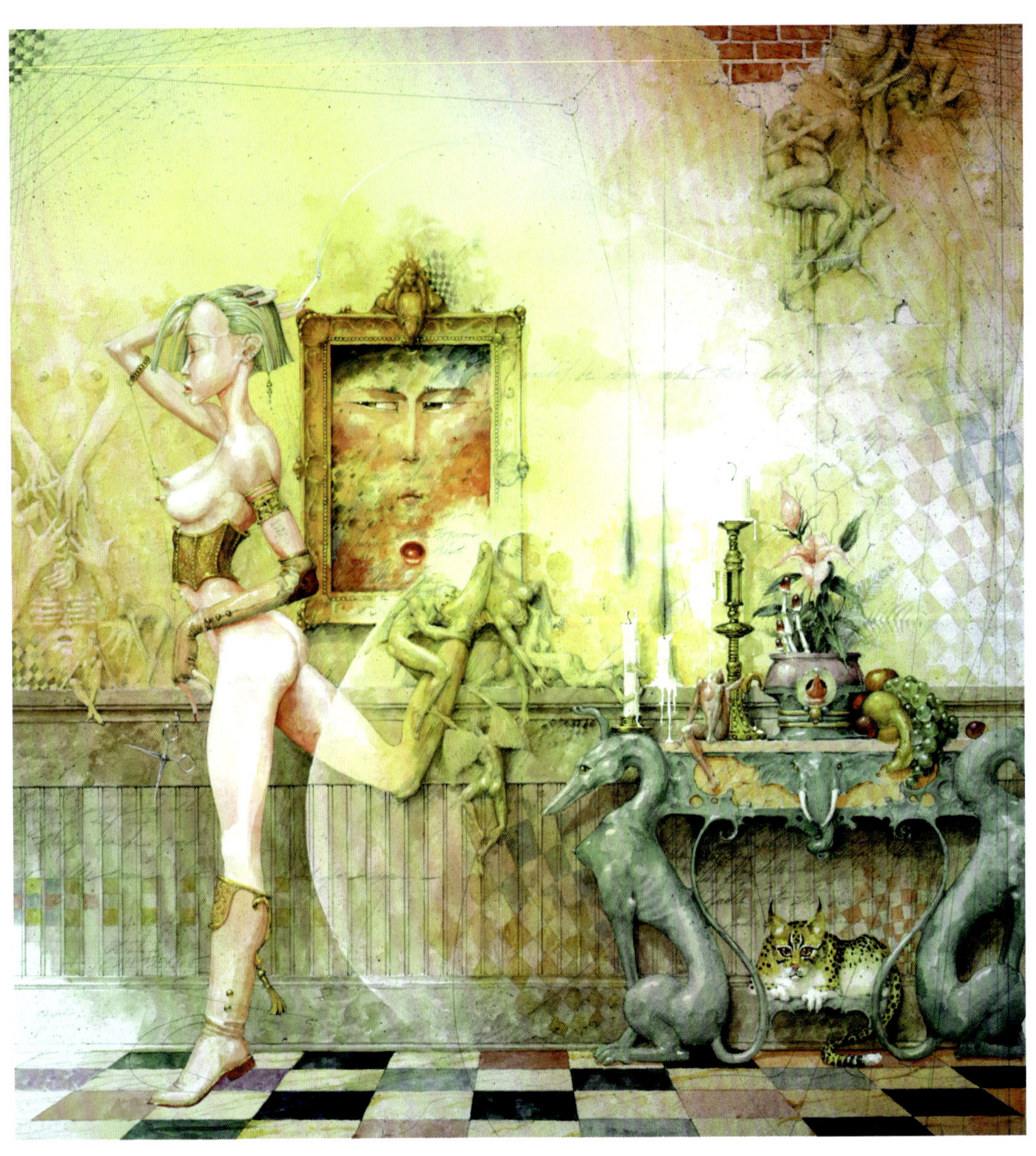

UNSOWN
1994, WATERCOLOR ON PAPER
18" X 16.75"

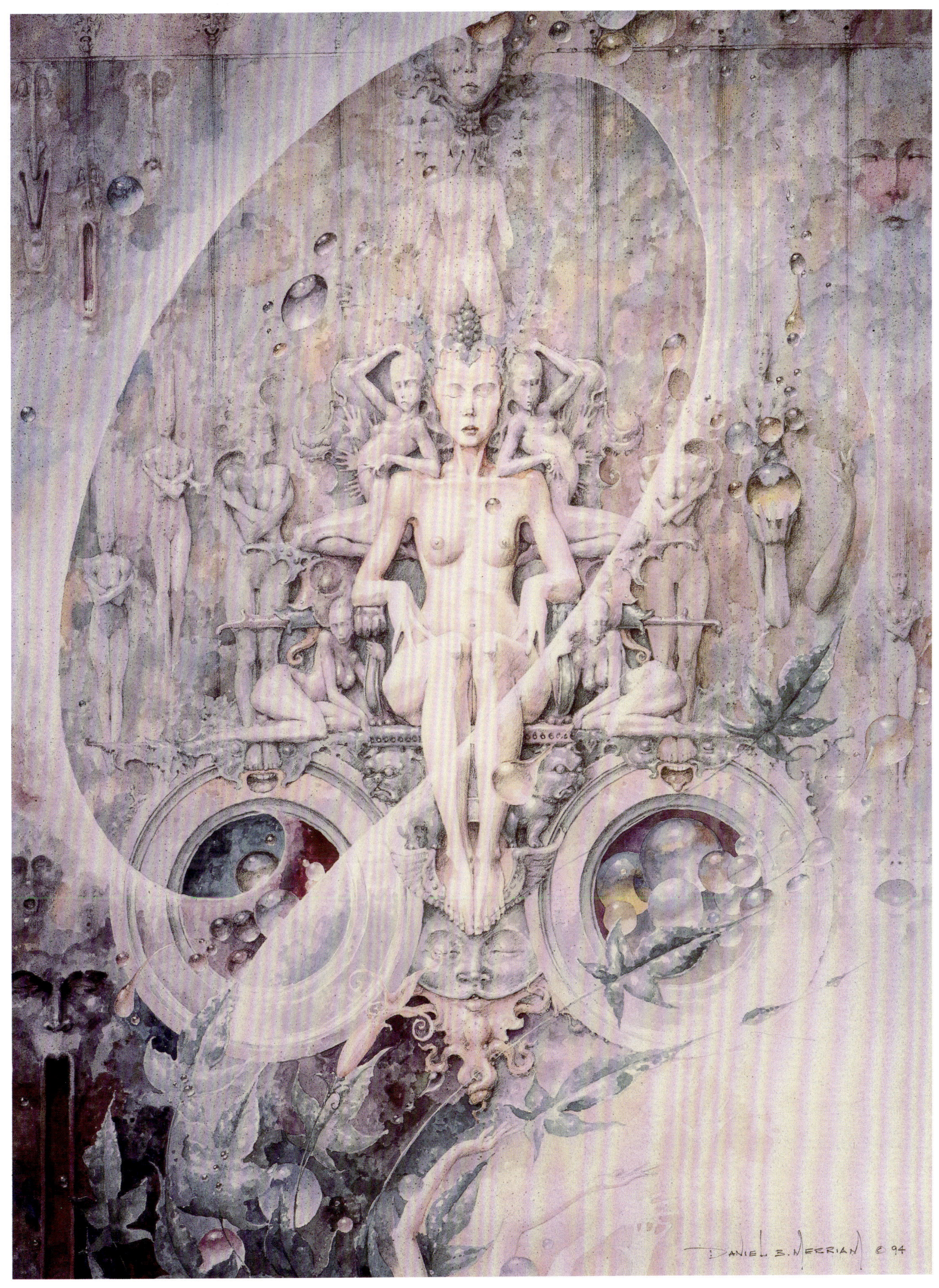

FACADE
1994, WATERCOLOR ON PAPER
A. 22" X 16"

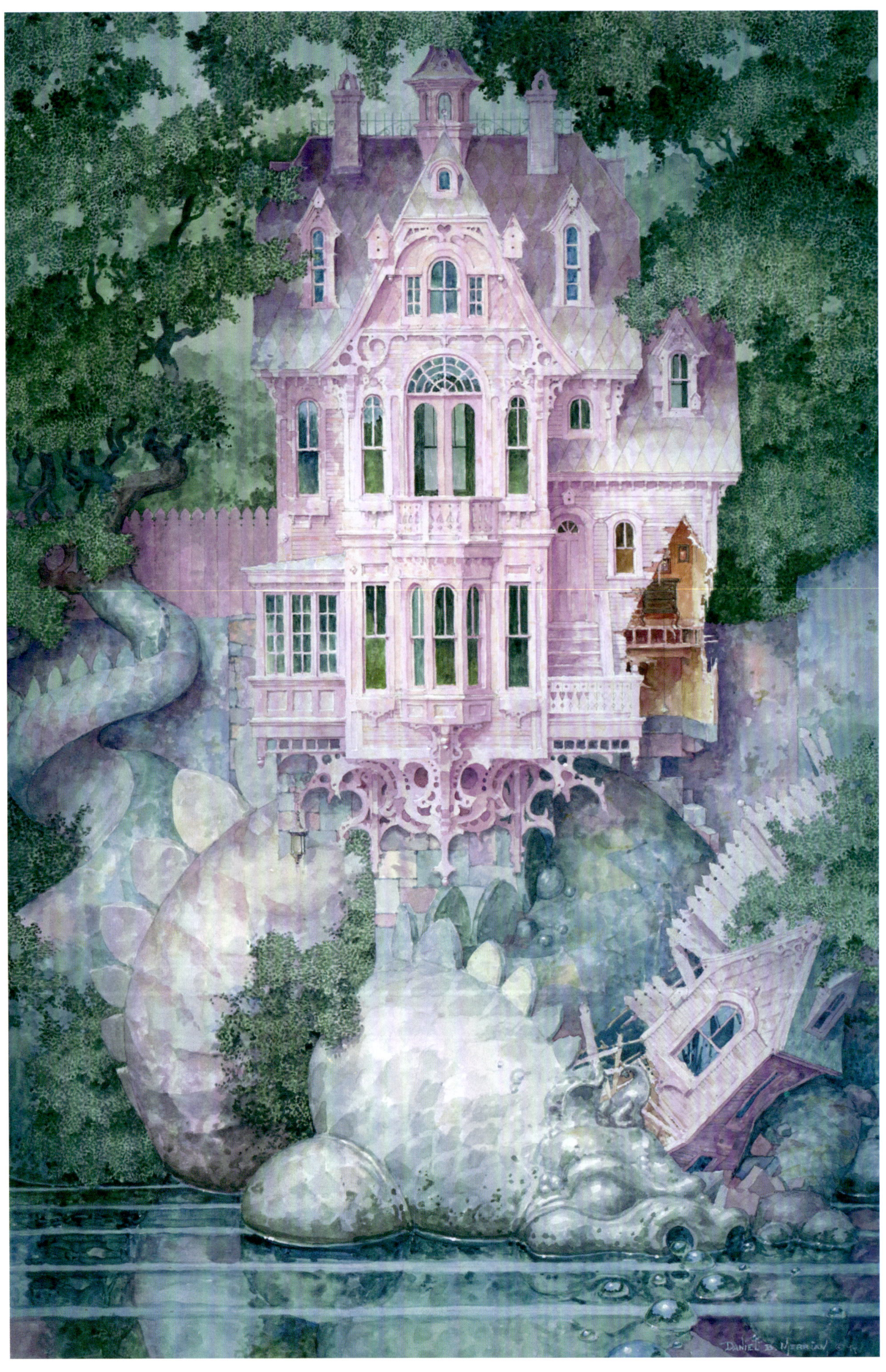

LIVING ON THE DRAGON'S BACK

1994, WATERCOLOR ON PAPER

22" x 14.5"

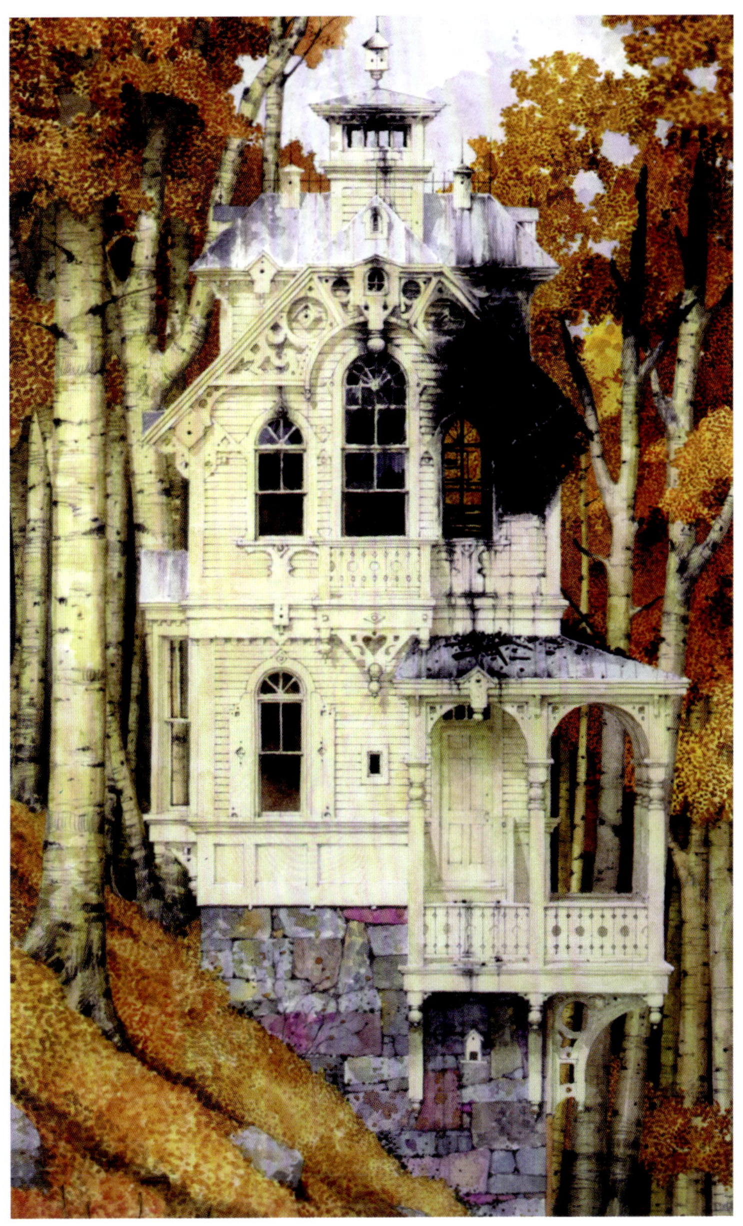

Autumn's End
1995, watercolor on paper
a. 18" x 10"

Design

Aside from color theory, division of space, and the economy of marks, there is a certain sense that has guided the hands of many artists throughout history. The styles of ornament have both differed and stayed the same. There is a power within the limits of this world. There is an intuitive guidance that allows form to develop naturally.

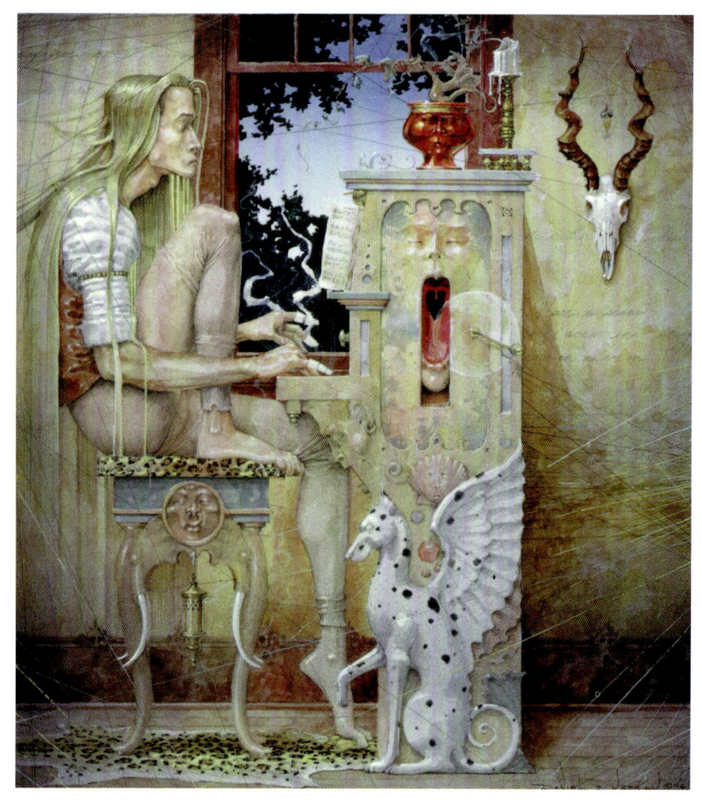

Piano Strings
1994, watercolor on paper
a. 14" x 12"

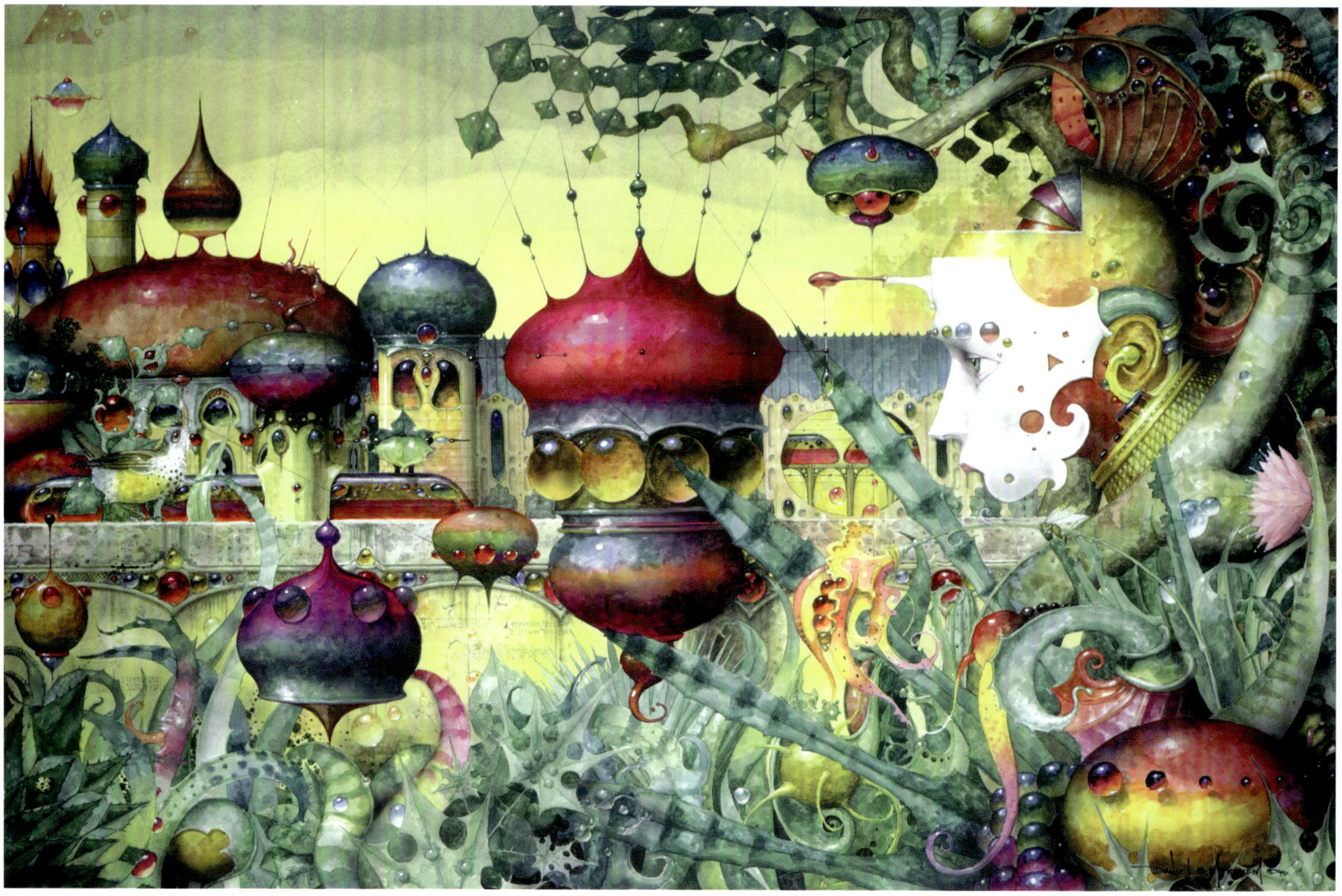

Long For This World
1995, watercolor on paper
a. 18" x 30"

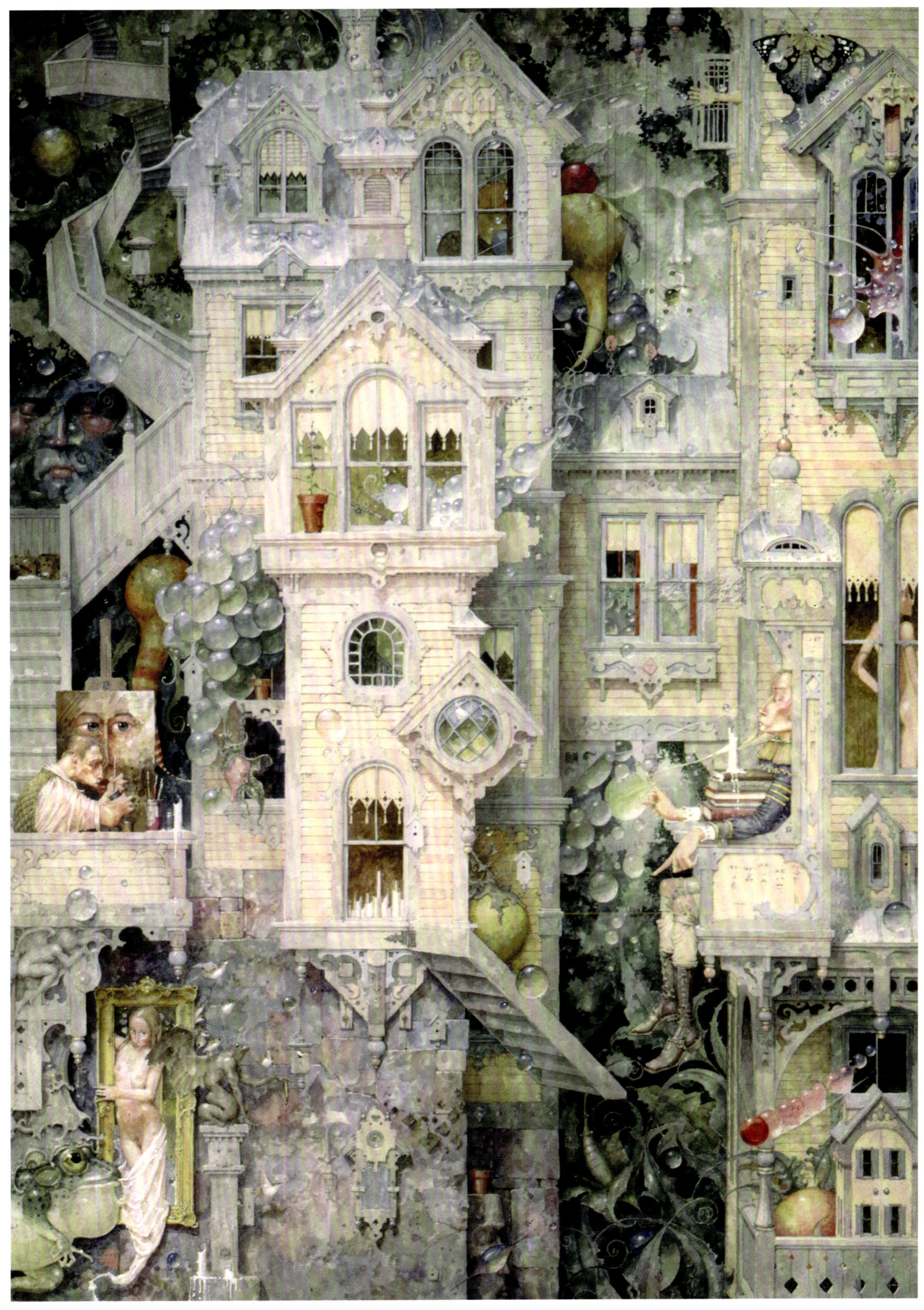

Window to The World
1995, watercolor on paper
a. 30" x 20"

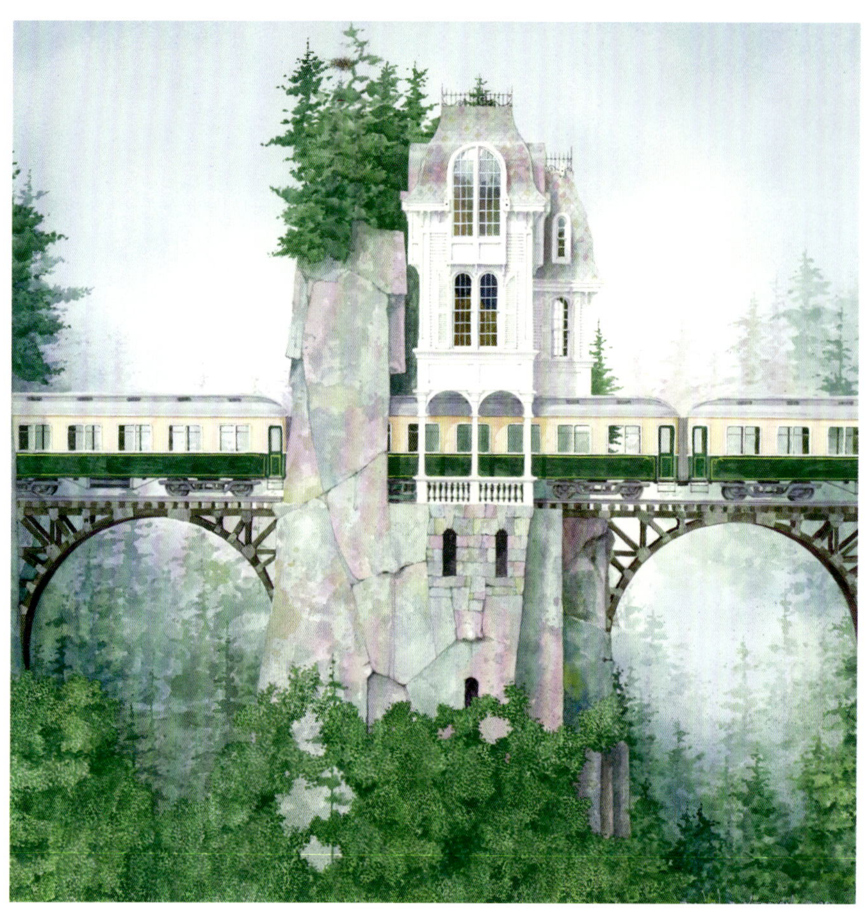

Passing Through
1993, watercolor on paper
16.25" x 16.25"

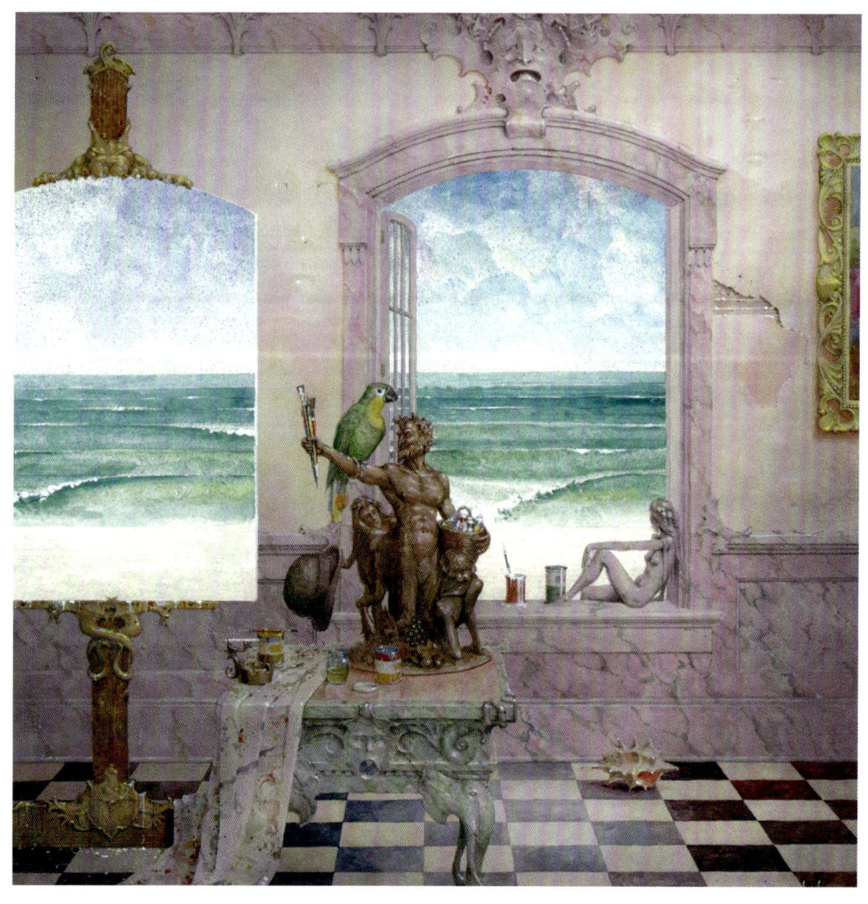

Ocean View
1993, watercolor on paper
18" x 18"

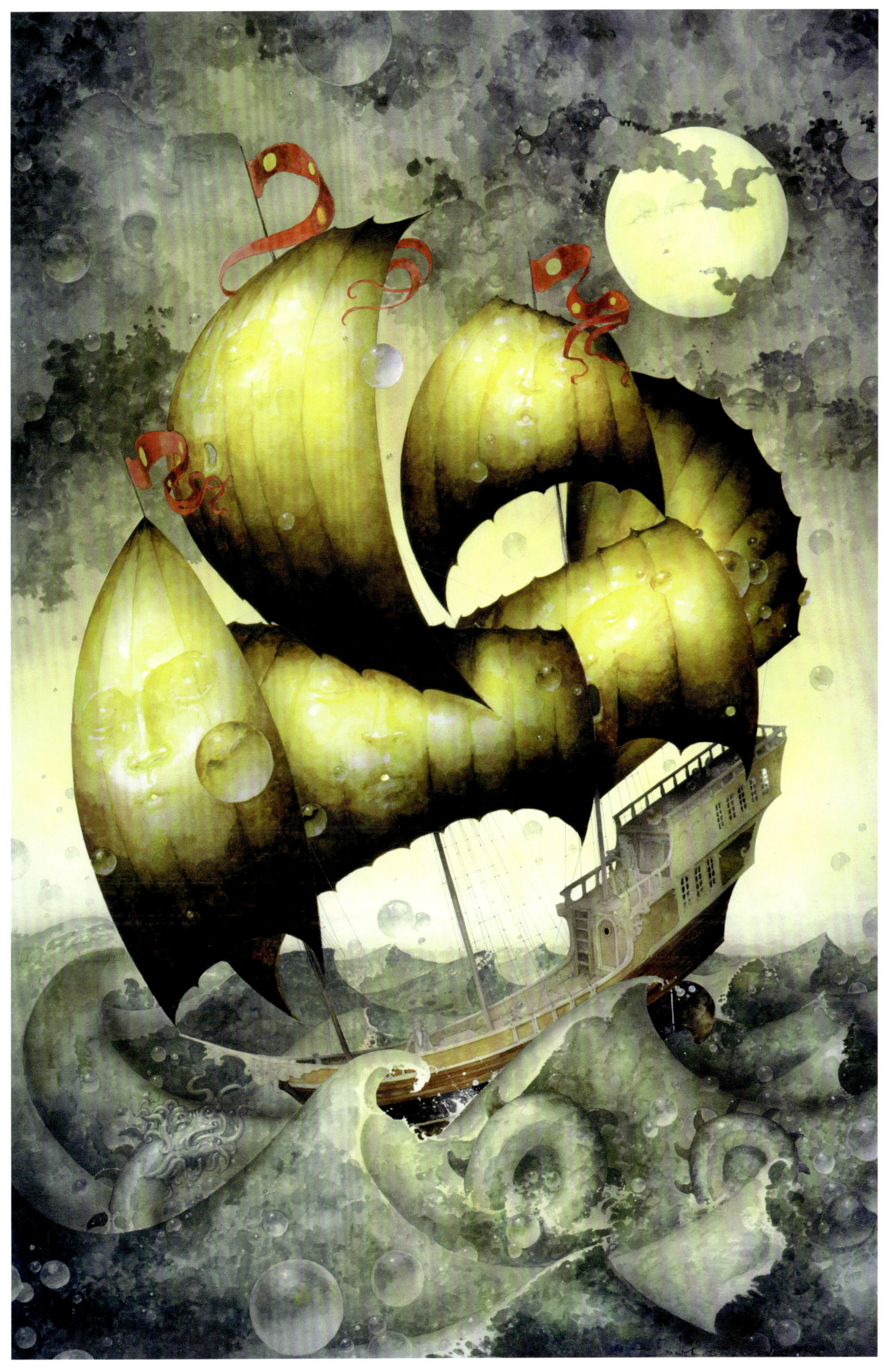

Winds of Change
1997, watercolor on paper
38" x 25"

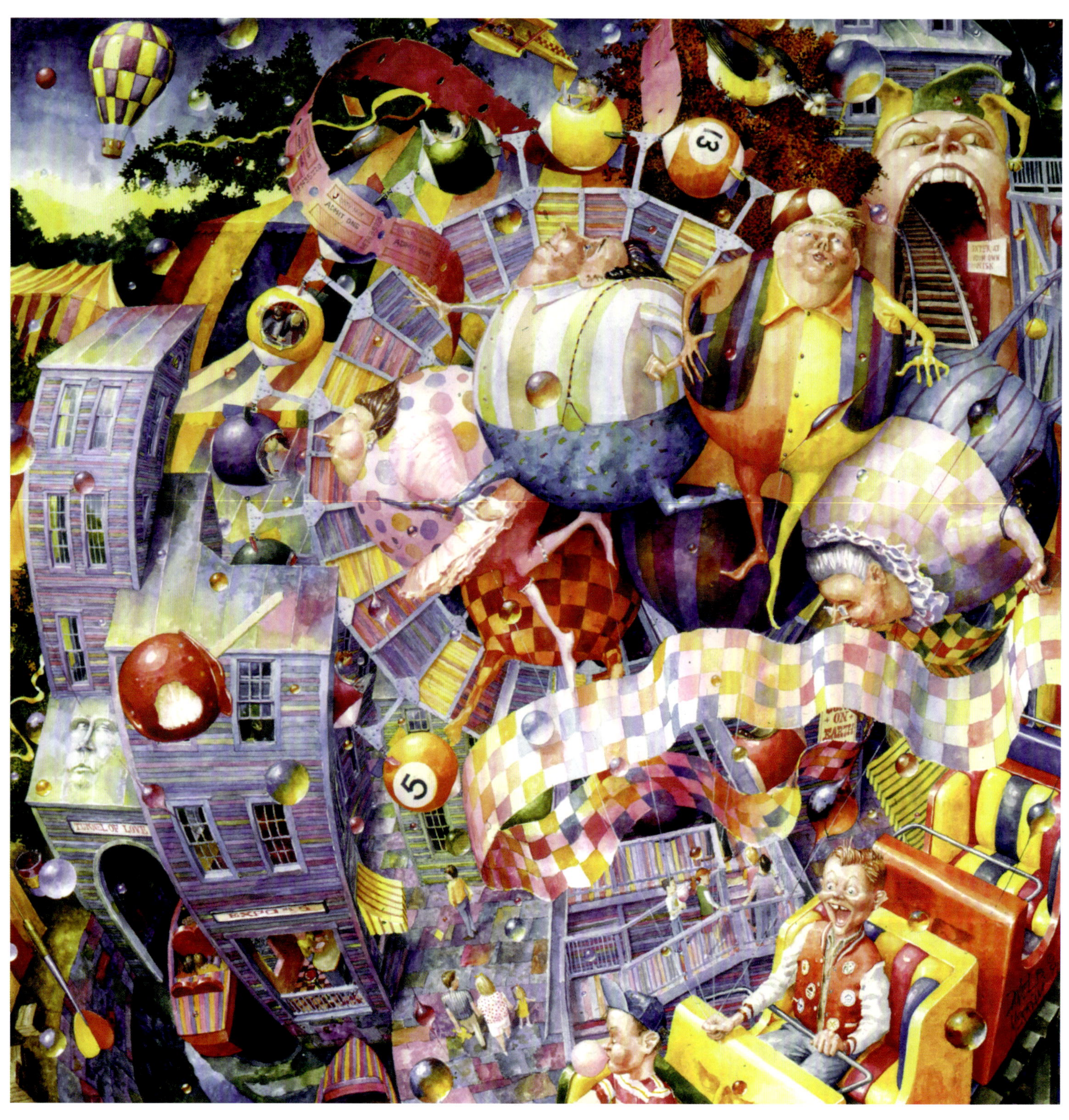

CARNIVAL

1990, WATERCOLOR ON PAPER

A. 22" X 22"

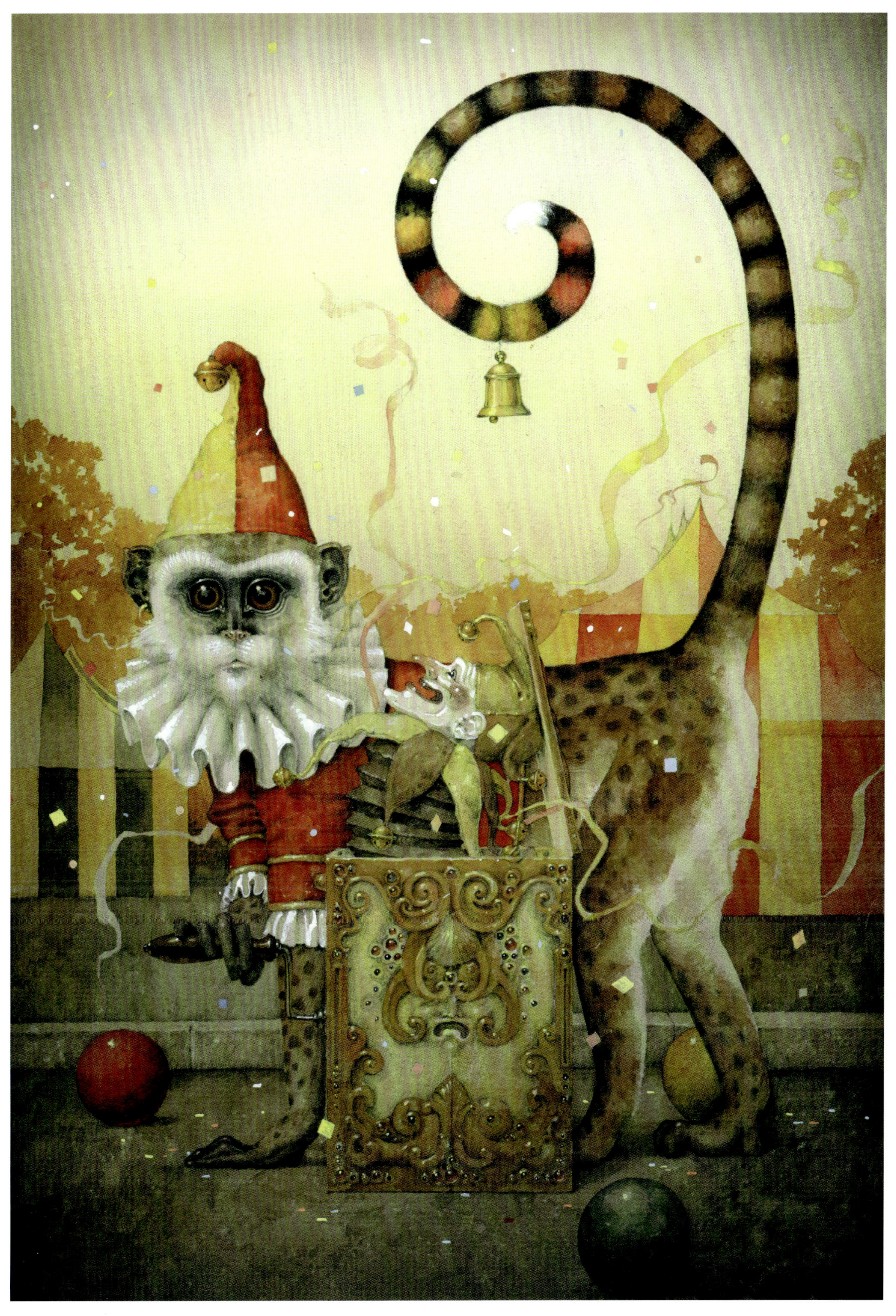

Jack-in-the-Box
1997, watercolor on paper
20" x 14"

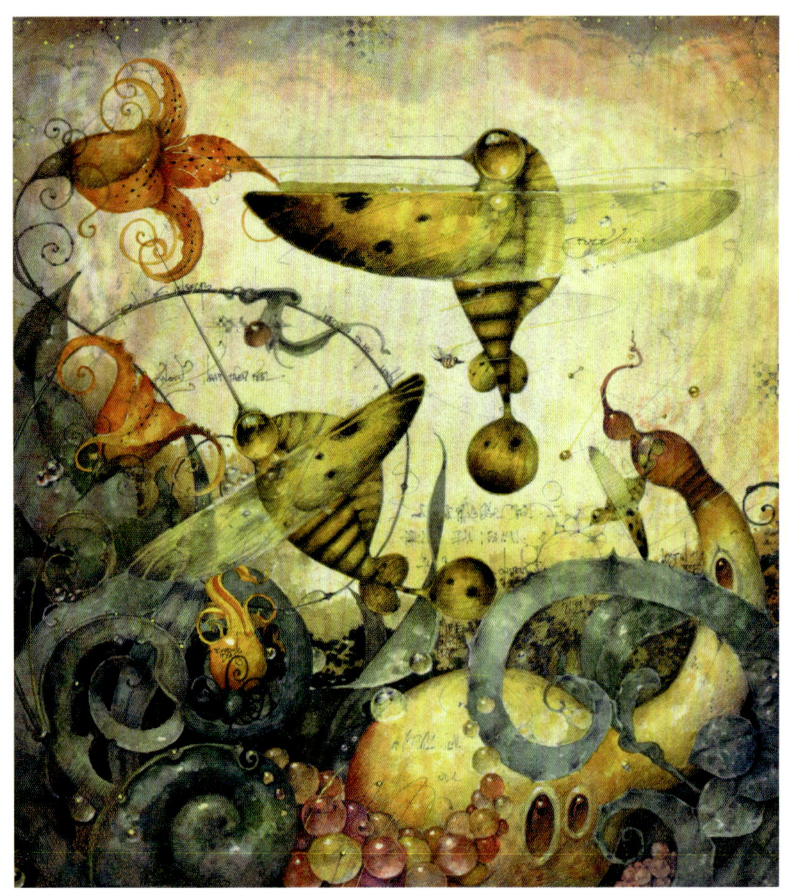

HUMMINGBEES
1997, WATERCOLOR ON PAPER
12" X 11"

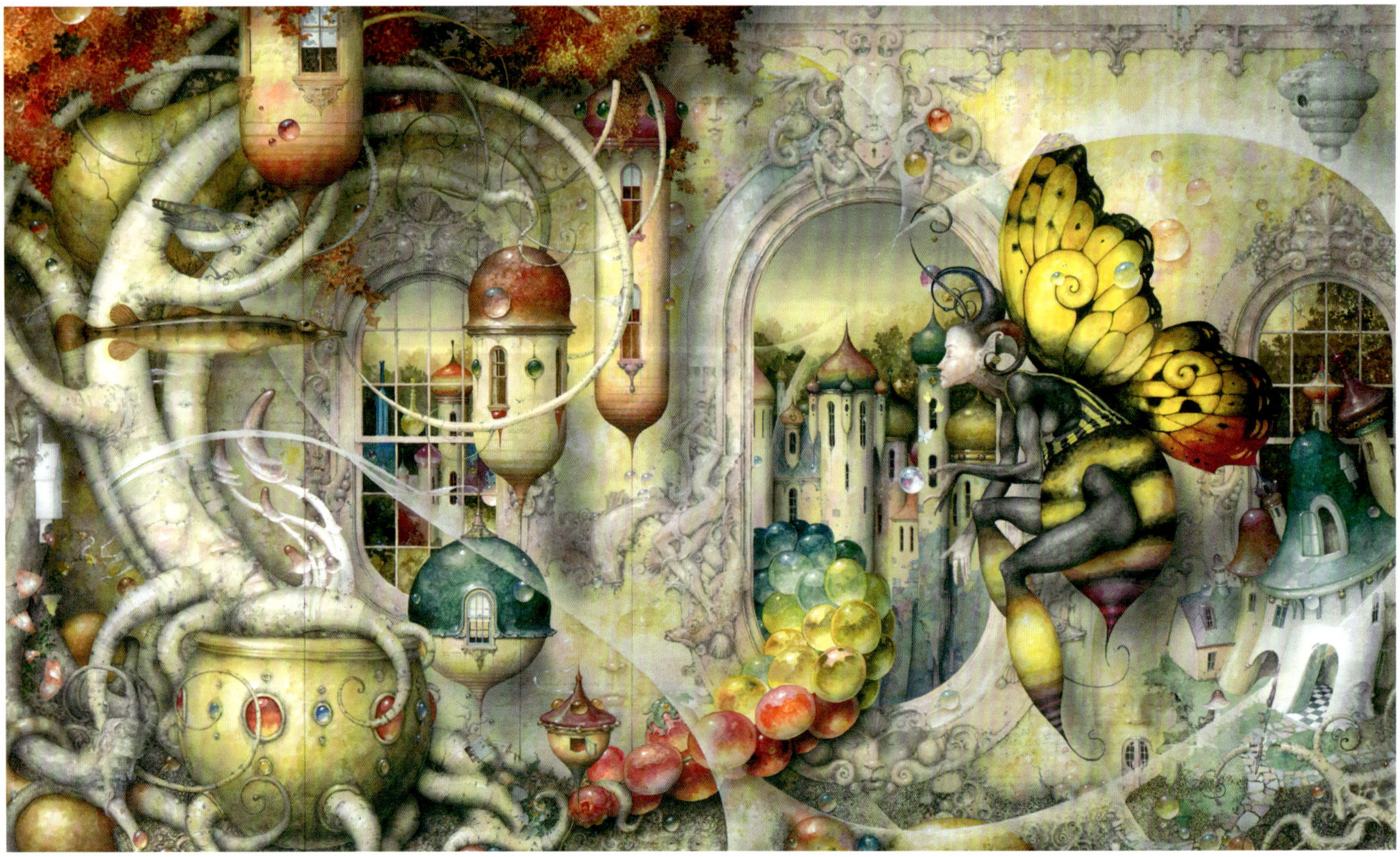

A WORLD APART
1996, WATERCOLOR ON PAPER
30" X 56"

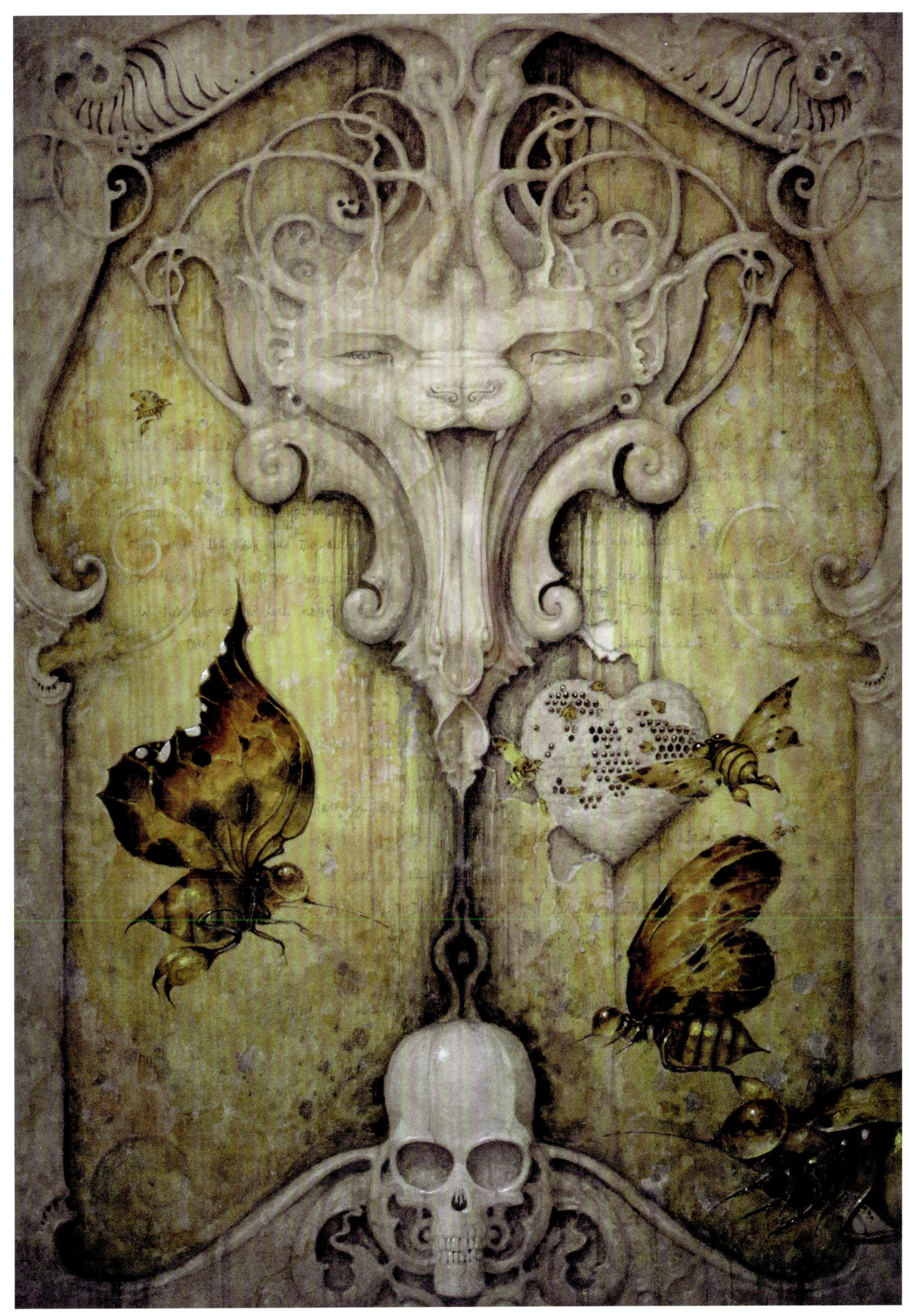

BITTERSWEET
1997, WATERCOLOR ON PAPER
20" X 14"

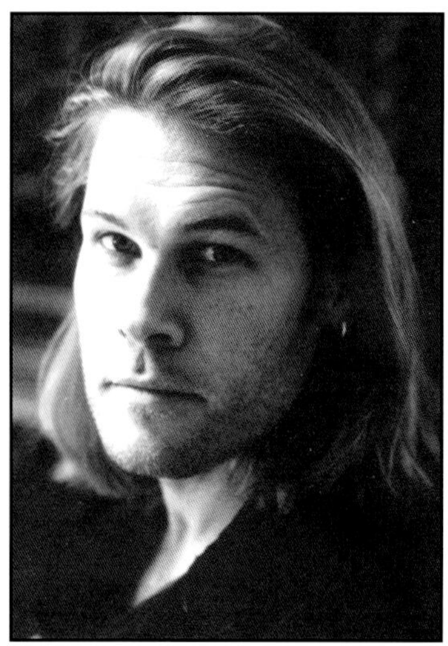

INFINITY

Cantilevered from my arms hangs the void of molten color, undetermined distance, changing its depth and girth tenfold by the second. My being, not sure what to make of this silent monster, swells a fearful tear in my eye. My tongue is laden with featherweight lead. My blood defies gravity, but my spirit cannot. Its mass seems to draw out what was deeply rooted certainty. Until tonight I could escape all but the memory of this undeniable beast, but now its existence has followed me into the light. With open eyes I try to shake it from my arms, but it stays with me from room to room. It has entered my body and become one with me, or, perhaps, I one with it. I find its burden heavy.

"Blessed are the meek, for they shall inherit the earth" --
and pray God they can carry it.

Perhaps the beast awaits always a new cognition. Perhaps it is the window to creativity. It was surely the window to my world. From this window I have looked upon the world. For me, art was the natural medium with which to fill that void, and its pleasure has fulfilled my life throughout. Its multidimensional repertoire of myths and meanings is limited only by the hours in the day and by my threshold of fright.

This is where I've found peace.
This is where I've found understanding.
This was and always will be my window to the world.

DANIEL B. MERRIAM

Special Thanks

Throughout my life, there have been certain people who have encouraged and supported me in my work. I feel the most appropriate way to thank them is to create my art to the best of my ability -- to bring to the world a sense of wonder, passion, and free spirit. I would like to take this opportunity to extend special thanks to the following people:

- Jacob Leferrier, for his recognition of my talent at an early age and for helping me take the first step into the public arena with my work.
- To the entire Hatch family, for their love and support during my early years as a painter.
- To Sal Scaglion and Dana Heacock, for their constant support throughout my career and their true concern for the art as well as the artist.
- To my good friend Yale Beebee, for his diligence and hard work in the oftentimes demanding task of publishing.
- To Susan Edwards, for her many years of friendship and emotional support, for being there for me at my best and my worst moments, and for always reminding me to protect my dreams.
- To my parents and the rest of my family, for their influence on my personal and artistic development.

And to all of the people who have collected my work or supported me in any way, thank you for joining in the celebration of my art.

Daniel B. Merriam

Index of Paintings

Index of Text

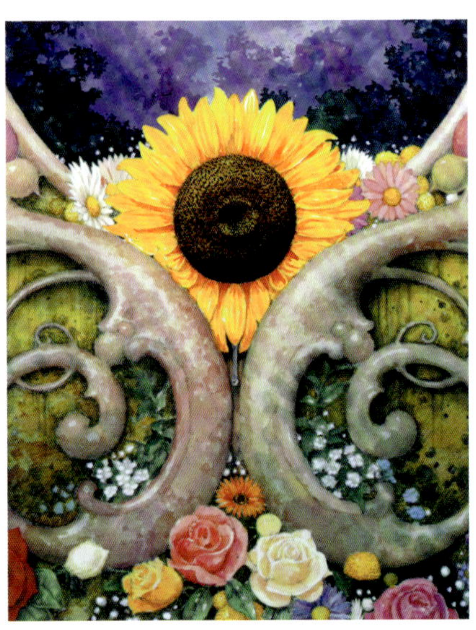

The Sunflower

She had a beautiful green stem
and the drops of wet dew would glisten
off her delicate leaves.
Her golden petals would shine with luminescence,
as sunbeams spread their warmth after a thundershower.
Her soft brown center contained an unending abundance of love,
which would overflow and soak the soft brown soil that bedded life.
God filled her heart, and she wanted to share this with the other flowers in the garden.
She wanted them to know what she did,
and if it took her death to let her companions see, then she would die.
The trembling flowers watched as the sky grew dark
and it began to rain.
A large boulder came down upon the sweet flower,
and she said to me,
I love you
and I said Mom,
I love you too.

Tiffani Marie Chapman

In celebration of my mom's life